TAKING UP THE REINS

TAKING UP THE REINS

A Year in Germany with a
Dressage Master

by

Priscilla Endicott

foreword by
Denny Emerson

Trafalgar Square Publishing
North Pomfret, Vermont

Dedication

*For Sheila La Farge who not only convinced me that I had a
real story to tell, but who encouraged me to keep on
writing until it was done.*

First published in 1999 by
Trafalgar Square Publishing
North Pomfret, Vermont 05053

The author has made every effort to obtain a release from all persons appearing in the photographs used in this book. In some cases, however, the persons may not have been known and
therefore could not be contacted.

Disclaimer of Liability: The author and publisher shall have neither liability nor responsibility to any person or entity with respect to any loss or damage caused or alleged to be caused
directly or indirectly by the information contained in this book. While the book is as accurate as the author can make it, there may be errors, omissions, and inaccuracies.

Library of Congress Cataloging-in-Publication Data

Endicott, Priscilla.
    Taking up the reins : a year in Germany with a dressage master /
Priscilla Endicott; foreword by Denny Emerson.
    p. cm.
ISBN 1-57076-134-5 (hc.)
1. Endicott, Priscilla. 2. Dressage riders—United States—Biography.
3. Dressage—Germany.
I. Title.
SF309.482.E53 A3 1999
798.2'3'092—dc21   CIP
[B]   99-44883

Illustrations:
The maps on pages 10 and 28 created by © 1999 Susan Berry Langsten. Any photograph not
credited within its caption is courtesy of the author.

Cover and book design by Barbara Homeyer
Typeface: Goudy

Printed in Canada

10 9 8 7 6 5 4 3 2 1

Table of Contents

Acknowledgments

I always wanted to "really ride" (as they say in the horse world) for Walter Christensen—to be for one little instant one of his star pupils, so that he would know how much the wonderful training we did together meant to me. But that high-level dream was unrealistic, given my age, my degree of talent, and general life circumstances.

So I chose another way to honor my Master Teacher and friend. I wrote this book. My aim has been to share my experiences in such a way that they might serve as an inspiration to others, and in this way, spread the word—Walter's words along with my words—and in this manner continue his work beyond his lifetime. I like to think that Walter might look down upon this book from wherever he is, flash that warm half smile of his, and repeat the words I used to treasure when he uttered them, "Ist gut, Priscilla," which meant it's good, or at least good enough for now. Whenever he'd say this, which was once in a while, I knew he was pleased and that would in turn please me enormously.

This book took time in the making. For five years I attended a weekly seminar called "Writing for Publication" at Radcliffe College Graduate Center. Gail Pool was my instructor the entire time. I could not have been blessed with a more generous, conscientious, and consistently available teacher. I hold a very warm spot in my memory for the other writers in the seminar—their support, encouragement, and criticism was invaluable.

Without my computer friend, Gary Miller, I would have had a hard time. This intuitive man entered my life when the manuscript was in its early stages. He understood immediately that I only wanted to learn enough "computerese" to allow me to get the book written and he tailored his help to this end.

Thanks to Kerstin Christensen. Without her assistance, I would never have been able to lay my hands on a few of the photographs taken abroad that I desperately wished to obtain.

I give special thanks to Carole MacDonald who so generously donated photographs taken during clinics at The Ark.

I will never forget my final months of getting my manuscript in order. Sybil Taylor came to my rescue, was always infinitely responsive to my needs, saw the subject from my point of view, and was great fun to work with—even through the hard parts.

Finally, I want to thank Caroline Robbins and Martha Cook for their enthusiasm for the book, their attention to detail, their taste, their style, and for the generosity they have both shown in letting me be involved in the fascinating process of being published.

Foreword

The world of American dressage in the late 1960s and the world of American dressage in the late 1990s is not the same world merely separated by a span of three decades. They are two very different universes.

My college's motto is the Latin phrase, *Vox clamantis is deserto* meaning "a voice crying in the wilderness," that cry presumably seeking knowledge, leadership, and guidance. The phrase aptly describes the state of dressage in this country for many years, despite such bright spots as our USET team bronze medal at the Bromont, Canada Olympics in 1976.

NEDA, the New England Dressage Association, was one of several vigorously active groups attempting to redress the imbalance between Western Europe, where intense discipline and intellectual rigor are traditions of the sport, and the United States, where, in the words of former USET Three-Day Coach, Jack Le Goff, "Americans want instant dressage the way they want instant coffee."

Priscilla Endicott's farm, "The Ark," in Harvard, Massachusetts, became a mecca and haven for many of us who were vaguely aware that we didn't know very much, and were "crying in the wilderness" for a valid approach to our various goals.

As an event rider, rather than an upper-level dressage competitor, my own ignorance was proportionally much greater than that of such luminaries as Michael Poulin, Lendon Gray, and Dorothy Morkis, who already had established the fierce work ethic and the ability to embrace minute detail that are needed for success in dressage.

Into this semi-wilderness stepped the towering presence of Walter Christensen, whose gentle demeanor and diffident smile belied enormous drive and intellect. We were drawn to him, many of us, as moths to a flame, but with infinitely more satisfactory outcomes.

All of this is by way of preface to Priscilla's logical extension and continuation of her personal quest. *Taking Up the Reins*, is her deeply personal, sometimes exhilarating, but also often painful account of her year of immersion in the world of German dressage, with all its nationalistic overtones, its structured hierarchy, and its often male dominated culture.

I've been involved in the three Olympic disciplines enough to know with complete certainty that of the three, Grand Prix dressage demands the greatest degree of precision, exactitude, and total commitment to meticulous detail. These are all traits I think Americans associate with the German mindset, perhaps to the point of stereotype. If Walter Christensen's stable was prototypical of national tendencies, those American stereotypes would be accurate. It didn't matter whether the exercise being performed involved perfecting a trot-halt transition or cleaning a stall. Everything had to be done exactly the way Walter wanted it. I saw for myself when I spent a month at Stall Tasdorf in the early winter of 1982.

High above the center of the indoor hall at Tasdorf, suspended by various pulleys and ropes, was a large iron ring. At Christmas, this ring was lowered, liberally festooned with greenery, and re-raised to form a Christmas wreath. The problem was that the ring weighed about 80 or 90 pounds, and was so unwieldy that it was difficult to raise it so that it was symmetrically centered and didn't tilt. Four of use, including Walter, struggled with the cursed thing for thirty minutes or so, directing many un-Christmas-like epithets at it, each other, and the Christmas season in general. No one appreciating its festive appearance would have dreamed how much sweat, effort, and exasperation lay beneath the surface of that particular iceberg. Perhaps, in this little vignette, lies an analogy to the iceberg below perfect one-tempi changes?

Another time, late in the evening, I chanced upon Walter vigorously sweeping the cobblestone barn aisle with one of those little handmade birch brooms, last used by normal people in the Middle Ages. I later mentioned this to Kerstin, Walter's Swedish wife. "Don't worry," she replied, "unless a North German goes to bed at night exhausted, he doesn't feel as though he's had a good day!"

This was the world of Priscilla's grand adventure, daunting enough for those growing up in it, and doubly so for "auslanders."

If you love dressage, you will want to read this book. Even if you're not immersed in dressage, but are fascinated by the process by which some people reach beyond themselves to achieve exceptionally difficult goals, you should read this book. It surely won't teach you how to ride; no book can do that. *Taking Up the Reins* can, though, open up a lost world, essentially that of the medieval guild system, with its complete and exacting emphasis on totality of effort directed toward the elusive goal of perfection.

Denny Emerson, Summer 1999
*Member of the gold medal United States
Three-Day Event Team at the 1974 World Championships,
Reserve Rider for the 1976 Olympic Games,
past president of the United States Combined Training Association (USCTA),
and United States Equestrian Team vice-president for Three-Day Eventing*

1

Pivotal Point

I wasn't thinking about the upcoming Mexican Olympics in July of 1968. I hardly knew that they existed. The four months of summer kept me busy with an energetic, growing family, an array of animals, particularly horses, maintaining a summer house and, at that time, my new love of the moment—three-day eventing.

Weekdays, I would spring up in the early cool of the morning to train in one of the phases of this exciting new form of competitive riding. The sport had been introduced only recently to the United States from England, and had immediately captured the interest of many Americans. The triple phase concept of three-day eventing—dressage, cross country, and stadium jumping—challenges everything most riders could ever want to do with a horse. Aside from testing the talent, daring, endurance, and courage of these animals, eventing requires speed. Most horses and many riders love a real flat-out gallop.

After hearing a number of exciting tales about riding in "events," I wanted to give this triathlon sport a try, even though I was in my late thirties and thrice a mother. Fortunately, right at this time a tall, slender, crisp lady with a British accent turned up in my life. Her name was Pamela Fitzwilliams and she was an experienced event rider. "I know all about the sport. I've done it for years." she said, and asked whether I'd like her to teach me. "When do we begin?" I said, without a moment's hesitation.

Half a year later, when Pamela and I were venturing out to small competitions in the New England area, I was given an opportunity to go to the equestrian events at the Olympic Games in Mexico City. The offer was totally unexpected and the Games were just days away. Pamela's enthusiasm took off at high speed. This was not an opportunity to be missed, she said. She knew all about the English, Australian, and American teams and could describe horses and riders in detail. Clearly, she insisted, it would be good for me to watch riders of this caliber, particularly since I was working so intensely at learning the sport.

Of course, she was right. I knew that. In fact, we should both go. But when I saw the tickets that had been arranged for us, I could scarcely believe my eyes—DRESSAGE. Unthinkable! Sitting through the dressage day in the three-day event competition would be quite enough. Schooling movements felt unnatural and confining and not at all in line with the "red-blooded" qualities we loved about our sport. After all—event riders claimed with considerable gusto—horses were built to run and jump, not trot and canter sedately around in prescribed circles, make subtle transitions, or stand quietly at the halt.

Dressage seemed so opposite in nature to the skills required in the two other phases. In the dressage discipline, the horse is confined to a ring and asked to perform a basic test with perfect obedience and precision. These requirements are almost antithetical to the athletic training demanded by three-day eventing. Thus, when an eventing horse is asked to work in dressage, the horse often reacts to the limited boundaries and rules of the ring with explosive behavior. Aside from the fact that event riders find these problems difficult, they don't really enjoy the restrictions and rules themselves. "Dressage just isn't any fun," I've heard many of them say.

Pamela and I made it to Avandaro, Mexico in time to see most of the three-day event horses perform their tests. For several days, we celebrated equine speed out on the wide-open spaces of what had once been a famous golf course. Standing in rain boots, deep in Mexican mud, we felt the wind in our faces, and watched the competitors, imagining ourselves in the saddle for every jump, fall, and thrill. Then, all too swiftly, the three-day event was over and there we were with our tickets to the Olympic dressage competition. The Mexican weather had switched from pelting rain to blistering sun. Could we bear to sit in the bleachers for an entire day? Would dressage at its highest level prove worth our while? At last, with nothing else on our agenda, we decided not to waste our tickets. If we didn't like it, we reasoned, we would just leave after an hour or so.

Pamela and I arrived at the equestrian site for dressage later than we had planned. Good heavens, the venue was as quiet as a church during a moment of silent prayer! But nobody's eyes were closed. What, I wondered, could hold the rapt attention of so many hundreds of people? As we tried to find our seats in the crowded rows of the bleachers, we felt like intruders. Faces turned toward us with indignant expressions, "How could you be late?" they seemed to say.

Finally, we settled into two perfect seats—the dressage arena with its low white fencing was directly in front of us. A contestant carrying the German colors was already in the ring and I noticed with surprise that the rider was elderly. He wasn't in his twenties, thirties or forties like most Olympic athletes, but well into his fifties, perhaps even his sixties—a good deal older than I was. The man was dressed in competition attire: jet black top hat and tail coat, snow white breeches, stock, and gloves. The only color in this penguin combination of black and white were several medals and a ribbon indicating merit affixed to his left lapel. This man had the longest, thinnest pipe stem legs, and his boots were polished to such a sheen, that had I been standing next to him, they could have reflected my face. A truly elegant sight.

An Italian sitting behind me, sensing that I was a novice informed me that the Grand Prix test being ridden was "very difficult." "Very," he repeated. Watching as the horse and rider went through their paces, I thought that I had never seen such precision. The competitor rode with perfect accuracy toward the dressage letters that bordered the ring. The figures in the test began and ended as if they had been measured. Five judges were studying the pair's movements. From time to time, one of the judges leaned out of his judging box. What could he be watching? Was it where the horse's hooves landed or the length of the stride? I remembered the meticulousness required in figure skating, in which the lines made by the blades in the ice were studied. Was this sort of exactness being demanded in dressage? Impossible! Certainly not with an animal.

Seldom in my life had I been so excited. What I was witnessing was no familiar walk, trot or canter. The lightness, airiness, and elevation made it appear as if the pair scarcely needed the ground. At one moment, the horse performed a high stepping, strong, rhythmic dance and the audience went, "Ah-h-h-h-h-h-h" with extreme pleasure. Together, man and horse made the work seem effortless. As hard as I looked, I simply could not see how the rider brought about such intricate movements.

Spellbound, I saw the horse perform a tiny circle at the canter, the width of which could have been no more than the spread of my hand. The man behind me whispered, "That's a pirouette and you'll never see a better one." It was tempting to believe such a moment involved magic. I wanted to clap and shout, "bravo," but the atmosphere was so quiet and respectful I knew I had to keep still. Finally the competitor came to a halt, doffed his hat, and saluted. At this, all of us bench sitters let loose with so much noise you'd have thought we were children just out of school.

I was amazed that we didn't frighten the horse and deafen the rider, but it was clear these two were experienced campaigners who knew how to accept applause. As the pair passed close by on their way out of the arena, I noticed the gentleman stroke his mount with obvious pleasure. The animal was now completely relaxed, head stretched far out and low. Anyone who looked closely might have sworn the horse was pleased, too.

Sitting in the bleachers that day, back in 1968, I had very little understanding of what I saw; yet I was so fascinated that I stayed in my seat the entire day. I was discovering that aspects of dance, music, poetry, and sculpture all seemed to be part of the beauty and harmony of dressage. Here—in a sport that I had regarded as primarily physical—was refinement, subtlety, and creative and intellectual rigor. I was filled with an excitement that I could barely contain. What an amazing challenge this discipline would be for a person who loved horses and wanted to ride until the last day of her life!

By the next morning, I knew that dressage would have to become part of my life. I didn't know how I would bring this about, I only knew I was determined to make it happen and I went home to find out more.

"Dressage," I learned comes from the French verb "dresser," to train (an animal or person), placing emphasis on work with the mind as well as the drill of the body. Although the art of fine riding goes back to the days of Xenophon in ancient Greece, dressage took root during the 14th and 15th centuries in the German, French, Swedish, and Swiss cavalry units. Riders encumbered with suits of heavy armor required well-trained horses to be effective in battle. The original purpose of what we call the pirouette (a 180 degree turn on the spot), the half-pass (a sideways movement), or an extension (a strong, straight, forward movement), were battle maneuvers to turn on a dime, to step to one side, and to line up for a charge with a spear extended straight out at an enemy.

When horses were outmoded as vehicles of war and cavalries followed more peaceful pursuits, the early masters of dressage emerged. These men refined their training into an art form, wrote treatises, expounded theories, and produced drawings of exactly what they had in mind. In this manner, all of Europe contributed to today's classical Western tradition of dressage.

One of the finest, contemporary examples of this tradition is the Spanish Riding School of Vienna, with its dazzlingly beautiful white Lipizzaner horses. The school's "Winter Riding Hall" was built in the 1730s by the order of Emperor Charles VI, as his tribute to the art of horsemanship. No more beautiful stage exists than this magical baroque riding hall in which the aristocratic Lipizzaners perform to music for their public. Each of these performances is an inspiring theatrical event, as is any great dressage presentation.

Actually, dressage has a lot in common with ballet, except, of course, in the case of dressage one's partner is not a human being. His aim in life may not be the same as yours. His willingness, interest and ability may have to be ignited, even nurtured to remain fresh and alive. Your connection to your horse friend needs to be deep and perceptive. This four-legged fellow can't say, "The hay I ate last night was slightly moldy. I'm not feeling my best, can we train for half the usual time?" It is up to you to detect the health, emotions, and moods of your fellow worker. Imagine the insight, (as well as the training) required to arrive at your peaks *and his* at a certain hour on a specific day for competition in an Olympics!

To achieve such a moment, to take a horse from the bottom to the top in his dressage education, requires seven to ten years of specialized training. In addition, it should be noted that both the rider and the horse can learn only as fast or as slow as the other can. Each is dependent on and supportive of the other. Learning this discipline is likened, by experienced trainers, to working with a series of interlocking building blocks. Nothing can be left to chance, no exercise commenced that is not prepared for, no movement requested that is not in the proper order of difficulty. The highest point in performance is reached when the horse and his rider each voluntarily offers the best of himself to the other.

When I returned from Mexico all set to begin learning this discipline that I had previously disparaged, I discovered how few riders in New England or even the United States had any interest in dressage. If they spoke the word at all, many pronounced it as if it were "dress-*age*" rather than "dress-*ajh*." After asking around, I found a smattering of dressage riders working on their own, and a few individuals who had managed to acquire high-level training. But basically, this classic equestrian art was unknown in America in 1968.

For a year or two, Pamela and I searched the surrounding states until we found a tiny group willing to share a day of instruction at my stable and to invite a speaker to my house. Eventually, this group began putting on very small local dressage shows. And then, in no time at all, we had grown to the point where friends suggested that we needed to form an organization. At our first formal meeting in 1970, someone said, "Let's think big and choose a name that represents all of New England." With no more than forty people sitting in the room, the idea suggested a bigger hat than we were ready to wear. However, we were an eager bunch and I was officially named president of "The New England Dressage Association." It was in this capacity that I was able to contribute actively to the early years of dressage in America.

Our beginnings were small and exploratory. Whenever possible, we invited Europeans both to teach us and to judge our shows. There was no doubt that this was the right time for dressage to take root in America: our wide-open spaces were disappearing and dressage can be practiced on small parcels of land. Too, more and more Americans were traveling to Europe where they discovered dressage as a popular form of riding. Simultaneously, a small influx of foreign riding instructors moved to this country, where they found a ready market. Some were well trained, others not. These men (hardly any women) began teaching for their livelihood, introducing the art of dressage to American riders.

You have to admire how diligently we "Ammies" sought out our teachers. Nuno Oliveira of Portugal, whose fame is now in equestrian history books, prepared a lecture presentation with films for our riders in New England. The occasion must have been one of his first visits to this country. A group of us who were to take lessons from him gathered in a church meeting house, and with the greatest fascination, watched images of foreign riders performing the most difficult of dressage maneuvers. His films did not apply to us. We were in kindergarten, not even equipped with the basics.

Europeans had a hard time understanding us. Some of our problems were ones they never had to consider themselves. For example: we had few models on whose performance we could base any kind of progressive standard; the correct concepts slipped away when our teachers weren't around; films were a rarity and even a good book with helpful pictures was hard to find. Our horses were often quite different, both in mind and body, from the animals bred in Europe specifically for dressage. In addition, our culture constantly reminded us that everything should be done quickly.

Major Hans Wikne, a well-known ex-cavalry man, instructor, trainer, competitor, and director of the Strömsholm national riding school in Sweden, perceived our situation immediately when he visited Massachusetts to give instruction. A small group had gathered in my ring for lessons. He rode every one of our horses, demonstrated how each of us should begin, and outlined the steps of progress that lay ahead. We worked for ten days and then made plans for him to pay us a second visit.

The following year, he shook his head halfway through my first lesson and said sadly, "You must go back to the beginning. We cannot go on to any advanced work until you have mastered the first steps." I was devastated. One entire year wasted. I had not understood enough myself on his first visit, nor had I received the proper help during his absence, to avoid faults which, in Europe, would have been picked up immediately.

Ten years of trying to learn dressage followed. When I got discouraged, and of course I did, I reminded myself that I had been told that in Europe, students of dressage often rode with supervision from their trainers every single day. Like dancers, they seldom worked alone. Under the circumstances, I reminded myself, I was doing the very best I could. But in my heart I was thinking, "Some day I will find a better way." And I did: enter Walter Christensen.

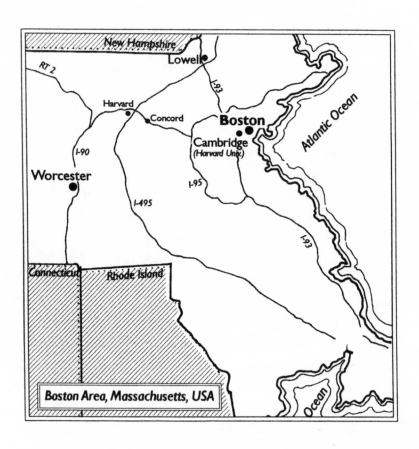

Boston Area, Massachusetts, USA

≈2

Enter Walter

The house that my husband, Russell and I shared and where I still live is one of the older homes in our town. This painted wooden farmhouse, dating back to 1725, is tucked unpretentiously into one of the round hills of Harvard, Massachusetts. It is surrounded by apple orchards and stretches of varying kinds of farm and forest land. Roads do not run straight. They are tree-lined, narrow, bumpy, and wandering, descending into sudden dips and climbing abrupt hills. Horses, sheep, and an occasional cow graze the fields. Several roads lead to points where the views are impressively vast.

On a fall day, in the middle of September in 1978, exactly ten years and two months after my trip to the Olympics in Mexico, a car arrived with the German equestrian instructor, Mr. Walter Christensen. He had come to conduct his first dressage "clinic" or training seminar, in this country. All I knew about my visitor was that he was a dressage trainer highly respected in his native West

Germany, where the best training was available. I knew too that Germany was the center of dressage competition. Few riders from any other European country were able to break into the tight, consistently held Teutonic winners' circle. The Germans had such a firm hold on the field of dressage that they seemed to own it.

Seeing the car drive in, I felt decidedly awkward. I wondered how we were going to manage since I had been told that Mr. Christensen didn't speak any English. Friends had warned me that Germans always shake hands. I offered mine promptly and gave this medium-sized, gentle-featured man a big smile. I wanted him to feel especially welcome. Immediately, Louise Nathhorst, the young woman who was with him, offered to interpret. She explained that she was one of his students from Sweden and that she was traveling with him as his assistant.

The arrival of Walter Christensen had been anticipated for weeks. People came to watch from miles around, from all over New England, New York, and Pennsylvania. They had heard that Walter Christensen would be spending three days at my farm. I had never met many of them before so I could only guess that the news had traveled far and wide because his visit was as important to them as it was to me. I suppose those of us who were scheduled to ride with him felt we had a great deal to learn, but I doubt that anyone had any idea of exactly what lay ahead.

The spectators had to have considerable curiosity or serious intent: watching a clinic isn't the sort of entertainment you pick because you have nothing else to do. Shortly after 7:30 AM, people hurried in through the huge door of my indoor ring, climbed up the tiers of the green wooden bleachers, and settled themselves in as if to stay. They went straight for the seats, saying little. Clearly, they felt that this was not an occasion for casual chatter.

The first hour lesson of the day at 8:00 AM was scheduled to go to me. At ten minutes before eight in the morning, I had walked my horse Inca up the dirt road to the ring, talking to him along the way. Inca appeared to like listening. Besides, I needed the companionable comfort of my old friend to keep me cool and give me confidence. With so many spectators watching and the German expert scrutinizing every detail, that certainly wouldn't be easy.

Meanwhile, Mr. Christensen had chosen to walk to the ring by himself, making a tour around our pond. Through the trees I watched him taking his time, looking here and there, inspecting whatever caught his interest. I had known him only a matter of hours, one evening to be exact. I'd already discovered he was a meditative type and was about my age—soon to turn fifty. My two dogs attached themselves to him as if they had known him forever. He had invited them to stroll with him this morning as politely as he would if they were his own guests. (He never did get around to inviting any people.) Together, the man and the two dogs made their way to the ring with the casual steps of those very much at home on this earth.

When Mr. Christensen arrived at the doorway, I was already mounted, walking Inca on a loose rein, giving him time to stretch out his muscles and accept my weight on his back. "That's Mr. Christensen," someone from the crowd whispered. I saw him take a long look at them as a group, then acknowledge their presence and take a seat on the small wooden bench next to Louise, who would assist him. He announced himself by clearing his throat, all the while studying Inca without giving me a clue as to his thoughts. Finally, he gave me a look that I took to mean, "You may begin."

Nine years of trying to learn dressage had taught me at least one thing: to start a lesson in a clinic with a new instructor by showing Inca's normal gaits. I began with the walk, praying that I could ride that well. Walking seemed to me simple enough. Later, I would learn that it was not.

There was no sound from the bench for a long time. Was Mr. Christensen waiting for something more to happen? Locked in my own physical tightness, I couldn't relax enough to feel Inca's body. We were two separate entities. Nervousness made me lose track of time. I asked if I should get on with my usual work.

"Not yet. Give yourself more time." Louise's English was easy to understand. She said that our walk needed to march right along. A good walk must not be fast, but must give the impression of having somewhere to go. I knew then that Inca must have been shuffling in his slow-to-get-started way. "Your reins should not dangle," was the next comment. "Make them shorter." "Have a straight line to the horse's mouth." "Now, be alive." "Be soft." "Sit up straight." "Drop your shoulders." "No, don't stand in your stirrups, SIT!"

By that time, I had decided to trot. It felt as if Inca and I were both stuck in mud. Feeling desperate, I goosed him in the ribs with my spurs. The tempo instantly became too quick. Mr. Christensen wanted to know why I was in such a hurry. Instead, I was told to look for the natural rhythm of the horse. Then I was left on my own.

Many American riding teachers keep up a running commentary as if they are being paid by the word. As this was what I was used to, I found the long silences that often followed in the lesson uncomfortable. Mr. Christensen's comments were short, occasionally punctuated by noises he made deep in his throat that were so explicit, he didn't need words. I translated them as mostly negative.

The instructors I had known stood in the center of the ring and made me ride around them. I wondered if Mr. Christensen chose to remain seated on the side of the ring because it was the German way. The fact that he sat there so still was unnerving, and having him outside the orbit of my work made our connection seem distant and cold. Then, when I rode close to him; I was able to see that he was intently observing our every stride. On occasion, he would turn toward the bleachers and ask for quiet; unnecessary noise was a distraction. It was not that he made a statement to the group, he merely turned his gaze in their direction and they instantly understood that they should concentrate along with whoever was working in the ring.

Mr. Christensen asked to ride Inca in order to get the "feel" of the horse himself. "Feel" to him had a special connotation referring not to any tactile sense or an animal's state of health, but rather to finding out as much about a creature as possible. "Feeling" a horse, for a man like Mr. Christensen, was an instinctive, deep reading. Within minutes of mounting Inca, he could sense any stiffness or physical hindrance, discover the extent of his past training, and be able to make a good guess as to how easy or difficult it would be to take on the horse himself. Later, I would learn that "feel" is the key element to good riding.

I explained—through Louise, of course—that I had bought Inca, a trained horse, to be my professor of dressage.

"How long have you owned him?" Mr. Christensen asked.

"Two years."

"And what are your goals?"

"To learn to ride as well as I can at the highest level of dressage," I answered. My dreams, I went on to explain, had been formed in Mexico. That was where I had seen the perfection I wanted to aim toward. I had thought an experienced horse would make learning easy. Speed the process. But, it didn't take long to realize that I needed lessons even to ride him. As for myself, I had come to understand that all my time in the saddle since childhood didn't seem to count either.

He gave me an I-know-what-you-mean nod. I had the feeling he already knew a lot about me and that somehow my "facts" really weren't very important to him at all.

I began riding when I was five years old, aboard a fat, black pony named Dolly. My legs were so short that knots were tied in the leathers so that I could get my feet into the stirrups. Most of all, Dolly liked to snooze, so we never really did much or went very far, but I was supremely happy just sitting there on my gentle friend.

Other horses followed Dolly, but none were quite as special until the appearance of Fregatte. This bay Hanoverian mare, imported from and trained in Germany, was offered to me with wonderful serendipity upon my return from the Mexican Olympics, by a friend who could no longer ride. Fregatte was handsome, impressive, and substantial. The truth was, her massiveness frightened me, but knowing I was incredibly lucky to have her, I lived with my fear until we became acquainted and I could relax. At that point, I even discovered that when my five-year-old daughter sat on her back, the mare would act as if she were Dolly reincarnated.

Fregatte was the great lady that started me on my serious pursuit of dressage. At the time, I didn't know enough to appreciate how well trained she was. Her real value only began to sink in years later. Fregatte was trained to do many dressage movements almost by herself. I would sit in the saddle, nudge her with my leg, hold my reins in the manner I was being taught, and she would give me a sense of what this form of riding was all about. Sometimes she would even initiate trained movements on her own, and due to her expertise I was able to ride in a manner years ahead of my actual trained ability. Tragically, I lost Fregatte four years later in a horrible fire, a holocaust that took five horses, a miniature donkey, and my entire barn.

Inca came into my life shortly afterward. I found him in Florida with his owner-trainer, Alex Konyot. I was searching for a horse that could be my teacher. I reasoned that since I had many commitments in my life and was not a born rider—as few people are—I needed an animal who could help me along.

Many riders need help getting used to a horse's vocabulary, habits and ways, especially when the creatures have previous mileage and training. A horse can both aid you immeasurably and still be hard to understand. Often, you feel torn between a variety of choices: asserting yourself, experimenting, doing the best you can while listening to your horse, and allowing him to tell you what to do and how to do it. True, you bought him because he impressed you with his fount of knowledge, but what combination of techniques and attitudes will bring out the best performance for both of you? And how do you arrive at this magical combination? Which of your choice of actions is correct?

In dressage, you need an observant third party—an expert instructor—to clear up your doubts, push you on, and say firmly, "This is the way to do it." For me, this role was filled by Walter Christensen. I was more ready for him than I even knew.

When Walter Christensen listened to me tell him how hard I had tried, he smiled and said, "Dressage takes time. You can't hurry it." The same statement was repeated to every one of the riders during his stay at my farm, not once but often, which made me wonder if "taking time" might not be the hardest part of this discipline for us Americans.

Naturally, we all hoped we would see Mr. Christensen on a horse, so we were thrilled when he asked to ride Inca that first session. In the lesson that followed, we saw why the German way of riding dressage receives world acclaim.

I tightened Inca's girth so the saddle wouldn't move when Mr. Christensen mounted. The man would never have been described as fat or heavy; partial to certain foods might have been the best way to think of his visible roundness. My stirrups were dropped to their limit to accommodate legs that were longer than I could have believed. Standing next to him I discovered we were the same height, both of us five feet ten; the difference was—legs. Signs of stiffness or perhaps discomfort were evident when he rose from the bench. He was, however, not the man to discuss such matters. His sense of privacy was as snug as his jacket.

Anticipation hung in the air from the gallery. We waited. Hard to tell for what. We probably didn't even know ourselves, but we wanted action of some sort. If I had to define that large group, I'd say we were physically oriented beings. Sitting and watching was not something we could ever do easily for too many hours a day, certainly not sitting and watching inaction.

Walter walked Inca quietly around. Dust particles caught in the rays of strong sunlight and hung in the stillness. I had the sense that Mr. Christensen was saying his how-do-you-do in a most gentle manner; we were present at an intensely private scene.

Walter and Inca fitted together naturally from the start. There was none of the usual tightness of neck muscles or tense looks you often see in a person with a new horse. I'd never seen a rider sit a horse like this Mr. Christensen. He didn't stir from the saddle, which is an art in itself. You might have said he was meant to be on a horse, even that he'd sprung up through the animal's back. As for his bodily position, it never even entered my mind to analyze it: he was just so right, with nothing unnatural, stiff or forced. He simply sat.

The audience in the crowded bleachers leaned forward. All were expecting elements of drama, big movements, some kind of fanfare, perhaps a kick of the spur, a whack with the stick, some obvious evidence of human mastery. The place became astonishingly quiet. Magic is easy to enjoy but it is hard to believe in. We were searching for clues.

Inca was a tall, leggy thoroughbred of English and Portuguese descent. I knew his body well, having patted, brushed, sponged, scraped, and blanketed as well as sat on it. But as Mr. Christensen continued, I saw that familiar body change. The length of Inca's frame became shorter, so that he rose higher underneath and in front of the rider. His chest appeared to have doubled in width and his neck developed a curve that I associated with the statues of horses rising out of the Neptune fountain in Rome's Piazza Navona. As Walter rode, Inca's head, instead of poking out in front, now was held in a position that formed a direct vertical line from his ears to his nose, showing off the white star on his forehead as if it were a headlight. In this position, his entire head assumed a noble look. It was truly amazing to see all these transformations occurring right before our eyes.

Next, the pair progressed into trot and canter. I recognized certain patterns and movements, but others I had never seen before. As Mr. Christensen explored the full extent of Inca's training, I thought that I was seeing the whole spectrum of dressage, not knowing that my eyes were those of a beginner. I had yet to find out that it takes knowledge as well as time to know where to look and how to see in dressage. Nevertheless, even my untrained eye could take in details of change in the way this dark mahogany bay of mine was working. Maintaining a square, compact body frame, he really began moving. With his front half lifted higher, his hindquarters reached farther under his belly and his back legs were able to take long, impressive strides. The result of the change in the axis of balance diminished any impression of heaviness. Thirteen hundred pounds of solid horseflesh went around the ring as if no longer earthbound. I thought Inca looked bold as a stag. My God, was he proud!

His facial expression astonished me. Every aspect of the face I knew so well was heightened, especially around the eye. He was a handsome fellow, and I had always loved the size and deep brown honesty of his eye, but now a new intensity, a light, gleamed there. The work he was being asked to do involved every ounce of his attention: he was being asked to think very hard. The articulation between the bony and soft areas of his nose and cheek sharpened and a map of veins lifted in high relief. As long as I had known Inca, his ears had been more or less stationary. Now they were moving antennae, cocking and flickering with every movement. He was listening. Was Mr. Christensen whispering or making some special sound? Riders do. I've heard professionals make cricket clicks, hisses, pops, growls, snarls, all kinds of non-people noises without ever opening their mouths. No. I couldn't hear any such sound.

Long, steady, quiet movements covered the floor in continuous symmetrical patterns. Inca's hooves could hardly be heard. They seemed to spring right out of the soft footing as if there were sponge underneath, instead of earth. But Inca himself made sounds—he grunted—he was making a true effort. Walter rewarded him with pats on the neck, moments of giving the reins, and a repeated, "jawohl." He let Inca know beyond question that he was doing well, extremely well, and that he, Walter was extremely pleased. The audience burst in spontaneous applause.

Lessons that first day proved harder for some people and easier for others. Even the most experienced among us, Denny Emerson, who had ridden dressage in the Olympics when a member of our three-day event team, had to struggle to make his jumper loosen his back and neck. I admired Denny for his willingness to learn. His interest in overcoming his ignorance and pursuing the correct training of basic dressage was evident, his enthusiasm catching. At one point, Mr. Christensen told Denny to ride a 20-meter circle. Neither Denny nor his horse had done this exercise before (not in the manner that Mr. Christensen expected to see it) and clearly, it wasn't easy for them. Suddenly, there were loud German words of protest. Louise translated "No square circles! Circles are meant to be round!" We spectators looked at each other, astonished that this foreign trainer was so persnickety about circles. We'd seen nothing wrong with the way Denny rode.

Denny sweated some more. This time the hoof prints kept to a circular figure of the correct size and those of us watching willed his thick-necked horse to cooperate. Denny must have thought it was going better when he looked over at Mr. Christensen for a sign of approval. But the German shook his head, "nicht gut genug," (not good enough).

Exasperated, Denny called out to Louise, "Don't bother to translate. I've heard those words enough to know what they mean." The audience exploded. Walter laughed too. He loved humor. He believed a good laugh made everyone ride better.

The audience identified with Denny's work—it was a clear visual lesson they could take home with them. All were encouraged by watching such a well-known horseman honestly trying as hard as he could, over and over again, without achieving immediate success. Many were having similar experiences themselves, and the idea that it requires patience to learn correct dressage basics was reinforced. Denny's persistence inspired us and it pleased Mr. Christensen.

After the lessons, Walter went for a walk to inspect the farm. He wanted to see how we kept our stable, what we fed our horses, and how an American horse shower stall worked. He examined the farm machinery, inspected our vegetable garden, studied the flower beds, took note of trees and was fascinated with the viciousness of 34 Canadian geese that had taken up residence in the lower pond. Was I aware that these big birds were trying to drive out two families of wild duck, he asked? He found the smaller birds' nests in the rushes and counted four eggs. He'd never seen a chipmunk anywhere in Germany and found it interesting that at home in Germany the squirrels were black instead of grey-brown like ours.

Louise assured me that Walter was content at our farm, The Ark. It was a beautiful spot. Much of the land was hidden from the road, which made it quite private. The landscape of Harvard, Massachusetts reminded Walter of northern Germany. Louise didn't agree, Harvard seemed to her much more like Sweden. Both of them were struck by the number of wooden houses they were seeing here, in contrast to Germany where the land had been so depleted of trees that all the dwellings in Walter's area were brick.

At the dinner hour, Walter reappeared from the guestroom and I knew as surely as I knew how to boil water, that not only had he unpacked all his clothes, he had put every item neatly away. There was an immaculate feel about his person. Not cold, crisp or threatening, just spotless and clean. Even his shoes were polished until they looked like the table we ate on in the kitchen. In European fashion, Walter was dressed more formally than most Americans, in a shirt, tie and V-neck pullover sweater. His sweater was the flat kind, best quality wool, probably Italian, and soft as moss, like the paths in my woods.

Louise spoke excellent English, having studied it for many years in school. Tilting her head like a little bird, she listened to the conversation carefully and repeated what was said so deftly that the stiffness and separation that usually exists with translation disappeared. In turn, eagerness to get specific meanings across found all of us using our hands and our bodies without embarrassment. The result was a childlike sense of fun and laughter as we began to feel comfortable with one another. Talk flowed. Louise told us a little about herself.

German became a third language for Louise when she heard about Walter Christensen and came to his training stable, Stall Tasdorf, in northern Germany. She explained that when she began as his student, she was a timid, inexperienced teenager, and for the first year, she felt that everything she did was wrong. The most difficult thing was that she spoke no German. "I didn't say a single word for two whole months," she said, "And I had to get used to such different food." When she returned home she discovered she'd been so worried by the whole experience that she had lost forty pounds. But still, she couldn't wait to go back; the training had far exceeded her dreams.

Louise described how she had first arrived at Tasdorf in a second-hand truck and trailer. "The Germans didn't know what to make of my used rig, but it was typical for Sweden," she explained, "At home, families don't start their children with brand new equipment. Vehicles are not status symbols."

As, she took her horse out of the trailer to his assigned stall, Mr. Christensen had shouted at her but she had no idea what he was saying. He wanted to stop her from allowing her horse to walk straight into the stall by himself. The right way, as he himself promptly demonstrated, was to lead the creature in, turn around, face the door and then remove the halter and lead. This method, he pointed out, prevents injury and accidents.

Louise said she had found it troublesome when Walter or his assistant raised their voices. She had to learn that shouting was the German way of taking control. Germans believe that when working with animals, actions take place so fast, that the people who handle them must hear and obey orders immediately. "Shouting is an accepted part of the German educational system, at home, in school and in compulsory military training," she said. But Walter isn't typically German," she added with considerable feeling. "In fact, compared to many other German trainers, he hardly shouts at all."

Why would she want to train in a country other than Sweden, we wanted to know? Wasn't there someone she could study with at home?

Oh, yes, of course, Louise was quick to answer, there were fine Swedish instructors, especially at the ex-cavalry school in Ströms-holm, but the best preparation for international competition was said to exist in Germany. Sources she respected had recommended Walter Christensen as an exceptional teacher and mentor. "I trust him implicitly," were her exact words. "He's become both my second father and a friend."

Louise was Walter's most talented and serious student. At twenty-four, she was thought to be one of the most promising young dressage riders in Sweden. An invitation to work, train and compete in the dressage stable of the Poulin family in Fairfield, Maine had recently brought her and her horse, Inferno, to America. Walter had urged her to make this move, believing that she and Inferno needed time to mature on their own, and that a variety of new experiences would benefit her.

The influence Walter and Louise had on one another was plainly reciprocal. Although neither knew it then, seeds were being planted that would bear rich fruit for the future. Louise was responsible for urging Walter to accept clinics in Maine, Massachusetts, and California. They agreed that night as they discussed the matter, that without each other, neither would probably have considered coming to the States.

"Some day," she said lightly, as if she were considering the option of a second cup of tea, "I will return home and ride for Sweden."

"You mean ride in the Olympics?" my husband Russell asked. We were impressed—that was certainly a high goal.

She nodded, "Yes."

Walter clearly understood the gist of our conversation. He nodded in a schoolmasterly manner, approving Louise's tale.

Wishing to wait on himself, he asked if he might brew himself a cup of tea. Walter's tea-making ceremony halted our conversation. It remains a vivid memory, in a way that someone's simplest actions often stay with us because they reveal so much about that person and his approach to life. Walter prepared his tea with unhurried deliberation as though he was engaged in a contemplative ritual. Or he might have been a chemist, the steps of the process were so clearly and cleanly defined: kettle boiling, water pouring, tea bag brewing, tea bag removal. His attention was fully absorbed in every detail in the same way his patience and observation focused on work with his horses.

Watching him made me realize how speeded up I was myself, often busy with two things at the same time. Here was a person who did not run his actions together to get on with life. He took time and he made time. I wondered, was this a quality he had brought to his riding or had the riding developed this in him?

Tea was fine, but in offering Walter what I thought of as our kind of food, trying to make meals a part of his American experience, my hopes of pleasing him went miserably wrong. When I set cornbread on the table, Louise explained that he had lived off cornbread as a child in the war and had never been able to face it since. When I presented, among other items, a salad of greens and mixed vegetables, he looked at the bowl with amazement; verdure of that sort was unGerman, he wouldn't venture a single bite. Fortunately, I was able to find in my refrigerator some slices of bread, some butter, a bit of cheese, and some ham!

Late in the evening, when our energy had flagged and our conversation had grown slow, I took a deep breath, turned directly to face Walter and said, "My dream is to learn dressage properly. Some day when I am good enough, I want to go to Germany." I was praying that Louise would repeat every word just as I had said it.

There was a pause in the relay. Then Walter smiled.

"Why not come to Germany now? Why wait? You're in luck," he said, "I have a stall open for Inca."

"Are you serious?" I asked. It was hard to believe I had understood correctly.

"That would be a good way to do it," he said in his matter-of-fact-way.

I sat there a moment, dumbfounded. How could I possibly leave home and Russell and my youngest daughter, Cricket, who was regularly competing as a three-day-event rider? She was living in Virginia and receiving instruction from one of America's top coaches and Olympic Team members, Jimmy Wofford. Russell and I tried to be at the competitions when she rode the big fences that, as her mom, took my breath away and left me in conflict between pleasure and fear. Another responsibility weighing on my shoulders was the New England Dressage Association, with which I was heavily involved as well as responsible. The Board was planning a program-filled year ahead, part of it initiated for the first time. A few moments of quiet reflection brought home how much I had packed into my life on an everyday basis. Besides, I knew no German.

It was with a sense of surprise, then, that I heard myself saying, "When do you think I could come?"

"Come in February," Walter said. I had four months to prepare for my year in Germany and one of the major experiences of my life.

3

First Day at Stall Tasdorf

Russell and I left home on a February morning to begin my journey to Germany, and right from that moment I made Tasdorf the center of my world. To my surprise, I had to buy four maps of Germany before I found one that showed the town, north of Hamburg, south of Kiel and west of Lubeck, in the north central farm area of West Germany. I couldn't imagine that Tasdorf would be unimportant to map makers, since it held so many of my dreams.

Here, at this tiny, abstract dot on the map, was a real town and a stall where Inca was already waiting for me. He had left home six weeks before my departure. The same little dot also spelled "Walter Christensen" to me. When I had telephoned from America for explicit directions, he was standing on top of the roof of his stable shoveling snow along with his stable crew: the weight of snow could be dangerous. Walter's Swedish wife Kerstin, (pronounced Chestin) told me that more of it had been dumped on Germany in

the last storm than had been seen in over a hundred years.

When we arrived on February 11th, the weather was gray, damp and cold. This first experience with winter in northern Germany reminded me of the damp cellar of my old New England house, where my sneakers developed a chill every time I walked across the cement floor. Mean stuff, this sort of climate. Mean enough for me to look twice at the dial of the car heater. It was on high but I could hardly feel the heat. Why was I cold, stone cold?

Russell drove with his gloves on, hands loosely grasping the wheel in the easy manner of one who truly loves to drive. I knew the Ford Escort would never have been his choice: it was, however, one of the least expensive rentals. A succession of grunts and a grimace or two preceded his acceptance of the situation, but from then on he steadfastly ignored any four-wheeled shortcomings. Since crossing the border from France, where we had been vacationing, Russell had been irritatingly forced into the slow lane on the major roads, reminded to stay in his place by all the big German cars.

In this country, left lane drivers seemed to be a special species of humankind with a deep hunger for speed and machine power. Whenever Russell chose to pull across the highway, to pass, or slow down to read a sign, he confronted anger. A blast on the horn from a Mercedes bearing down fast from behind was no sociable "Hallo," but a warning, "Achtung! Go where you belong!" I noticed, too, that left laners kept their eyes fixed dead ahead. They passed by us, their heads in profile, reminding me of the frames in an old-fashioned filmstrip.

Traveling well-marked roads adds extra pleasure to motoring in Europe. We had found all of our destinations easily except for this— our last one. Finally, the sign for Einfeld/Neumünster appeared above us. We slowed down. Lined up. The left lane and the right lane alternately merged into one single exit lane, an orderly, defined system, reminding me that regimentation was part of the German culture. We experienced a kind of patience in the line-up of waiting cars that we'd never known back home.

Hidden behind the enormous, imprisoning piles of snow, Einfeld, the town next to Tasdorf, existed for us only as driveways. The narrow, winding country road we were on curved up to the sky. Out of words, Russell and I had retreated into our separate selves as these final days of being together wore on. This was not unusual. I had discovered that remaining silent is a way of living together with which you can become comfortable. We had learned to read each other quite well over the years. I wondered as I sat there, if he would understand if I broke the silence and told him I felt all alone in the world and that I was hardly in the car at all. Instead, I was a child walking down the street trying to be brave, holding my thumbs in tight little fists.

The entrance to Walter Christensen's stable appeared on our left. I spied it first. The huge wooden sign, "Stall Tasdorf," was wearing a snow hat. The hat was a peaked roof built to protect the sign on which "Stall," for stable, appeared in block letters and, "Tasdorf," painted in script, suggested mobility and creativeness. Perhaps everything here was not all rules and regulations. I wondered whose idea the sign had been. In two days I would see it pulled up by rope until it disappeared into the peak of the roof. An oversized horse transport would pass unscathed underneath, further demonstrating the sign's clever design.

We entered a driveway that was as straight as a ruler and found ourselves facing a large, rectangular, cement block building. The long side abutted a parking place where several compact automobiles had been parked as neatly as shoeboxes in a store.

I had arrived.

I did not want to think anymore. I picked up my purse the instant Russell came to a halt. Opened the door. Got out fast. Was he wondering, "What's the hurry?" Perhaps he read me as being eager or excited. I can't remember taking the steps that brought me to the big, wooden stable door and the smell of horses. I gave my name to a young man and asked for Mr. Christensen. We were expected.

Walking toward me was the one person I knew in all of Germany. Walter greeted me with a handshake that reminded me of an old-time, wild west cowboy making a fast draw. It was a full arm motion. What spoke to me about this form of salutation was its readiness, the totality of a hand reaching out and expecting mine. Walter's fingers were both gentle and strong, their skin unexpectedly soft. The handshake told me his mind was on me: I had walked into a real welcome.

We paused awhile, looking at one another. Was he as I remembered him, I asked myself? I didn't want to find any change in him; I wanted him to be exactly as I expected, or I would be even more apprehensive than I already was.

I noted how wrinkled Walter's skin appeared: crows feet extended into his hairline. Wrinkles accentuated the smooth fullness of his cheeks, which in America had seemed rosier than they did now. I noticed how blue and alert his eyes were as he looked straight at me. When he smiled, wide, broad, and honest with a touch of impishness, his fifty years became five.

"Komm, da oben im Casino," he said in words that I could not precisely decipher but could guess at because he waved his hand with a gesture of invitation. Would we please come with him? His wife was waiting for us in a room above.

He removed his spurs, placed them next to his riding gloves on a high ledge as tidily as a man arranging his desk, and gave a half salute in the direction of a blond rider near the entrance of the ring who had been watching us from the moment we appeared. I saw authority shift from Walter to him. As we walked, the wall directly to the left caught my eye. Round medals, the size of a person's hand, covered every inch of available space. I looked carefully and saw the dates and names of German dressage shows. So these were the awards given out in this country. They must have been won by riders at this stable. Impressive, I thought and marched straight into Walter as he carefully wiped the stable dirt from the soles of his boots!

Back home, five months before, he had scuffed his boots on the doormat of my porch and I had bumped into his backside there, too. Once again, I didn't know how to say excuse me in German.

The words, "Enschuldigen Sie mich" were too much to remember. My head was so full of other thoughts. There was nothing to do but laugh, feel awkward and silly, and let the moment pass.

Russell and I climbed eight steps and followed Walter through a green door into the casino. The name "casino" made me think of Reno or Las Vegas, not the observation room of a riding establishment. Did spectators here gamble while they watched the horses? Apparently, a room with large viewing windows facing into the indoor ring was customary in Germany—ideal for clients, parents, and riders looking at horses for sale. It kept people from wandering into the ring and fitted in with their desire to gather and talk for what seemed to me amazingly long stretches of time. Conversation, as it is practiced in Europe, was a custom that I would get used to with time.

Stall Tasdorf's casino was tavern-like in its decoration: it was filled with hunting memorabilia and one wall was covered with horse pictures. At the far end was a bar and all along the observation window were cloth-covered rectangular tables set with fresh flowers where customers could sit and imbibe whatever they chose. The kitchen in the back served hot drinks, simple snacks and on special occasions, a slice of cake left over from a stable party the night before.

To my surprise, on entering the casino for the first time, I found *The Salute*, (the magazine of The New England Dressage Association) displayed on a table. As one of the editors, I had been responsible for this issue: I had written articles, gathered others and helped to plan its contents. How far away home suddenly seemed! How safe and predictable life had once been. I reminded myself that even if my courage was only the size of a single oat, I must take firm hold of it.

Kerstin, Walter's wife, was sitting at a table with a cup of coffee, waiting. I didn't know it then, but Kerstin would become vital to me in the year to come, lightening moments of discouragement and despair.

"You look just like your picture," were Kerstin's first words when she came forward to welcome me. I liked her right away. She was firm, straightforward, and not shy. Best of all, she spoke my language. She began by apologizing for her English, which she claimed not to have used since the year after she graduated from school when she worked as an au pair in England.

Like Louise, Walter's interpreter, Kerstin was Swedish, and she certainly looked it with her clear light skin, blonde hair, blue eyes, and younger-than-her-years face. Kerstin exuded the sort of loveliness and good health that made me think of clear lakes and forests with very tall green trees. She seemed out of place in the casino's still air laden with the stale smell of old cigarette smoke.

When Kerstin asked if we would like coffee, Walter said, "Ruhe," (calm down), in a tone of marital exasperation. Though I didn't know what he was saying at the time, I would find out soon enough—it was a word he repeated often. I would also come to see that these two had totally different human rhythms and I would wonder how they could get along. Even at this initial meeting, I was already aware of the difference between them. Walter pulled our chairs away from the table calmly, indicating for us to sit down. Kerstin remained standing, her empty cup in one hand, a picture of energy. I half expected her to run instead of walk in the direction of the kitchen to order Russell's hot chocolate, Walter's tea and my coffee. But, of course, she didn't.

The table arrangement left no question which seat was Walter's: the one with the arms. Even as we talked, I was aware that part of him remained out in the ring. Although his expression responded to everything we said, his attention seldom left the horses being worked in the arena. When his assistant, or "bereiter," rode up directly in front of our ring-view window and gave him a questioning look, Walter nodded briefly to him, expressing his opinion through the glass. Apparently, he was indicating to the young fellow that he had done enough for today with one horse and should get on with the next. Walter then pointed to his watch, meaning there was much to be accomplished before midday.

Russell was emptying his pockets of the paper-wrapped sugar lumps we had collected from the hotels and restaurants we had visited in France. The loot, although typical for most horsemen, represented outrageous thievery. The stable cook, coming to take our order, stared with the same pop-eyed expression as the stuffed owl on the wall behind her. "Guck dass an" (look at that), she gasped in disbelief.

"For Inca," Russell said to her, as if Inca's name would justify the situation.

"Ja-a-a-a," okay, she responded, still clearly disapproving.

"Stall Tasdorf is like a big family," said Kerstin, referring to the strong smells coming from the kitchen. I sensed that she was embarrassed by the hearty odors and needed to explain that the apprentices, or "lehrlingers," lived in rooms behind the casino and next to the kitchen and dining room. Normally, Walter and she ate breakfast and lunch with the stall's crew. However, today they would show us Neumünster and then the four of us would dine at an excellent fish restaurant next to the brewery. I imagined that Kerstin was the kind of woman who tried very hard to do everything not only well but elegantly, difficult when cabbage was cooking and potatoes were pan-frying only fifty feet away.

"But before you do anything, wouldn't you like to see Inca?" Kerstin asked.

Yes. I wanted that most of all.

Russell and I went out to find Inca in one of the two smaller buildings behind the main barn. Health restrictions had required that he be quarantined for ten days, and now he was waiting for a sale horse to move out and give him a stall in the main barn. I felt sorry for him when I heard he was the only horse out back, but Walter said there were advantages to his situation. The stalls faced the out of doors. The upper doors were left open. Horses living in the back breathed fresh air and had a view of the surrounding farmland. Walter reminded me that once he was moved inside, he would work and live indoors until late spring. I hadn't thought about such changes when I came here and wondered how it would feel for Inca to lose the freedom of going out in his field everyday.

Germans think in the most practical terms about their dressage horses. They view animals as investments of both time and money. If they are let out, which many are not, every horse is given his own paddock, meaning he is alone and in no danger of being caught by the flying hoof of another. Nor are they allowed to build up a head of steam and run madly about: a few bucks, a roll and a bit of a gallop are tolerated, but no more than that. Question an owner about these rules and you get an are-you-crazy look. Why would you allow a horse the chance to injure himself when you have put months, even years, into his training?

To me, however, these restrictions seemed strange. What about grass? I asked Walter. I'd always assumed several hours on grass was the best way to take care of a horse: it is good for the mind and good for the physical condition, the most natural offering in the world—therefore, the best. On this point, Walter was immovable: a half an hour of grazing was maximum, otherwise the horse ingested excessive water into the system causing him to become sluggish, dull, and fat. What could be worse for an athlete? Walter predicted that Inca would undergo considerable physical change, most noticeably in the neck, and would gain muscle throughout his entire body. He promised me that there was no need to worry, Inca would be quite content with his new regimen.

It was hard to believe him, but it was not for me to tell such an experienced man that Inca had an inner fire he might not suspect. That he could heat up like a kettle on a stove, then explode in all directions. How could such a horse possibly tolerate life in a stall with only one hour in the ring for daily training? Paddock time had been law in my barn forever. It was going to be interesting to see how my temperamental fellow would take to German life.

In our search for Inca's whereabouts, Russell and I came across a manure pile that was worth a photograph. We would have walked right past the heap if it hadn't been for the steam rising off its top. No odor assailed us, due to the cold. The mound, half straw and half manure, had been forked into a cement area as deftly as if someone was bent upon creating a layer cake. Friends back home needed to see this, I thought. On a later day, I would watch the neighboring farmer collect the pile and spread it as fertilizer on the surrounding tilled acreage. Walter would comment when he noticed my interest in his stable management, "Nothing goes to waste here. Everything finds a use in one way or another."

Then I saw Inca. My friend was half-asleep with his head hanging out of the box. He looked in our direction and studied us, not yet quite sure who we were. This was one of the dearest faces in this world to me. I had been thinking about him so often that my memory of him had faded, probably from overuse. Without realizing it, I had forgotten many of his fine lines.

It seemed as though years had passed since I had filled out Inca's health documents, obtained his passport, bought his ticket, packed up his black steamer trunk, blanketed him and driven down to Kennedy Airport in New York. The transport requirements stated that he had to be in the ASPCA shelter at least six hours before departure. I was hardly able to live with myself when I said goodbye to him, knowing that he was ignorant of what was about to happen to him. I anticipated that he might become extremely anxious during the trip.

Inca crossed the ocean in a Lufthansa airplane, traveling in a high-sided, wooden standing stall that was forklifted into the plane and rolled into place next to several others. Horses travel in what is called a pallet, a unit that usually contains three stalls together. The thought of all this was frightening, but I was told that horses do not seem to mind as much as you think they would. In fact, they are constantly shipped everywhere in the world for breeding and racing purposes.

Animal travel is considered quite safe. I had assumed I would have to sedate Inca, but I was told horses travel better when they have all of their normal senses about them. However, I was also warned that there is an ever-present danger that a horse may become frightened, throw himself down in his narrow box and not be able to get up again. True, attendants do stay in the cargo area in case of trouble, but often if there is a problem, a sedative does not work. And problems can be contagious: when one horse panics, he can cause all the rest to lose their heads and therefore it can become necessary to put the panicked one to sleep permanently.

Hearing about these possibilities caused me deep concern. "How often do these things happen?" I asked.

My shipping agent reassured me that he had never lost a single horse, so I signed on the pink sheet. There was no choice.

Inca's seven-hour flight landed him in Amsterdam, where he was picked up by the Holtzner Pferde Transport and driven to Stall Tasdorf. The entire trip, door to door, took just under thirty hours. I was kept informed all along the way. I wondered how horses can tolerate such an experience. But they do. And mine did.

Animal greetings are such spontaneous gifts. Most creatures come to you freely and openly, each in their individual way, like children. They don't make bargains or extract promises; all that matters is that you are there for them. When I said "Inca" the second time, he was instantly awake. Surprise crossed his face and then recognition. No sun ever came through the clouds in a more lovely way. His eyes glowed and then he leaned as far out the door as he could, trying to come toward me. But I wanted more of him. I made him step back and take his weight off the door so that I could open it, go in and hug him hard. He loved attention and as long as I would stand close to him, he would stand endlessly by my side. He was a true people horse—human contact was his goal.

Horses learn quickly that sugar comes from people's pockets. Inca's excitement reached a high pitch when he saw me put my hand deep in my pocket. His ears were bent as far forward as possible, signifying urgency and tension. I removed small bits of paper from the sugar lumps. The rustle aroused every fiber, made his lips and the tiny hairs that grew out from them quiver with anticipation. Clearly, he found my fiddling round with the treats hard to understand. How could I be so slow? Inca was running short of patience.

The stall Inca had been given was roomy, about twelve-by-twelve feet was my guess. It must have felt comfortable, even cozy to him with its deep bedding of straw. This was a luxury he didn't get at home, good quality straw being hard to find. I had always been sorry to have to use shavings. I missed the clean, sweet smell of straw and some of its other good qualities as well: a horse will snack on straw between mealtimes, which relieves boredom and gives him something to do besides picking up bad habits such as chewing on wood or tearing at his blankets.

I wondered if Inca missed other horses or friends at home, and I tried to imagine what he thought about hour after hour. Yet, though I worried, when I peered into his food bucket there wasn't an oat in sight, a good sign that he was handling the changes in his life. He might settle in more easily than I would.

We humans seldom stop a moment to reflect on the choices we make for the animals who serve us. We decide their careers without considering their natural preferences. I am sure that given a choice, Inca would much rather have been a jumper than a dressage horse. He told me this quite plainly when I first began riding him. We came upon a fence that had been erected in the arena, and he thought there was a chance we'd go over it. He couldn't wait to jump, and he had naturally good form. He snapped his front legs right up tight under him, rounded his back, and kept his hind legs out of the way. Jumping made him feel great. Of course, he'd charge toward the obstacle too fast if he were allowed to. His rider had to set the appropriate pace, understanding that Inca's behavior was due to the mercury of Thoroughbred temperament, because a horse, like a human, responds instinctively to that for which he has natural skill.

Whenever I'd congratulate myself about what a great life I was giving my friend, I'd have to be honest and guess that dressage must have felt just like school: repetition, exactness, geometric figures. Nevertheless, our work may well have been the wisest career choice for a fellow with Inca's build. He was a large horse, 16.3 hands, with the long slender legs of his breed, and compact, small hooves that were delicate and tender. Landing on a stone bothered him terribly. I don't believe he would have lived a quality life for twenty-three years if I'd let him pursue jumping as he wished.

The first time I met Inca, I could see within half an hour that he was talented in two fields. Alex Konyot had exhibited the horse's courage, power, and ability by asking his daughter Tina to ride him over obstacles that made me whistle in admiration. Minutes later and with a different saddle, Mr. Konyot mounted and showed me all the movements he had taught the horse. Right there was the knowledge, the discipline, the concentration, and the control I'd been seeking. Furthermore, every detail of Inca's body spelled refinement. No wonder I fell in love with him. No wonder Walter would say to me, "You are lucky if you own a horse like this once in a lifetime."

When Russell and I returned to the casino after our visit with Inca, I wasn't ready for sitting. I wanted to walk, run, ride a horse, fly like a bird, do anything but stay in one place. I had been so busy working, planning, and packing in recent months that I had given very little thought to what it would be like when I actually arrived. Now, I was like a motor in high gear, eager to explore my new world, but I could see that the Christensens were wanting to sit down for a chat. They seemed to have something in mind.

So we settled down to drink a "kannchen" (small pot) of coffee, two cups of blackness with Wagnerian impact. At last, Walter, sipping tea, revealed that he had important plans for my horse. He wished to discuss them with me through his wife. As she translated, he listened to every word, adding grunts as if her voice were his.

Kerstin began by saying how pleased Walter was with the way Inca and he had been working together in the short time since the horse's arrival. Inca's training was going so well, he wondered if I would let him ride my horse on the following weekend, the 16th of February, in the Neumünster Winter Dressage Show. She explained that this was one of the first important competitions of the famed German indoor winter circuit. The show grounds were only ten minutes away from Stall Tasdorf, so that getting there wouldn't be much of a trip. This competition would provide a marvelous opportunity for the horse to be seen and marked by the some of the best judges in the dressage world.

Walter heard my gasp of astonishment and misjudged it. Believing that I was disappointed not to be able to ride Inca immediately myself, Walter pointed out that his experience in the competition ring would actually help him to train me. But I wasn't even thinking of my own training, I had gotten no farther than my vision of Inca entered in a German dressage show. I was brought to a halt in disbelief.

Inca was not qualified to compete in Germany, but because of a special invitation by August Christian Horn, manager of the show, Walter could ride him as a guest, or "vorreiter" (first rider), for the morning showing of Intermediare II. The Intermediare II is a high-level test, one level less than the Grand Prix test ridden in the Olympics. The vorreiter rides the test immediately before the class begins as a reminder to the judges of the specific movements involved as well as the sequence that will be followed in this particular test. It is considered an honor to be a vorreiter, and he is also given the advantage of being marked without actually competing in the test. In effect, the vorreiter gets a trial run.

Judges are kings at a competition. Every score they give is important to someone. The five dressage judges of these highest levels sit separately and must mark everything that the test asks for exactly as he or she perceives it. Judges hope that their marks come reasonably close to one another. Nothing enrages a competitor more than big differences of opinion. Wide variations affect an audience as well as the entire atmosphere of the show. Questions flow: which judge is right? How can the same movement be judged so differently? Is there no standard? Are politics involved?

Walter's question, "May I show Inca?" far surpassed my dreams. I was amazed, "Yes, of course," I answered immediately. Studying Walter's face, I saw he was pleased. I also noticed that he looked more strained than he had in America. His hours of teaching and training were no doubt the easiest for him, but here at Tasdorf, he also had to cope with endless decisions and long hours, caring for both horses and people. He needed patience to listen to his riders talk endlessly about themselves and their mounts. I was beginning to appreciate what he meant when he said how much like a vacation being in America had been for him.

Russell gave me a nudge to catch my attention. "I'll bet you've never seen riding like this before," he said pointing at the viewing window. Even he, a non-rider, was staring into the indoor ring, visibly most impressed.

Ten horses were being worked in the ring at one time. Back home, that would have been too many for the space, but here no one appeared to be crowded. Every rider seemed to have a program or a plan he or she was working through. Each sat in the saddle as if glued. To my eyes, I was looking at a totally professional scene; no amateurs anywhere around. I took a deep breath and reminded myself to stay calm. This is what you've always wanted, I told myself, you've finally arrived at the place where you'll learn everything. You are looking at home plate. In the riders before me, I saw mirrored the images of my own future perfection. Kerstin stood at the window beside me to point out who was who. Tasdorf, she said, was an international training stable. The younger riders were the apprentices, the girl on the gray was from Denmark, the two other girls were both Swedish, the boy on the chestnut was from Holland, and the others were German.

Three mature women rode among them, training just as hard as the "lehrlingers." These ladies were among the customers who came to ride regularly every morning. I tried to imagine riding among them, but gave up my fantasy before anyone could notice I was off in a dream. Then, half bursting with enthusiasm, half afraid of the answer, I asked the question uppermost in my mind: "Walter, when will I ride?"

Walter and Kerstin looked at me with surprise. Had we misunderstood each other? Hadn't I just given Walter permission to ride Inca in the show? Of course. How silly of me. My logical self knew that at this time, with the competition so close, it would be best for Inca if Walter was his only rider. If I rode him too, it might be confusing for the horse and might upset the work the two had done in the last weeks. Walter and Kerstin were visibly perplexed that I could even entertain such a thought; they were not sure how they should deal with me.

I stood at the casino window pretending to concentrate on the ring while I sorted out my emotions. Which did I really want more: to see Walter compete my horse or to begin riding myself? I couldn't give up either. I wanted both.

It was shortly before noon and the casino was coming to life. The gathering customers didn't even need to place coffee orders, each one apparently asked for the same thing every day. The ladies were hearty and especially friendly in their greeting, the way people are after they have accomplished something they love to do and are feeling at peace with their world. Someone suggested we should add a round of drinks to the coffee, to celebrate my arrival and to warm our insides. A conversation started about handbags. I couldn't understand the discussion except for the general subject, but I had on my smile and I nodded along with the rest. Russell left to confirm his return airline tickets by telephone. Looking for something to do, anything at all to be part of the group, I reached for the champagne bubbling in the glass set down in front of me.

"Wait!" Kerstin's hand on my arm stopped me. "Don't start before the person who is offering the round of drinks. That's the custom here."

"Oh, I didn't know," I said embarrassed, "but I'll learn," I assured her. Turning my wristwatch around, I stole a glance at its face. At home, the time would be shortly before six in the morning. Friends who owned horses would be thinking about getting up about now and here was I, sitting in riding heaven drinking a glass of champagne.

It was in this mellow mood that I made up my mind about Inca. Why not be patient, I told myself. After all, although I had thought about him every single day, I hadn't been in the saddle for weeks. Surely, I could wait just a few more days and be rewarded with the pleasure of seeing Inca compete.

Competition

I n the week that followed my arrival, Walter worked with Inca, preparing for the big day at the Neumünster. Finally, at 6:30 AM on a clear Sunday, Russell and I were on our way to this renowned show.

We had no difficulty finding the sport hall, having ferreted out its location across the railroad tracks and just beyond the center of town the night before. The building's great cement body looked like a beached whale and a huge sign said, "Pferde Show," (horse show) in letters as big as workhorses. Cushions of air were under my feet that February morning; grabbing Russell's hand, I wanted to be a kid and skip with excitement. If my personal rainbow included steps to heaven, they would be made of cement and painted like the steps in the Neumünster's Holstenhalle.

We joined the crowd at the entrance and inched our way forward to the ticket takers. I counted almost as many dogs waiting in line as people. Their owners introduced their creatures to everyone around like favored children, often proudly whispering a small command. Instant obedience. The dogs' expressions showed they liked these moments. Being obedient brought them a tail wag's worth of praise and attention. I decided they were the most peaceful beings in line.

I found myself looking at the German people with new and appreciative eyes. "Don't you wish we could take our dogs around with us at home? I find it so companionable," I whispered to Russell. We wondered whether it was love or discipline that kept so many dogs standing quietly in a small area without causing a rumpus. I myself could hardly keep still.

"Be patient!" my husband urged, knowing that his suggestion would have no effect at all. Then he put a restraining hand on my shoulder, catching me red-handed crowding the people in front of us and willing them forward while maintaining a look of sheer innocence on my face. Not that there was any place for them to go except to shuffle six inches forward every half minute. "We'll make it," Russell promised. "There's time."

"But these folks are probably just spectators and don't have a horse that's about to show," I pleaded loudly, wishing someone would overhear me, understand English and say, "Oh, if that's the case, go on ahead."

Kerstin had told us that the Tasdorf "family" sat in the same section every year and would be easy to find. Once we'd gotten inside the bowels of the hall, Russell and I looked for letters and numbers on signs. The proper stairway was easy to find, and we popped out from the subterranean depths as eagerly as a pair of chipmunks emerging from a hole.

Climbing straight upwards the height of two floors, we found the Stall Tasdorf customers and their families in one cluster of seats and the lehrlingers sitting together in a row.

Kerstin was relieved to see both of her Americans. "You didn't get lost," were her first words. Seats had been saved next to her, and when she had arrived earlier with Walter she had obtained a program for us. "Where's Inca?" I wanted to know instantly, and she told me he was down in the warm-up area. She had been pleased to note that Inca was taking in the different sights and was acting neither upset nor nervous. Walter had planned to allow extra preparation time for them both, not knowing what he would be up against. He preferred working alone for the warm-up and had sent Kerstin to join the others. "It won't be long now," she predicted, "Dressage classes always begin on time."

Having never considered a horse show an occasion to wear town clothes, I was surprised to see that Tasdorf's young apprentice riders were quite formally dressed. Each boy sported a shirt, tie and jacket and had so wet-combed his hair that in some cases, lines of hair stuck together like rows in a newly tilled field. The girls had transformed themselves into young ladies in skirts or pant suits. I suspected their lapel pins and scarves might be on loan from Kerstin. It was plain to see that anticipation and appetites were running high. Food was clutched in every hand and youthful faces glowed.

Noting my observation of the group, Kerstin pointed out that some day, one or two of the apprentices might be lucky enough to head a business. "We try to encourage them to present themselves well," she said, "small details in Germany can make the difference between success and failure. Besides, it's important to present a good image for our customers and our stable too."

I could tell that she was proud of her young people. In a sense, they were her family, and she was particularly pleased that day. Apparently, Walter had lent out two neckties and a jacket. When the moment came to dress up, the town-style clothes that the boys were required to bring from home sometimes no longer fit. These growing youngsters, especially the boys, often found that the stable's steady hard work and solid food served three times a day furthered unexpected rapid changes in their bodies.

Russell and I took our seats quickly, aware that the spectators were unusually silent and respectful. They obviously knew a lot about dressage. When a mistake occurred, several thousand people groaned, and even though it was practically under their breath, the noise echoed like a roll of thunder. The spectators never clapped during a dressage test, but the recognition of a brilliantly performed movement sent out a shock of electricity that surely must have traveled right down to the ring.

Like so many birds lined up atop a barn roof, we waited high up in our tier for Walter's class to begin. Of course, Inca's name did not appear in the program, as he was "Hors concours": not in the competition. I wrote "Inca" in myself, making clear, intense, round letters for posterity. I had every intention of reading the program ten years hence and remembering precisely how I felt.

The overhead light shining down on the ring caused the sand of the arena to appear extraordinarily chaste and white. I found it a frightening stage, but as the competitors came through the passageway, they displayed a coolness that I envied. Their experienced behavior filled me with questions for Kerstin. I wanted to immerse myself in the entire experience from every side. Was the seasoned German dressage rider ever nervous in competition? Did she think he took a final big breath, as I would have, leaving the warm-up and entering the huge arena, or did one grow used to spaces like this? Could you feel those thousands of eyes fixed on you? What did she, Kerstin, suppose went through the rider's mind during the two or three minutes before the judge's bell rang?

Kerstin had ridden dressage competition herself but claimed an amateur status. She tried to answer me from the tales she'd heard from others. Every answer she gave boiled down to one: the true competitor shuts out every distraction and focuses his mind on riding the horse.

If he even notices the pots of flowers brought in for the occasion and placed around the twelve dressage letters, it is only in passing. That the ring he is about to ride in is 60 meters long and 20 meters wide with a low white fence surrounding it not more than .3 meters high is a detail that is as deeply implanted inside as is his name. However, if the floral arrangement set at the arena's in-gate gets in the way of the tight circle and left-handed entrance he had planned back home, he might use the minute or two before his entrance to decide on a viable alternative.

If there is one thing the seasoned rider is specifically aware of, it is the arena, the "vier ecke" or four corners, as it is called in Germany. As he waits at the arena entrance, he looks out at his testing ground, seeing the footing, dragged flat as a freshly made-up bed, and a centerline that has been raked by hand. Just in that second before entering the ring, he might picture himself and his mount presenting a fault-free straight entrance, a perfect halt, and beginning steps that would earn him a much sought after score of 10. Then, he hears the bell informing him that the judges are ready and the next eight minutes belong to him.

Vorreiter Walter Christensen and Inca were announced over the loudspeaker in tones I might have heard in church. Just as they appeared, a flashbulb flared from a distant corner. Flashes are not allowed, of course, but people occasionally disobey the rule. I instantly worried what the effect would be on Inca. A woman in a front row seat dropped her purse. Its contents fell out and rolled for a long distance. Men wheeled in barrels of beer for the drink concession behind us. Somewhere a metal door slammed shut. Two children argued. I had thought the hall was quiet when I sat down, but once Inca appeared all I heard was noise. Instinct urged me to hush people circumspectly, but no one beside myself seemed bothered. Kerstin's eyes were fixed straight ahead and Russell was leaning far forward in his seat. Walter and Inca circled the arena halfway down each long side as the competitors in the class before them had done. Tapping the rhythm of their gait on the program in my lap, I noticed that my fingertips had gone numb with excitement.

Inca took a good look at the flowers. Walter generously allowed him plenty of time. The pair of them seemed like toys way down there. So small. Even vulnerable. Yet, at this moment I was intensely proud of the two of them. I felt as if I'd swallowed a mountain.

The judge at the table behind "C" rang his bell. The sound system intoned, "Bitte beginnen." Walter entered at "A," halted and saluted. The chief judge rose, doffed his bowler hat and sat down. Russell looked over at me. I looked at him. We shook our heads. Who would ever have thought this? The test commenced.

The pair began softly, almost tentatively, as if Walter had asked Inca for that dance. They seemed to gain confidence as they rounded the far corner. When Walter asked the horse for more energy in his gait, he responded instantly. His series of bounds were round, full and big; the moment of suspension was a moment of ballet. Horse and rider held each other's complete attention as if by mutual agreement. In the half-pass, Inca floated laterally across the ring and Walter appeared to have made no effort to accomplish the movement. Together, horse and rider coursed around the arena as if on air. I could hardly believe that this was my Inca.

Because I had watched Walter train Inca in the stable, I had seen them achieve a sensitive, working connection, but he had warned me that there was still a lot to discover. If the test were not to go well, he did not wish me to be discouraged, because, he said, in competition anything can happen. The Intermediare II has twenty-five separate movements; each one following hard on the next. Walter rode every single stride. Kerstin said, "Good," under her breath several times, "all right" occasionally and then "not so good, but maybe the judges didn't see it," once or twice.

Then it was over. I was caught between laughing and crying. The crowd burst into applause; we clapped as hard as we could and stamped our feet on the cement floor. The test had been quite correct even if, in Walter's words, it was not "confirmed," which meant he had felt tentative moments. It had been what a vorreiter's test should be—a promising ride for a first time out.

The official Intermediare II class began and a stream of riders competed for hours. I told Kerstin that if we had a class at this level back home, we'd have been lucky to have six competitors. She allowed as how there were many more good dressage riders in Germany than in any other country. That morning, names that had become familiar through magazine articles in the States became real people to me. I watched Karin and Herbert Rehbein, Dr. Josef Neckermann, Klaus Balkenhol, Harry Boldt, Uwe Schulten-Baumer and dozens of others. I was thrilled with them all.

At the end of the day, Walter showed me the five copies of his test with judges' marks of 1 to 10 along with their comments. If Inca had actually been in competition, his points would have placed him seventh. Therefore, in a show of this quality, Inca had done extremely well. Unusually well for a beginning. As custom dictated, it was time to celebrate.

By nightfall, however, the Neumünster triumph was behind us, and a different reality grabbed me by the collar and shook me hard. No new adventure or distraction could put off Russell's imminent departure. Vacation was over for him. He must get home and sit behind his desk as head of the Ashland, Massachusetts, high school English department once again. The next morning, while the sky was still dark, we climbed into the car for the drive to the Hamburg airport. I had anticipated the trip and our last "good-bye" until I was worn out with emotion. In addition, I was fearful about finding my way home alone on an unfamiliar autobahn.

We stood together, bodies touching, in front of the Lufthansa check-in ticket counter. My world felt frozen: outwardly, I was trying to assume my new role, while at the same time my inner voice was crying out, "Why am I staying here alone?"

"Mother," my youngest daughter's voice came back to me, "this is your dream coming true."

I remembered too, Russell's words of encouragement, "You'll never be able to live with yourself if you don't take advantage of this opportunity," he had told me back home. "Think what a good rider you'll become. Besides, whenever I can, I promise to come and see you."

We watched as his suitcases moved away on the black conveyer belt; heard the loudspeaker announce immediate boarding in two languages. After a short walk to the gate, he hugged me for the last time. I felt the warmth of his skin, the roughness of his English tweed jacket, and then he stepped into the booth for his security check and was gone from sight.

There was no time to dwell on Russell's absence. The next day, Walter, Kerstin and I sat down to a second consultation in the casino. Inca had been invited to a show by Hermann Duchek, the Manager for the International Dressage Show in Holte, Denmark, a town just outside of Copenhagen. Once again, Walter asked my permission to compete Inca from March 7 to 11.

The advantage of this show was that riders would come from many more countries than had been represented at Neumünster. Inca would be measured not just by German standards, but by truly international criteria. Moreover, I would see Christine Stückelberger

The Ark. Our horse farm in the town of Harvard, Massachusetts. Walter Christensen's much anticipated clinic brought in horses, riders, and spectators from all over New England. Photo: Carole MacDonald

Preparing for our visiting German dressage instructor, Russell manicures the farm driveway. Meanwhile, I am in the kitchen preparing—as it turned out—all the "wrong" kinds of foods. See page 25 for more on our culinary differences.

Walter's first visit to Harvard: I'll never forget—he was sitting on this sofa in our living room when he popped the question (which of course had to be translated), "Why don't you and Inca come to Germany to train?" On the sofa left to right, Walter Christensen, Louise Nathhorst, and our most faithful clinic house guests, Denny and May Emerson. We were enjoying our evening after-dinner ritual— watching wildlife documentaries, which were Walter's favorites and an excuse to stop struggling with two languages.

Following his ride, Denny observes the other lessons. When Denny put his hands in his pockets and got a far away look in his eyes, I never knew whether he would come out with words of profound wisdom or one of his "great stories," (always humorous, sometimes shady—in both cases translations were attempted for Walter's sake). Background: one of our most regular clinic observers, Sally Swift.

*Clinic Time. Judging from the expression on Walter's face, he
must have been considering how much we riders needed to learn of
the ABCs of dressage and how much he could leave us with in just
two weeks of instruction. Photo: Bill Ewing.*

Walter is getting to know Inca and loves him. "You get a horse like this once in a life-time," he kept saying.

That very "special" Stall Tasdorf entrance gate in Germany. The center panel could be lifted upward to allow the passage of hay trucks and huge horse transports.

A bird's eye view of Stall Tasdorf. The horses were stabled in the long arm of the L-shaped building that surrounded the arena. The casino, the stable kitchen, the "büro" (office), and apprentice living quarters were in the short arm. To the lower left was the barn where hay was stored and Inca was first quarantined. Every time I went to see Inca, I was freshly impressed by the truly Germanic tidy state of the stable's manure pile in the concrete rectangle between the barns.

When Kerstin said on the phone that it had been snowing in northern Germany, she wasn't kidding. Here I am in my yearlong Ford rental, parked up against the snowdrifts at Stall Tasdorf. This compact wagon treated me well except when a red light appeared on the dashboard and I had to struggle to decipher the German instruction manual, especially difficult as mechanical problems are foreign to me even in English.

Walter and Kerstin Christensen. This is the couple that I grew to know well—"the team" that made Stall Tasdorf the respected and busy stable it was.

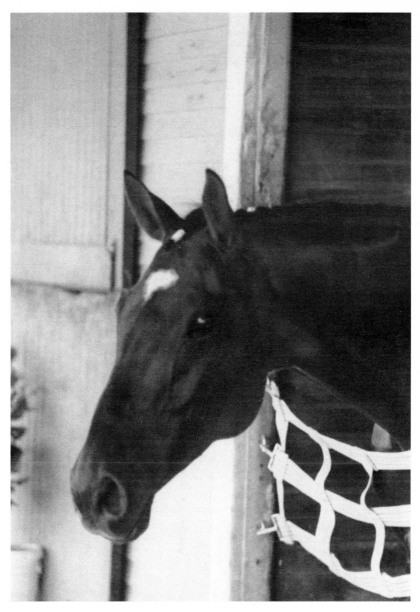

Is there any question about Inca wanting to say, "Hello there!" I've been waiting for you?"

Inca knew I would always arrive with a treat—apples, carrots, sugar, and grapes (grapes were his all-time favorite).

Looking down Tasdorf's long stable aisle where the metal doors clanged with an eerie sound when they were closed. Notice: not a wisp of straw on the floor, just the stable dog. Photo: Foto Huck

and her horse Granat—the pair that held the dressage World Championship title. Tales about Granat were legion. This wonderful bay Holsteiner was almost a fable to me, and had I known where to lay eyes on him, I might even have walked to Denmark on my own two feet.

Of course I gave Walter the permission he asked for, but it did mean there would be two more weeks during which I would not be able to ride Inca myself—two more weeks of preparation for Walter and my horse. So, for the duration, I curbed my impatience and thought about the upcoming trip. Walter told me that the Danish show would offer a large variety of breeds among its competitors. With a wide spectrum of types of horses to be scored, Inca might fare well, even better than he had before. The judges would have to weigh the power, elegance, and often impressive size of the popular European warmblood against the beauty, lightness, and spontaneity of the Thoroughbred. It was clear that Walter had hopes and there was no telling what might happen.

Competitors came from Finland, England, France, Germany, Switzerland, and all parts of Denmark. The only horse listed in the Holte program from the United States was Inca, misspelled "Inka." There were well-known enough names to send my excitement almost over the edge; Christine Stückelberger with Cameera, Kyra Kirkland and Piccolo, Elisabeth Theurer and Mon Cherie, Dr. Neckermann and Sunnyboy, Herbert Rehbein and Gassendi, Elizabeth Becker and Electron, Tove Jorek-Jorckston and Lazuly, Britta Iverson and d'Artagnan.

Three stalls had been assigned to Stall Tasdorf. One was for Inca, one for another horse and the third for tack, hay, grain, and lodging for Halle, Walter's Danish lehrlinger. Halle was thrilled to have earned the privilege of grooming for the weekend. Caring for two horses was, to her way of thinking, a light load. She anticipated watching much of the show. Still, the physical conditions of her job seemed to me to be trying. I could not believe how accepting she was of them, almost oblivious. Halle had the flu. The cement sta-bling area was cold enough to turn my words into smoky clouds. I couldn't help but think how soft and well cared for I was and won-der uncomfortably how in the world she would survive.

I discovered that the purveyors of food would not open their food stands until the competition began. Halle did not expect a motel room, a heated bathroom, a warm supper, a cozy bed or even a cup of tea. I offered to share some of my comfort. She shook her head firmly; everything was fine. She had brought along crackers, cheese, and an apple for supper. Extra horse blankets were available to cover herself on the narrow, folding metal cot. It was out of the question to leave two valuable horses and go to a motel room.

"You never know," she said, "I've heard stories about drugging and inflicted injuries at shows. Herr Christensen told me that under no condition was I to go off anywhere for too long." The conditions of Halle's apprenticeship were imprinted deep in her mind. In fact, they appeared to give her self-esteem.

Just as we were speaking, the door to the arrival and unloading area for horse transports was flung open. There was a blast of cold air and a shout sounding something like a German "heads up!" or "beware!" followed by a frantic clatter of hooves.

"It's Granat!" Halle pulled me back into the safety of her bed-room stall. Granat appeared on the scene head high (well above mine), mane flying, eyes wide, legs flailing, tail up. The man who was leading him with two lead chains attached to the halter was flying, too. Four metal shoes struck patterns of sparks on the floor. The poor attendant's legs could hardly move fast enough, but at least he was adroit at keeping himself out of harm's way. I was happy not to be standing in the aisle.

Granat's attendant was the brother of the horse trainer, the renowned Georg Wahl, and he accompanied the hard-to-control animal to almost every one of his shows. I was told Granat's rider, Christine Stückelberger, always rode the horse under the watchful eye of Georg, who was her life partner as well as her trainer.

The creature was a presence no one could miss. His passing down the narrow aisle caused Inca to canter in place in his stall, showing pink in the cave of his wide nostrils. He broke into a sweat under his blanket so that Halle had to take it off and replace it with a spare.

Unlike Neumünster, at Holte I was able to watch Walter in his warm-up. I could actually stand in the area as long as I wished and watch anyone I wanted. I felt as if I were backstage and I enjoyed the informality. Walter appeared to be well known among all the people. He spoke to almost everyone, and Inca walked neck and neck with so many famous horses, I was tempted to beg, "Stop and let me take a picture." But of course, I didn't. The respect and pleasure with which Walter was greeted made me proud to be with him. Although I knew no one and spoke to no one, I felt involved in the competition and walked around feeling extraordinarily happy.

Here in Europe, the fine, chiseled lines of the thoroughbred set Inca apart from the more round-bellied, large-rumped, wide-chested, heavier-boned, shorter-legged and muscular-necked breeds raised for dressage. True, he had already added brawn to his neck and the angular lines defining his shape had grown more rotund. Just as I was thinking he looked less like a racehorse than I'd ever seen him, Halle piped up, "Doesn't he look well?"

She stood next to me watching Walter go through a few of the more difficult parts of the upcoming test. I sensed that Halle wanted me to comment on Inca's braids, so I complimented her on them, counting thirteen, all even and tight. She had done him up like a professional. Having his mane braided in this fashion revealed the elegant arch of his neck, which in turn carried the eye to the rich, dark brown sheen of his coat. Halle had brought out the natural oils of his skin with intensive grooming. I wondered aloud how Halle could have worked quite so efficiently with such a feverish flush to her cheeks, but attention paid to her rather than to Inca irritated her, and she muttered, "I'm fine," as if her health didn't matter at all.

From my behind-the-scenes viewpoint, I was able to observe how different riders acted in those last minutes before they were to compete. A few became square-jawed and determined looking. They went into a kind of other-worldly trance and would have trampled me unseeingly had I been in their way. Others made the transition more easily. Seconds before he entered the ring, Dr. Josef Neckermann threw a kiss to his elegant wife as she stood on the balcony in her mink coat. She looked down at him with a radiant smile.

I knew something was about to happen when I heard the spectators titter; it was as if they had said, "Watch this!" A Dane whose name I couldn't pronounce rode into the arena wearing a top hat twice as high as anyone else's, much like the one worn by the cat in Dr. Seuss's children's book, *The Cat In The Hat*. When he reached the point of "X," he halted, made the traditional salute and, with a theatrical gesture, raised the top hat straight up in the air and brought it smartly back down on his head again. The crowd roared with laughter. He let the spectators know by the grin on his face that he'd had fun too. After that, it took the audience in the big hall nearly a minute to settle down to silence, but the rider continued riding his test as if he'd done nothing special.

By the time it was Granat's turn to appear, there wasn't an empty seat in the house. I felt the audience's anticipation. Even the concession workers had ceased their various duties and were standing behind the upstairs glass window looking into the ring. Georg Wahl appeared first, walking through the passageway that led into the ring area from the practice hall. It was comical, after all our anticipation, to see just a human being enter such a large space. Almost everyone knew who he was and that he trained Granat. That knowledge made him nearly as interesting as his horse. Wahl looked carefully around as if to assure himself that the way was sufficiently clear: no children running around, no dogs off the leash. Then, he beckoned for his student and her horse to follow.

Granat entered the competition area looking like a dragon, and Christine made him circle the outside of the arena as all experienced competitors do. I held my breath. When the pair flew past the judges' booths, she gave them a nod, then headed back toward the entrance of the ring. I listened to the loudspeaker announce their names. The bell rang. The pair went in at a powerful collected canter. I wondered whether Christine would be able to halt at the point of "X" in front of the judges for her salute—but she did. Taking the reins in her left hand, she very carefully dropped the other hand down by the horse's side in the gesture that is the traditional woman's salute. I held my breath. Would Granat stand still? Yes, for the brief moment required, he stood before the judges looking as classically beautiful as a living equestrian statue, then they were off. Movements and gaits braided smoothly into one another and Granat ate up distance as if it weren't there. I could see that Christine was keeping control with every fiber of her being.

I didn't watch the test. I watched Granat. He was a God on four legs. His blonde, elegantly petite rider sat on top of him with a kind of fierceness that convinced me that she too believed he was more than merely a horse. When they came to the final movements, at about the time most horses would be flagging, Granat attacked the difficult moments as freshly as though he had just begun. The crowd waited for the final salute, and then, as the two were leaving the ring, several thousand people as one unleashed their pent-up approval. Granat whirled. He looked wildly for a break somewhere, anywhere, to escape from the noise coming at him from every side. The spectators read his state of mind and instantly grew quiet. Not one of them wished to push glory into disaster.

Shortly, before Walter was to enter the competition area, Halle removed the white wraps that Inca had worn to protect his legs in the warm-up, and then toweled away his rivulets of sweat. Turning to her boss, she wiped his boots and asked him if she should take his whip. No, he told her, not yet. He would keep it until the bell rang. After that he simply waited in silence and I couldn't tell from where I was standing next to Halle whether he was concentrating or totally distracted. I did see, however, that he was pale.

"Is Herr Christensen all right?" I asked her.

"He's all right," she responded, but I thought I heard the implication of something more in her tone of voice.

The bell sounded. The announcer asked Walter to start. He began the collected canter. Let the whip drop from his hand. Rode a tight circle outside of the entrance of the arena, and then turning close by the "A" marker, proceeded down the centerline. Inca came to a good square halt. I took a deep breath of relief for both of them. After he had doffed his hat, Walter slowly gathered his reins. I thought he took too much time, but wasn't sure. They struck off at the trot. Something appeared different about the two, but I couldn't tell what. Every step seemed hard work. The first movement was a lengthening of the stride: Inca should have flown. He was good at that. But suddenly he lacked energy and his usual spark. The second movement required lateral work. Not easy, but in practice Inca had shown no problem. It was difficult to establish what was happening because the pair was almost performing well—and yet—

they weren't. I had never seen Walter be . . . what was the appropriate word . . . maybe, tight? The third movement required suspension. I could see practically none. Were Inca's brakes on? The test should have flowed from one movement into the next, should have been a song from beginning to end; instead it had turned into a litany of varied exercises. The root of the trouble lay not so much in the few small mistakes the pair made in the geometry of the test as in the loss of their harmony with each other. They'd had it in the warm-up and in the final seconds outside the ring, but from the moment they entered, it was gone and could not be restored.

The expression on Walter's face when the seven long minutes were over and we were standing back in the holding area told me the full story. Walter had had an attack of nerves beyond his control. "I lost Inca," he said flatly, "it's all my fault and I'm sorry."

Halle handed Walter several lumps of sugar. He patted Inca and gave the horse his treats. I saw that there was no anger in this man. He himself accepted the full responsibility for the way the horse had competed. They received the marks they deserved and I never did check out their standing in the class.

When we were away from other people and Walter had gone to change his coat, Halle informed me quietly that her boss had never found competition easy. Both customers and trainees at Stall Tasdorf were aware that riding in a show often made Herr Christensen physically ill. It was common knowledge that if he turned up as white as his shirt, the cause was "nerves and a weak stomach." The Neumünster Show had been a welcome exception. Perhaps he was more relaxed in the position of "vorreiter," or maybe, since the opportunity to show at Neumünster came at the last minute, he didn't have time for an attack of nerves, or again, his confidence may have stemmed from the fact that Inca was so new to him.

It never occurred to me that Walter could have such an extreme reaction to competition. I ached for the man; where previously I had elevated him to the role of my unique and special teacher, I now saw that like all human beings, he was vulnerable. Knowing what he did about himself, perhaps he had expected too much. Or maybe he had hoped one good experience would follow another.

I was deeply grateful that after such a difficult ride, Walter handled himself so beautifully. Sadly, and too often, I've witnessed competitors react to similar situations in abhorrent ways, frequently using the whip on their horses to vent their disappointment, humiliation, anger, and frustration. Such behavior was utterly foreign to a man like Walter.

The memory of the Holte show stayed with me for a long time. It brought a deeper tone to the colorful mix of beauty, talent, excitement, and glamour to which I had responded so completely. Suddenly my dream of riding looked different: complicated and serious. I wondered what the lessons in Tasdorf would be like, how I would do, and what else I might discover.

5

Square Pillows

Less than two weeks after my arrival, I moved from the Park Hotel in Neumünster to an apartment over a garage with two furnished rooms and a bathroom that Kerstin had found for me. It was here that I would learn about more than riding; I would learn about myself.

One of my hardest lessons would be learning to live alone. My growing up years had been a succession of boarding schools, camps, colleges, and then marriage. Although I was almost 50, it was not until I moved into that German apartment that I realized I'd been surrounded by people all of my life. I had no concept of having my own space or independently establishing a routine. Rooms as I knew them were for everybody, and who and what was in them was often determined by others. I had never given a thought to empty rooms—that is, empty of people.

As Kerstin and I hauled my suitcases across the black and white tiling of the entrance hall, I was nervous, feeling the weight of my thoughts. The few times I had thought about living in Germany, I had envisioned renting rooms from a friendly local family, speaking German, eating German food, learning German ways, duplicating the cozy kind of scene I was used to at home. I had never considered taking on a whole apartment and probably would not have done so, but single rooms close by the stable were scarce.

At the moment, I was embarrassed at feeling helpless, even childish, in comparison to Kerstin, who seemed almost frighteningly capable. I was quite sure if she'd known what was racing through my head she would not have understood. Kerstin broke into my train of thought with laughter as she hoisted her part of my load up the steep staircase, "Did you bring stones from America?" she asked. I didn't let on how glad I was to have brought so much of home with me.

The rooms I walked into cried out in their emptiness. Not wishing to seem ungrateful, I immediately murmured, "How nice," and noted that the furniture was "basic." Although I made no comment, I saw there was no color, no softness, no cheerful detail, no relief from starkness anywhere in the rooms. This was surprising, since the apartment was over the garage of a house that I found impressive, even lordly. It was one of the nicer brick houses in town, meticulously set among beautiful old trees and flowering shrubs. The apartment, however, was as impersonal as a packing box. If these rooms were going to be my home, beyond question they would need books, pillows, plants, and lots of me.

After Kerstin left, I opened my cases and began spreading myself out in the smaller of the two rooms, which offered a bed, a table, a desk, and a chest. The decor was limited to two tones, stark shiny white on the woodwork and a flat white on all plastered surfaces. I found my clock and placed it with some books on the bedside table. There were no pictures on the wall, so I spread out my photo album accordion style and took a long look at Russell, my three daughters, Katrina, Francesca, and Cricket, the farm, and the various animals. Then I arranged my letter opener, pens, paper clips, stamps, and writing paper carefully on the desk. The clothes closet took me by surprise. Such an enormous space was a discouragement. It was still going to look empty even after I'd hung up everything. For one minute, I felt as if I was losing my battle against emptiness, and then I remembered the old trick of arranging each hanger so that it hung slightly separate from the next, thereby making a closet seem full. I buttoned every shirt and blouse right up to the neckline and ironed out the wrinkles. Next, I placed my shoes below, each pair a bit apart as if they were soldiers standing at attention. When it came to the softer goods like sweaters, I made stacks of exact heights on the shelves and rolled up my socks into colored snowballs and placed them in a drawer. My riding boots, spurs, gloves and whip were taken to the hall.

The neatness I had created everywhere acquainted me intimately with my space and gave me comfort. I gained a kind of simple pleasure every time I looked at my handiwork. Later on, when feeling lost, alien or alone in my new world, the rooms, and particularly that closet, stabilized me, returning me to a sense of my own presence, bulk, and visibility. In general, my possessions took on double lives, acting as reminders of the past and reinforcers of the present. Even though these objects were inanimate, their familiarity imbued them with an almost home-like existence.

As I settled in, puttering around the apartment, evening fell and suddenly I became powerfully aware of something else that was totally unfamiliar to me—silence. There, on a side street where few cars passed, separated from my landlord's quarters by a long utility wing, my isolation was brought home to me. In the profound stillness of my rooms, I looked back on the pandemonium I had been accustomed to—the activities of my family, the demands of animals, the phone calls, friends, and endless projects—all took on a cherished glow.

Now, here I was, alone enough truly to hear, for the first time, the sound of just me. I listened in amazement, to the sounds I made, wondering just how one person could be so loud. When I investigated what it took to be noiseless—tip-toeing around, giving each piece of furniture a wide berth, even opening my tiny refrigerator gently like a thief—I still heard my own breath. Did other people's breathing dance around inside of them so frantically? When I silenced my breathing, I wasn't breathing at all.

Perhaps a radio would help, I thought. I wouldn't even have to understand what was being said, I'd hear voices and there would be music. And a phone; there was none, but perhaps one could be ordered. Ever since my days at school, I'd depended on this lifeline to the world. Before Russell's departure, we had promised each other the luxury of regular phone calls to take the edge off separation.

Only later did I discover that in Germany, telephones are hard to come by. Kerstin suggested that I use the one in back of the bar in the casino, which was used by the apprentices and customers. Or, I could drive to the Neumünster Post Office and use the public phone there.

My vision of waking up in the morning for a weekly call home or catching Russell for a long conversation before he fell asleep, was not to be. I laid pen and paper by my bed for making lists and faced the thought that I might even end up talking to myself.

On that first day, I decided to keep a snug rein on thoughts that might pop up and unseat me, even make me wish I could jump the paddock fence and . . . and . . . well, I never let myself quite finish that thought. Instead, I entered each day holding tight to the dream that had brought me to Tasdorf. By nightfall, I would fall into my bed, lay my head on the pillow, and surrender to the relief of sleep.

Pillows were a subject I could laugh about. I wrote about them in letters home, describing in particular my initial night's experience at the Park Hotel where my bed was endowed with two big, square pillows. When I first encountered these pillows I didn't know what to do with them. I tried to sleep on them both. Then I chose one and wrapped my arms around it. Tried cradling it. Tried flattening it. Tried plumping it up. Tried giving it two valleys and one hump. All the while wondering exactly what the Germans did. Smothering a giggle, I pictured Walter in his bed. After a night or two, rest eventually became so essential, I could have slept on the floor using an umbrella for a headrest. At last, I tossed one outsize square pillow away, hugged the other and got through the night in peace.

Thus, when I first saw the apartment and looked at the bed with its square pillows, I had a moment that was like the sun breaking through dark clouds. "Well," I said to myself, "that's one difference I've already coped with!"

Though living alone never did become easy, I found ways to make time spent in those rooms tolerable, sometimes almost pleasurable. And with each passing day, I saw how much I needed this apartment and my solitary hours within it to hibernate and to renew my sense of self.

I was probably one of the few people in Germany who didn't look forward to time off every week. I measured my time penuriously, feeling that each day that I couldn't ride or at least watch riding was squandered. I had the uneasy sense that such waste was unfair to those I'd left behind in America. Furthermore, I was restless and eager by nature and "free time" was a concept that was completely new to me.

At Stall Tasdorf, "Ruhetag" (rest day) was Monday. Hearing this,

I instantly decided that I would spend Monday mornings with my horse. It would be quiet in the stable, the perfect time to graze him, brush him, clip the coarse hairs on his nose, scissor the shape of his ears, thin his mane and maybe even trim his tail. At home, I brought Inca's tail fully to order each week, finding the grooming process peaceful and pleasurable, especially when not rushed. It reinforced the relationship between me and my animal and taught me a great deal.

It was not always so, however. Twelve years earlier, when my riding teacher Pamela Fitzwilliams arrived for our first lesson, she was aghast at how I readied my horse: I was simply giving him a once-over with the brush to remove any visible dirt. I remember Pamela stating in her British voice, a voice that instantly established rules, "A horse is not a coffee table. Dusting is not enough." This was one of my first encounters with the kind of real discipline that can surround horses, the sort of discipline I would later encounter at Tasdorf.

Pamela herself represented a good model for me. Never sentimentalizing her horse, she epitomized the deep pleasure a person could get both in working with an animal and in keeping their company. Watching her groom her own horse, Caper, was an eye-opener. She went about the process with elbow grease—using the whole of her long body, she showed me what a real brushing was, a kind of deep muscle massage in which several brushes with different length bristles and varying stiffnesses were employed. She disclosed the old British tradition called "strapping," rhythmically slapping the horse smartly over his neck, back, and rump with the flat side of a length of leather. "It's toning," she explained, "Brings out the inner oils from the body and builds muscle." This was the best way in the world, she claimed, to keep an animal fit. What she left unspoken was that she was putting in time with her horse and that just being with him was what she wanted to do.

When I asked Walter's permission to be in the barn early on Monday mornings, he looked at me with a perplexed expression on his face. Monday was "time off," he explained, speaking to me in exaggeratedly slow German and making broad gestures. Clearly, he wanted to be sure that I understood Stall Tasdorf rules. The routine was set, he told me the horses were fed twice instead of three times, their stalls were cleaned, and then they were left alone. For one entire day of the week, he said, horses should be left to themselves, disturbed as little as possible by people.

Although I didn't like it, Walter's reason for aborting my plans intrigued me. Maybe he's right, I thought, filled with respect by the care he was taking of the horses in training. After all, wasn't it to learn such new things that I had journeyed to Germany? I was trying to encourage myself, in much the same way that a mother encourages a child.

On "working" days, I soon learned to go about my business in the stable like everyone else. I telescoped my grooming into a daily fifteen minute session that got me into the ring on time for my lesson. When the ride was finished, I untacked, brushed Inca clean, and returned him immediately to his stall. With customers, apprentices, a stream of visitors appearing, and about thirty-five horses constantly in training, I always had the feeling that I needed to keep moving and find ways to make myself useful.

Like a typical American, I assumed that I could just pitch in and be part of the scene. In Germany, such an approach was not always acceptable, due to the scheduled and structured way in which life was conducted. I had not been at Walter's stable very long before I learned this cultural lesson in a way that was truly embarrassing to me.

One morning, my eye fell on the twig brooms that were used to clean the stable. The twigs are gathered at the stem end and bound to a broom handle, and what I found particularly intriguing was that where they splayed out, every one of them curved in the same direction. I really liked the resiliency of the twigs, the alive bounciness that made it seem as though the broom itself liked to work, and I wanted very much to try one out. Moreover, I thought that I might contribute to the labor in the stable by helping to clean the floors.

Walter swept the aisles every day. In fact, there was no job that the workers did that he did not do himself. More than once, I saw him give lessons in sweeping. "If you are going to do it . . . then DO IT," he'd proclaim, and then off he'd go, broom in hand, sweeping the passageway spotless. Afterward, he'd hand the implement to the apprentice with a nod that meant, "Here, your turn."

I suspected that Walter picked up the broom for several reasons. One, to escape from someone who wanted to talk at him. Two, to think some matter through quietly off by himself. Three, because he honestly despised dirt.

Naturally, I wished to please my teacher and to show him that I, too, hated dirt. Sweeping, I thought, would be the perfect way to demonstrate how much I appreciated Tasdorf. So, one day, after I had put Inca away, I picked up the broom. To my surprise, I found it heavy, heavier than a corn broom. The handle sat well in my hand, giving a feeling of substance and balance in spite of its twiggy bend. After a few moments, I established the proper motion to work with; it helped to picture myself out in the fields cutting hay with a scythe. The wooden broom was exactly the right implement to go after sand and dirt on rough cement and I was thrilled to see the aisle become spotless. Returning the broom to its appointed spot, I went on to clean tack.

Suddenly a furious shouting rang out. A man's voice. Walter. The sound of him reverberated through the stable like an alarm bell. The lehrlingers stopped what they were doing and came running. The riders in the ring halted instantly and turned toward the door. Customers, sensing commotion through the sealed windows of the casino, stood up and came close to the glass, "What's wrong?"

"Who has done this?" came the roar.

As soon as I could put the saddle soap down and dry my hands, I came out of the tackroom to see what the excitement was about. I had to jostle my way through the gathering of bodies to get in the front row.

Walter was standing like Napoleon, boots wide apart, just inside the ring.

There, at his feet, was the sand, dirt, straw, and dust that I had gathered in the aisle and swept into the ring. My leavings lay like a fan before the shiny toes of Walter's boots. The atmosphere was stone heavy.

One by one, the apprentices shook their heads and turned away. "Not me," each one said. Finally, I was standing there alone.

"I did it, Walter."

"Du!" (you).

Walter heard me but was unable to forgive me. He seemed to find it impossible to fathom my logic, or perhaps my lack of it. How could I ever have done such a thing? Think what would happen if everyone swept straw into the ring. How would it look? The ring was our work place, he pointed out. Straw was meant to be picked up and deposited in the muck bucket in the far corner.

At first, I was angry that I had been treated in such a way; from my point of view, I had been humiliated in front of everyone. But as I thought further about the incident, I realized that for Walter, details in stable management were not personal but functional. It had been my bad luck to make a mistake.

Naturally enough, the question of cleanliness didn't stop with the ring. It took on forms and facets strange to me. Walter's view of cleanliness and his meticulous attention to every detail struck me as picky, small, and not always necessary. However, I put down such thoughts as not worthy of the "higher education" I was getting. All the people who rode at Tasdorf fell under Walter's inspection. He saw everything: a missing sleeve button, a twisted rein, an animal's foot that needed shoeing, a person's expression, and of course the horses' training. Not that he was intrusive. He was simply there, observing. "Wait a minute," he'd say, "That doesn't look right."

This "it doesn't look right" approach had its effect and influenced us all. I tried twice as hard to be aware of everything going on around me and was especially careful to prepare my horse and myself. Perfection became everyone's game. To my amazement, I discovered that it was considered good fun and fair play for any one of us to point out another person's sloppiness. This was one of the few ways, during my stay in Germany that I perceived everyone to be on an equal footing.

One morning, I happened to be watching one of the customers enter the ring. Before she had even put her foot in the stirrup to mount, I heard a meaningful "Oh-h-h-h" from Walter's assistant. In a minute, I saw what had caught his attention. The lady had not removed one long piece of straw from her horse's tail. She was immediately reminded of the price for such misdemeanors; Tasdorf tradition decreed that straw in the tail cost a round of drinks in the casino for the entire crew, clients included. The woman laughed good-naturedly as did Walter's assistant, who was pleased with himself, and both took the incident as a joke.

It occurred to me that such an expenditure might not be taken as lightly by an apprentice as by one of the customers. How right I was. Not long after, a lehrlinger said to me, raising her eyebrows in knots of concern, "You'll see. I'm never going to get caught. I could-

70

n't afford to buy for everyone." And for the whole of my stay at Tasdorf, she never made that particular mistake.

From my first day at the stable, I was impatient to begin formal study of German, and Kerstin quickly arranged for me to have private lessons twice a week with a German teacher who lived right in the village of Tasdorf. "Don't expect a college professor," Kerstin warned me. Frau Kunze had taught young people for many years and was in her first year of retirement. She was tutoring one or two students for high school and college preparation and had time to take on "the American."

The first day that I met this intense sparrow of a woman, her presence literally pushed me toward the lesson table in her living room. I was told in which chair to sit. After a few suitable moments arranging pencils and papers, Frau Kunze drew a long audible breath and faced her first English-speaking pupil with a zeal that made me move my chair four paces away, pretending my long legs required more room. I soon discovered that though my teacher was a mite hard of hearing and a bit over-zealous, she was as kind as anyone I'd ever met.

Frau Kunze talked straight at me too loudly, but most distinctly, for one and a half-hours. She gazed at me intently the whole time and pursed her lips forward so that they came away from her teeth and could enunciate freely. The upper lip had a few tiny hairs on it that shone in the overhead light when Frau Kunze pushed her lip upward under a slightly sharp but still authoritative nose. I leveled my gaze straight back at my instructor. To look away even for a minute might be considered inattentive. The thought crossed my mind: "Here we are, two birds in a bird house. I'm the one being fed the worms."

"We will not speak one word of English at our lessons," she

informed me in German, and talked on without a break until she looked at her watch and said, "It's time to stop." My head ached. No one in my life had spent as much time talking to me in German and for some reason that I couldn't fathom, I'd understood practically all that she said.

I took my written work assignment and a children's book with as many pictures as text back to the quiet of my apartment. She instructed me to buy Duden's Dictionary, do my homework in pen, and take the time to write clearly. Frau Kunze found my handwriting illegible and asked if everyone in America wrote the way I did. I admitted that after I finished my formal education, I had developed my own style. The expression on her face told me that from that day forth I was to go back to big, round, open, legible letters just like hers.

In no time at all, word got back to Kerstin Christensen that Frau Kunze was pleased to be teaching the American lady. She referred to me as my Mrs. when she talked about me in the little village. I knew that she took my education very seriously. Often, my lesson began with food of some sort. I was given a piece of cake, a cup of soup, a taste of this or that. "You *must* try this," she'd say, all a-twitter, as I came up with excuses that she refused to hear. She suggested outings together. I sampled herring where it was a specialty, sat in on a wedding ceremony (uninvited), attended a local fashion show, and visited a textile museum and several historical spots, all the while being lectured non-stop by a voice that carried at least 300 yards. We were stared at unabashedly by anyone around. I pretended not to have any idea we were cause for notice.

During our first months together, my teacher did little to prepare me for the social situations I was facing. We began our study with a steady stream of very easy-to-read books. I learned that the rooster on her side of the ocean said "Kike-riki" and the dogs, "Wau-wau."

Then we moved on into the rest of the animal nation, now depicted with smaller pictures and more lines of advanced text.

It was natural for me on the Monday day off to visit the small zoo, know as the Neumünster Tier Park. I had gained new knowledge about its inhabitants through my reading, it was a comfortable way to pass the hours, and I enjoyed getting the exercise out-of-doors. Most of all, I loved the creatures who came right up to the bars when I practiced my new vocabulary trying to talk to them. Late one night when Walter, Kerstin and I were leaving a restaurant where we had dined with some visitors, Kerstin asked me if I had enjoyed myself, in spite of the fact I hadn't dared to say a word. "Right now," I told her, "I get along best at the zoo."

Gradually, Frau Kunze and I approached other subjects: my husband Russell, her husband Ewald, my three daughters, her son, my life in Germany, and her vacations. Frau Kunze loved to talk. I sometimes had to remind her that I needed to talk too. High on the list of her conversational priorities was the ever-continuing subject of birthdays. In Germany, birthdays are considered major occasions, public property, more important even than national holidays.

Frau Kunze's harping on birthdays should have forewarned me that I might not be able to hide my own upcoming birthday. When I brought up the subject of birthdays to Kerstin and told her that Frau Kunze had already invited me to hers almost a year from then, Kerstin showed me the birthday diary she kept that included all of her family, her friends, the workers in the stable, even her dog and Mannix, her horse. "What about you?" she asked. "When is your birthday?"

"Friday," I admitted. It was then Wednesday.

She leapt at the fact like a cat on a mouse. How unthinkable of me to hide a birthday, and my fiftieth at that! No question but that it was cause for a major celebration. Right then and there she invited me to my own party. Such spontaneous planning was typical of my new friend: she was always happy when there was a party to think about, eager for places to go and forever wanting to make things happen.

At ten to five on April 24, I left the refuge of my apartment and wandered slowly up to the casino, dressed, as she had suggested, "a bit elegantly." The tables had been pushed together to form one long length. Bright tablecloths, vases of flowers, colored napkins, and four huge cakes transformed the room into a place of celebration. Everyone came in and we took our places. I was dismayed to see that I was to sit at the head of the table and sighed with relief when Kerstin put herself next to me. I knew I could count on her to laugh and talk in her vivacious way, making it seem as if this party was the most special two hours of the entire year. For all of Frau Kunze's help, I still could not come up with small talk. The entire staff of Stall Tasdorf was present, including the cook. Walter was late.

"Oh well," I thought, "he'll be along," half wanting him to be there and half wishing that he might not feel duty-bound to come. I knew that Walter really wasn't a party man, but this was his territory, and I knew too, that he'd walk a mile for sweets.

In time, he arrived. Tea with lemon, an ashtray, and two of the cakes were placed before him. "Schwartzwald Torte! "(cherry cake) Kerstin!" Walter's voice rang out like a hammer on an anvil. "Du weist, ich hasse Kirchen," (you know I hate cherries). He shook his head in sudden misery like a little boy, shoved his chair back and declared that he absolutely could not eat cherry cake. He eyed each one of us with challenge in his eyes, as if we had created the hateful fruit ourselves.

The sound of forks on plates and all the other noises of eating and drinking had became noticeably louder. The young people ceased talking and looked steadfastly down at their plates. The cook quickly jumped to her feet, rescued the lemon cake, the cinnamon apple cake and the mocha-chocolate cake from the other end of the table and removed the offender as if the cake itself had been at fault for being there. Kerstin launched into a new subject.

I was stunned. My previous feelings of paralysis about my German social skills ebbed away, and were replaced by an enormous disappointment. Looking down the table at all the faces, I could tell that the young people hadn't liked the scene any more than I did. For several moments, if I could have spoken for us all, I would have said we felt let down and leaderless.

The teacher we'd all come to respect, the man some of the young people looked up to as a second father, the mentor they turned to for help in planning their futures, the master to whom I was devoting a year of study, had become a child—a rude, self-involved, unhappy child.

So unexpected was Walter's tumble from the heights to which I had elevated him, that I could not forgive him in a sane, easy way. That night, as I lay sleeplessly mulling over the implications of his behavior, more and more questions began to arise for me. Did the master's guise hide a spoiled man-child? What else might be hidden? The incident of the broom came back to mind—should I have considered it a warning? This streak of unpredictability in Walter's nature concerned me deeply. Would it show up in the ring? Get in the way of his expertise? Had I crossed the ocean only to find myself with the wrong trainer after all?

By morning, I was wondering if I could learn from a person I was no longer sure that I admired or even trusted. As I reviewed the scene yet again, I began to think about the reactions of the apprentices and Walter's "bereiter." These young people had been with him for a long time—they knew him better than I did. Even before my party had ended the previous evening, they appeared to have put aside the incident, forgotten it and forgiven him. Were they perhaps wiser than I?

Clearly, student idealism had pushed me to want perfection from my master teacher. In a way, I'd thought I'd found it. But was such a concept useful to me or fair to Walter? Stepping back from my emotions, I asked myself a number of impartial questions: Had Walter disappointed me as an instructor? No—I could not think of a single occasion. On the contrary, my admiration for his teaching abilities was increasing almost daily.

Had he been a steady, thoughtful, and aware human being as long as I had known him? Without question! In fact, it was these very characteristics that had drawn me to him in the first place.

Given all of his unusual and positive qualities, I realized that I could easily allow Walter a moment or two to be less than his best self, without any blame or concern. I didn't need a God or want one.

Early Lessons

The morning I first mounted a horse at Stall Tasdorf, I'd been in Germany eighteen days. Putting my foot in the stirrup and mounting the horse framed itself in my mind as an event. Not an achievement, mind you, more the notion, "At last! I've begun." Of course I was wrong. I had, in fact, been learning from the moment I had arrived but, being a physical person, I thought of learning in terms of being on a horse. The prior eighteen days had given me more than enough time to build up a case of both excitement and anxiety. Waiting to begin had been an Olympic test of patience that I hoped I had survived with sufficient grace.

I had seen dawn drive out the darkness that Tuesday and had risen especially early so that I could dress with the care I might have taken when going to a good restaurant for dinner. My models were the ladies I joined for coffee in the casino, who appeared every day fully made up, wearing shirts with creases pressed sharp as dressage whips and sweaters that always looked new. The previous evening I had laid out what I intended to wear and buffed my boots to a gleam that I hoped would elicit comment. When I arrived at the stable, in keeping with my mood I parked my car much more precisely than usual, and full of joy, entered the stable door. How long I had dreamt of this day!

However, the appointed hour did not turn out as I expected. A horse I had never noticed before was brought into the ring. Was this horse for me? Walter explained that an unexpected matter had caused him to change his plans and ride Inca himself very early. Deeply disappointed that I wouldn't even see my horse work and surprised that I wasn't to ride him, I asked, "How did it go?" Whatever his answer was, I never heard it. I was too busy struggling with the rising tightness behind my eyes. I forbade myself to cry.

"Gut," (good) he said, nothing more. Then I saw that I was to get on the horse in the ring and be put on the longe line. The longe line, I thought indignantly, was kindergarten work. I didn't consider myself a beginner but rather a person who needed to learn the right way to ride dressage. Should I inform someone in the stable that I had been in competition at home last October and did not need to be treated like this? True, I hadn't won my high-level class, but I'd placed 7th against a solid field of professionals and team members in a large class that had run most of one morning. Perhaps I needed to reiterate some facts to Walter.

Thinking more highly of oneself than one has a right to had no place in a school such as Tasdorf. Whether Walter was simply unaware of my attitude or chose to ignore it, I never knew. In Walter's lexicon of basics, longeing was the primary "A" in the alphabet of learning. It was the foundation upon which all further attainment rested.

Walter explained to me that as his first step in training, a rider is placed in the correct position and learns the correct seat. I duly swallowed my pride, got on board my assigned horse, and shortly realized the wisdom of his words. Back home I had been put on the longe on occasion, but never with the focus and continuity I now experienced.

At Walter's orders, the reins and stirrups were taken from me. This, I was reminded, was the most effective practice for obtaining the correct seat. I was instructed to sit squarely on my saddle, drop my legs down as far as they would go, sit up tall, and breathe. There was no need to think of anything other than the correct body alignment and staying in balance with the horse, because in longeing, the control of the horse is handed over to an assistant. This "director of activities" holds the lengthy canvas longe line in one hand and a long whip in the other. He works the animal in a circle around him, using voice commands, subtle tensions on the line, and occasional flicks with the whip. You can see this kind of exercise in circuses, usually executed by a team of equestrian acrobats.

Gradually, (and it takes time) I was able to feel the way I gripped with my knees, allowed my legs to ride up, leaned too far forward, stuck my left elbow out, raised both shoulders and put my chin out, to name only a few of my discoveries. A half-hour session riding the three gaits, lengthening and shortening the steps within the gaits, making transitions, and practicing several body exercises to induce relaxation was as concentrated and complex a training as I have ever been put through. Old habits were rooted out one at a time and new ways began to flourish like spring corn. Some commands I heard were as body encompassing as "Straighten the spine," while others were minute, "Move the little finger." What amazed me was that whether or not I could maintain them, the corrections always made my riding feel better, even natural, secure, and certainly stronger. I wondered why I had ever sat differently.

I had read that many Europeans began dressage training in this manner. So that I could see my goal, Walter showed me pictures of the correct classic riding position in his bible, *Das Gymnasium des Pferdes*, (The Training of the Horse), by Gustav Steinbrecht, (a book that at that time was not translated into English). Yet, as important as it was for me to find the correct seat, he made nothing special out of my search. Perhaps he knew that focusing too intensely on my lacks would not hasten my discovery, and that someday the right things would simply happen. "To sit is so natural," he said with a smile that suggested I be patient. "Just sit as if you are sitting in a chair."

I studied my teacher closely until I saw what he meant. Some people sit *on* chairs, others *in* them. Walter definitely sat *in* his. He sat in such a way that if an earthquake struck, shifting the floor and the chair, Walter would not only have remained in his chair, he would have moved *with* it. Watching him, I understood viscerally a major equestrian tenet: moving with a horse, with his every stride, is the result of a deep seat.

Few people are like Walter; few come to riding with a natural seat. What is easy for some is complicated for others. It doesn't take trained eyes to spot someone who has such a gift. It's obvious, pure, and "simply right." The rider is never left behind by the horse, never gets ahead of him, but always stays with him. The art is then artless, the way it should be.

One day, I was finally presented with Inca. At first, I was excited—whispered to myself, "It's him. It's really him!" Then I noticed that my mouth had gone dry and I could hardly take a breath. A lehrlinger held him still for me to mount, and as I lifted my foot into the stirrup, I felt surprisingly awkward, even unbalanced. Giving a hop, I got aboard—and there I was in my own saddle. We walked into the arena. I tried to sit heavy, look around, loosen my jaw, and find a smile. But all the time, I felt oddly out of sync with my old friend. Where was that glorious moment I'd been dreaming about, I wondered, where was that easy, beautiful first ride on my own horse that I had originally envisioned? As I went into my first working trot, I began to realize how my focus had changed and to understand that there were many important steps I would have to take before my idealized picture could become real.

For the next three months, I remained working on the longe line several days a week, riding either Inca or a series of other horses. Around and around I went in a circle about the size of a nightclub dance floor. Every time I was given a new horse to sit on, I noticed that I was so tense I could hardly think. Without the reins or the stirrups, I grabbed the horse's mane or put my hand under the front of the saddle and held on for dear life. Periodically, I'd chastise myself. How could I have such intense reactions when I was on a prescribed circle, unable to go anywhere? Why was I so frightened?

The answer of course, lay in the fact that I was forgetting Walter's "ABC." Thus, when I was given a young horse chock-full of energy and unexpected leaps, I gave the other riders in the ring a "performance" they thoroughly enjoyed. They laughed. I didn't.

Assigned to instruct me on the longe was Marin, the smallest apprentice in the barn. She may have been tiny, but she was as fierce as anyone twice her size. Marin convinced the horses they'd better respect her and step lively or else they'd find out what they should have known in the first place. Marin was one hundred percent serious about wanting to make her horses think about work when it was time to do so. She also wanted me to respect every exercise we did and to maintain total concentration.

I was to stop hanging on and learn to trust my body's instinctive ability to stay with the horse. It's hard to dare this, however, when your horse puts his head down so low you're sure he'll either step on his lower lip or grab the occasion to buck you off. Marin put on the face of a headmistress. Even though I was thirty years her senior, during those long moments, she overrode my fears and I was her charge.

We walked, trotted, and cantered; changed gaits in swift succession; practiced transitions. My legs grew longer and I sat taller. I began to feel the sides of my horse and knew precisely where he placed his feet and whether his stride lengthened or shortened. I sensed my buttocks widening and softening, found I had a pair of sitting bones deep inside that could telegraph instant messages to me. As a test of growing awareness, Marin would ask me to tell her the exact moment when the horse's inside hind foot stepped under his body. She saw to it that I practiced saying, "Now!" until I got it right. I was learning that my attention had to become double-barreled, always including myself and my horse.

When Marin returned to her family for a ten-day holiday, I was placed under the care of Halle, the Danish lehrlinger who had explained things to me during Inca's competition in Denmark. Walter gave her specific instructions to help me progress in my riding. The basics remained the same, only now the emphasis was on transitions. The first time Halle asked me to bring Inca down from a canter into a walk without saying "whoa," I wondered how I'd accomplish this without reins. "Sit deep and heavy," she told me, "Slow your body down." I followed her instructions and steeled my mind to think "slow-w-w-w-w-w," hoping my horse would get the message.

"You see!" she said triumphantly when Inca settled to a walk, visibly pleased with herself and the two of us.

Here was precisely the example Walter had been wishing for me—clear evidence of the influence of the rider's seat. We repeated details over and over again until the patterns of my response began to be reliably correct.

I grew to appreciate the simplicity involved in having neither stirrups nor reins nor the responsibility of my animal. Longeing broke down the separation between me and my horse. Some moments were delightful. I felt like the child who, while learning to balance on his two-wheel bicycle, suddenly finds he can stay upright and still keep going. "Look, Mom, no hands!" he shouts.

Finally, after this initial period of working solely on the longe line with one or the other of the lehrlingers, lessons with Walter were added to the learning process, and suddenly, Inca began coming up with surprises for me to manage. I suspected that they were his reaction to the new discipline in his life. When I rode him in the warm-up, Inca would look for something, almost anything, to give him an excuse to be startled: a spot on the wall, a footprint on the ground, a pile of fresh manure, or someone standing in the doorway. He would snort and became distracted and stubborn. With a wild horse's shrill whistle, he would claim his right to independence, saying, in effect, "I am going to do exactly what I want to do!" In the ring, minutes would often feel like hours, with Walter's voice growing steadily more insistent. "Do something!" he'd call out. "Ride a circle! Anything!" Meanwhile, Inca's head would be high as a camel's and his body frozen. I knew, of course, that he should be reaching down for the bit, loosening his body, and growing round. Yet whatever I did, during those first warm-up moments he would inevitably hold himself against me.

Thanks to Walter's tutelage, the horror of these ineffective warm-ups did not last forever. By the time I had been under his instruction for a month, I was able to devise a plan that stopped Inca from plunging ahead with ideas of his own and persuaded him to listen to me. The strategy I developed was centered on flying changes of lead. Flying changes are like switching the leading leg when dancing the polka step. Of all our dressage movements, flying changes were

Inca's favorite, so I asked for them often, as an incentive. Immediately following the changes, Inca became more obedient to my directives. Because of his Thoroughbred build, the movement was easy for him and he therefore executed it with great pleasure. All he had to do was fling his long Thoroughbred legs deep under his belly without any visible effort whatsoever. I, on the other hand, hoped that the ease with which he accomplished this maneuver wasn't too obvious and that I'd be admired for having made it all happen with such panache. Flying changes made Inca inordinately proud of himself. With each stride, he would make a sound like a frog's chug-a-rum, asking everyone in the place to take a look. Amused by Inca's directives, Walter used to smile appreciatively and say, "He really is a show off!"

Of course, the road to mutual understanding was not without bumps, and we advanced in fits and starts. I had not expected this slow rate of progress and was frustrated until I came to terms with my impatience and understood this was the reality of learning dressage. As might have been expected by a more experienced horseman than I, Inca had repeated spells of resistance in the beginning. The first of these was the longest. It lasted about a month, during which time he refused to give in and follow commands. For example, he would not bend to the left as much as he did to the right. Under Walter's influence, I began to notice that bending his body wasn't easy for Inca. Moreover, he was being asked to re-balance himself and use himself in many kinds of new ways. I began to realize Inca was doing hard, hard work. On some days, all he had to say for himself was, "I'd rather not!" His frustration expressed itself in rivulets of sweat. To prevent the reins from getting so wet they would slip through my gloves, Walter would summon a lehrlinger with a sweat scraper to the ring an extra time, once in the middle of the lesson and again at the end. By the second month, Inca's resistant spells with me gradually grew shorter, until in some cases he would hold out only for a matter of minutes.

At last, I was learning to ride. Nevertheless, on the days when the horse and I did not work well together, it was hard to view my longe with Marin or Halle as anything but humiliating. Had I come to Germany simply to work under them? I imagined reasons that put them at fault for bad days, making excuses for myself.

Most of all, I resented having my awkward moments occur in plain view of the entire stable and especially everyone in the casino. Why was I required to longe precisely when so many people were around? Being longed clearly singled me out as a beginner. I noticed that other customers were seldom longed, and felt that the exercise was reserved especially for me and the newest apprentices. It was not until almost a year later, a few days before I left Germany to go home, one of the ladies in the casino remarked that she wished she had been put on the longe the way I was. She had reached a plateau in her riding and needed to break out of it and progress. "Don't you feel you gained a lot?" she asked, and told me she was planning to bring up the subject with Walter. Never once had I guessed that I might have been envied my longeing experience; how wrong my assumptions proved to be concerning the thoughts of others!

In those early months, while I was working with Marin or Halle, Walter rode Inca almost every day for at least part of the hour. Inca's demeanor showed that he knew he was a pupil too. His eyes had taken on the serious intent of a graduate student, and like me, he had both good and bad days. The bad days were times of resistance, when he continuously said "No!" to moving forward or to working on whatever Walter would ask of him. There were times when Inca's energy level decreased, especially by the end of the week. Sudden changes in the weather influenced his attitude enormously. Overall, however, the dailiness of intensive training kept him involved. Matured him. If Inca were a human pupil, I'd have described the change in his behavior in just a matter of a few weeks like this: "He sits right down at his desk now, and without gazing off into space, promptly gets out pen and paper. He knows why he is there and settles down to work."

I wondered if he thought about his work afterward, the way I did. Walter treated Inca as if this were so. "Let's put him away now," he'd say from time to time, "let him think about it."

Those two shared a beautiful respect for one another. At times, I was a mite envious. Walter spoke about Inca or to Inca with appreciation, as though he held him in the highest esteem. Inca responded by trying very hard for Walter, by concentrating and showing that he was thinking things through. When he was led into the ring, he wanted to walk right over to Walter as soon as he had a chance. All Walter had to do was call, "Inca, Inca" very softly, as if he were calling a friend. After work, Inca's eyes followed Walter whenever he came through the stable aisle or appeared anywhere near his stall. He would watch the man steadily until Walter passed out of sight. There were days in Inca's training that his body language fairly shouted with pride, "Look at me!" and Walter would ride him with a smile on his face.

Frequently, Walter would talk to Inca. He had a spare but intriguing assortment of nicknames and short comments that popped out during lessons. I'd overhear him remark, "That wasn't so hard, Old Man, was it?" A few minutes later, in a note of triumph, he'd say, "You see? I told you, you could do it." I suspected he spoke in a combination of Platt Deutsch, the north German dialect, and a few unmentionable bits of slang. The only time I ever asked one of the German lehrlingers what Walter had just said, he laughed, turned red in the face and said, "You don't really want to know." That ended my request for translation. Unlike some professional trainers,

Walter almost never spoke angrily either to his horses or even about them. "Du alte schlummy Gummy," was one of his most repeated and reprimanding phrases, meaning "You lazy old rubber band." I tried those words to see if they held magic and found that if there was magic, it belonged to Walter.

By April, I was beginning to think of both Inca and myself as athletes. He was obviously reaching his prime under the daily work out; I was surprised to see how much Inca could sweat during his hour. He lathered up faster than I had ever known him to do when he was put to intensive work. Walter said I shouldn't worry, that his body was taking time to get used to the enormous effort of bringing new muscle into play.

To watch Walter teach Inca was equally a lesson for me. Often, he would initially exaggerate his demands in order to make them clear to the horse. These were the moments when communication between the two was most visible to me. I tried to remember every detail I picked up, which of course was impossible, Yet, I came away from every session with a definite impression, a mental picture and a plan, or a part of one, that I used when it came time for me to ride.

To master German and study dressage at the same time seemed more learning than anyone should attempt. But I had no choice in the matter and concluded that since I was in Walter's country and not he in mine, I had to weave in his teaching vocabulary along with my attempts to learn dressage.

From the very first day, every word of instruction I received was in German. I could only try to understand as best as I could. Walter expected me to learn his language, and there was no indication at the time that he had any interest in learning mine. I listened to a succession of instructions: sit tall, lengthen your legs, elbows in, chest open, shoulder blades together, thumbs up, hands together, head up, look out between the horse's ears while walking, trotting or cantering. In addition, I was instructed in preparing, executing and finishing precise figures. What a struggle! I wondered if Walter had any concept of my inner chaos. However, there was no alternative but to press onward through this avalanche of incomprehensible words. There were times when he wished fervently for me to make a correction, that although I couldn't understand the words, his tone clearly demanded, "Do it now!" I despaired. The German language was definitely a thorny patch. "What in all the world had he said?" I wondered. I tried something, whatever seemed most right under the circumstances.

It must have been during a lesson in the first weeks that I heard Walter distinctly call out, "Noch mal." This meant, "Do it again." But I was still fully anchored to English, so that when I heard the "N" of "Noch mal," I associated it with the "N" of "No," certainly negative. I went through every fault I could think of, trying to correct each of them. Meanwhile he kept repeating, "noch mal." He was baffled. It seemed so simple to him. Why couldn't I do the exercise one more time? It hadn't been badly ridden the first time. He only wanted to be sure I could ride it the same way again.

At one morning training session, before I even began to walk, trot, or canter, Walter asked me, "Which direction is easiest for Inca to work in?" I had no idea. How does one tell? Next he asked me, "Are you left handed or right handed?" "Right," I replied. And that was when I learned for the first time that horses have left and right preferences, exactly like people.

Walter pursued the subject further, asking me to see if I could discover which side Inca favored. We proceeded through the three gaits. Though I tried to sit as softly as a wet sponge, I couldn't feel the difference in my horse's preferred side.

My goal, Walter told me, was to ride Inca into evenness on both sides. In time, I finally was able to gain this skill, but at that moment I was baffled. Watching my struggles, Walter announced, "It will come. But for now, remember this point, begin your work on the left. When that's good, change over to the right. Don't try to hurry your perception, a good rider makes the training as easy as possible for herself and her horse."

The speedy "American" in me wanted to fight time-consuming learning details; I would have liked to ignore Inca's left or right and get on with it. At such times, I tried to hold a conversation with myself to quiet down and get back on the right track. I would remind myself that great performances are made up of moments in which every tiny detail is perfect.

Walter's teaching style, I was discovering, often did not involve words. On certain days, he made only three or four comments the entire time I was riding. I was as sensitive as his horses were to his whereabouts, and I always looked for him when I was in the ring. As I passed in front of his bench by the door, I could feel him watching, and I'd hear an occasional confirming clearing of the throat. This position by the door kept him out of the draft but in touch with Tasdorf's activity: he could hear people arriving, the ring of his telephone, noises made by horses in their stalls, and any ruckus whatsoever in the stable aisle. Moreover, he could also have an eye out for who stepped into the casino and which apprentice ducked outdoors for a smoke. Thus, he calmly kept his finger on Tasdorf's pulse, all the while maintaining his acute observation of the horses and riders training in the ring.

At first, I found Walter's watchfulness and lack of commentary disturbing. Lessons during which he said the least were the days I asked myself the most questions. Surmising that Walter wished me to figure out my problems on my own, I began to watch the other riders and check myself against them, as a way of seeking out my own answers. Sometimes, I wished my teacher wasn't so watchful and that I could sneak off and have five minutes alone. But that was hardly ever possible.

Walter's avoidance of my questioning looks and his minimum use of words were aspects of his teaching technique that I had to work at to understand. In the evenings, I would go home and review my difficulties with the lesson of the day. Frequently, I would sit on my sofa bolt upright, shoulders back, eyes forward, hands together and thumbs upward, reliving the morning's riding, repeating certain dressage movements and critiquing myself with as professional an eye as I could muster.

These review sessions turned out to be useful. However, there were always those "down" days when I couldn't turn Walter's silent lessons into anything helpful. Black thoughts sat on my shoulders and jeered at me like crows: "Walter didn't watch me. He didn't care. My work wasn't worth commenting upon. My horse has talent but I have none. Maybe, I'm wasting his time. Maybe I should go home."

At these times I wished for a friend in the same position, someone with whom I could share horse talk in a productive and supporting way. If I had been handed the clay of creation just then, I would have fashioned a friend who was seriously bitten by the dressage bug, so that we could talk about where we had come from and what we might expect to do with our horses when we returned home.

Not being able to speak the German language brought a strange kind of isolation; it distanced me from other human beings even when we shared the subject of horses. I, of course, wanted to talk endlessly about each day's riding like the lehrlingers did. The other clients, interested as they were in learning, brought a far more social and family agenda to discussions. At times, the linguistic void between myself and others was startling and even painful. I never could tell a joke or make someone giggle. In fact, I couldn't even be myself. In the groups that gathered in the casino, which sometimes included the regular riding ladies and sometimes did not, I felt invisible. I'd sit in silence and listen to the rhythm of their conversation, marveling at the loudness and the energy with which Germans talk. I almost never heard, "What?" or "Pardon me, what did you say?" Their voices climbed steep hills and slid into valleys with astonishing rapidity; there was not a single monotone among them. After the initial, "Guten tag" and handshake, which I had learned to take as earnestly as any true citizen, I'd hear, "I'm sorry but I don't speak English" (said in English). The few people who had learned English at one time claimed they were out of practice, and returned to speaking German. Thus, at first, life seemed unendingly serious. I even wondered if while I was learning to ride, I might forget how to laugh.

When I made halting conversation with the lehrlingers, I noticed that they had their own kind of language. It was a sort of stable slang that they used among themselves. Their sounds were especially strange to my ears. They could have been spitting out pumpkin seed husks. On the other hand, the neighboring farmers who appeared in the stable on work errands and held long conversations, mainly with Walter, had a manner of speaking that was as robust as they were. I was told this was a dialect known as Platt Deutsch. I liked the beer belly richness of their words and the music of the men's voices as they slid up and down the scale and made amusing sounds. From their faces, I'd assume they were being jocular, but when I sidled up as close as I dared, I'd see that they were dead serious. Walter knew a certain amount of Platt Deutsch and spoke it in the stable, to everyone's glee. So, when I came in one morning, plunked myself smack in front of him, looked him in the eye, pumped his hand vigorously and said, "Moyn, Moyn" (Platt Deutsch for good morning), with as much gusto as I could generate, he burst into delighted laughter. My daring pleased us both. The incident showed me that I should trust my ear and made me sing a cricket song deep inside. Several years later, Walter would tell me that he had been impressed with my willingness to try to speak his language, even though I sometimes sounded like someone stumbling over stones.

In the spring, while I was still in the early part of my stay at Tasdorf, the visit of a newly married California couple and their trainer taught me to see Americans from a German point of view. They came to Walter's establishment as potential buyers for one of his horses. I distinctly remember the particular Saturday they arrived.

It began quietly in the casino. There were few outsiders around. "Would you like to join us?" Kerstin said, inviting me to sit down with the American guests. Perhaps she felt she needed my help as an intermediary: I had heard that on more than one occasion, she and Walter had not been able to make sense of the way Americans behaved on a buying mission. "You people go about looking for horses in such a different way than we do," she had once remarked.

Curious about these differences, I had asked her to explain. "Americans are always in a hurry," Kerstin began, "while Europeans plan on spending time in their search. They take months. Often, Americans don't really know what they are looking for—they want to try this horse and that horse. Those of us who have horses to sell get the feeling Americans want to sit on every horse they see, even when they have no intention of buying. As most of them don't ride well, we don't like to have them sit on a horse they're not seriously considering."

Aside from complaints about excessive riding, German sellers resented the wholesale manner with which Americans approached business matters. When Walter took my countrymen through his stable, they asked for the prices of horses they clearly could not have been interested in. "Horses are not pieces of furniture carrying price tags around their necks," Kerstin said. The vehemence in her voice told me exactly how the two of them felt.

Kerstin explained Walter's approach: "First, we find out what the customers are looking for and then we pick out the kind of horse we feel is right for their situation. If they watch a horse being ridden, try it out for themselves, and finally say they like it, then we discuss the price. Often, the horses Americans buy are quite different from what they originally asked for. Sometimes, they fall in love with a creature and insist on buying it even though it is exactly what they should not get." Did this happen, she asked me, because Americans were emotional buyers who bought on a whim, or because they were suddenly attracted by a color or a certain quality that they saw in an animal?

"Hard to tell," I responded. After some thought, I told her that perhaps the problem lay in the fact that we were truly novices in the whole field of dressage. Our unusual actions and decisions were the result of a lack of education. In other fields, I believed we were clear and hardheaded.

From Kerstin I learned that in general, German horse dealers assumed that all American buyers were wealthy. This was partly due to the fact that the exchange rate had worked to our advantage ever since World War II, a state of affairs that the Germans viewed as grossly unfair. Thus, many Germans felt justified in taking advantage of Americans, resorting to seller hi-jinks and unloading horses too unsound or poor in quality for the more savvy European buyer. "This animal is plenty good enough for America," was the by-word among certain types of dealers.

By sharing some of this information with me, I knew Kerstin was giving me an overview of the horse business in Germany as well as an understanding of how sales were conducted at Stall Tasdorf. She also provided me with an insight into the intensely competitive nature of the business they were in. I was beginning to understand why Walter had to work so hard both to make money and to stay at the top of the field.

Kerstin wished to know how she and Walter might work more successfully with Americans. Was it a question of improved communication, she wondered? It certainly looked that way to me. I could see several areas where an understanding of the difference in culture and circumstances would improve matters. Walter, on his end, expected time and careful negotiation to be an integral part of the process of buying and selling a horse. American buyers, however, were probably coping with time restrictions, travel, fatigue, and difficulty with the German language. They were not prepared to sit down to lengthy introductory conversations. The average American wishes to get straight to the point.

Americans were frequently the subject of conversation at Tasdorf, and ever since my arrival, I had been thinking in a new way about what it meant to be an American. I discovered that over all I was proud of my American heritage, a fact I'd never known or thought about before. When I heard American popular music being played, I was dying to say, "That's ours." I wanted to talk about my country to anyone who would listen, and I wanted to explain Americans as much as I wanted to explain myself. It bothered me to overhear German comments like, "Americans are a bit crazy, a little stupid and rich." I hated the way Germans sometimes talked about us as blundering into the dressage field, filled with dreams, without knowledge, without training, unable to see the depth of the commitment involved. If I protested, or attempted to explain, I heard, "We're not talking about every American, just some of them. Anyway, you are different! You understand." I wasn't so sure about that last statement. Perhaps I was beginning to understand. It would take time.

And so, on that spring morning when Kerstin invited me to sit down with the American buyers from California, I was not only overjoyed at the chance to meet my compatriots, I was eager to see what would transpire. Kerstin introduced me to Hilary, a well-tanned blond, who crossed her pair of gorgeous legs and said she was relieved to meet another American. "We can talk English," she said with relief. "You'll never know how good that feels to me." She and her husband, John, were newlyweds and were spending their honeymoon looking for a horse for him. "He's wonderfully talented," Hilary informed me, "Everything he puts his mind to do, he does well."

I looked at John and decided that whatever he did for a job, he could always moonlight as a model for shirts and ties, tight jeans and toothpaste. I was proud of these beautiful people and wanted to say to Kerstin, who appreciated such things, "Aren't they gorgeous?"

Skipping any preliminary conversation, John's American trainer let it be known that his client had taken up riding a year and a half earlier. John's success, this leather-jacketed, bone-serious trainer immediately informed us, was so phenomenal that he had persuaded his pupil to take extra time away from the vice-presidency of a software firm and give himself a trip to Germany. They were looking for a horse who could take John all the way to the Olympics. He spoke with a certain terrier-like tenacity. Alarmed, I thought, good God, are these three about to embody the stories I have been hearing about Americans?

Walter remained purposefully unreadable. He nodded his head as if taking a long time to consider the qualities of his sale horses. Kerstin pulled me aside as I went to the ladies room. "Have you ever heard of this trainer?" she asked, "Or do you recognize the names of these people?"

"No," I replied, "but our country is so big, my knowing or not knowing names doesn't necessarily mean a thing." Such a concept was hard for her to imagine. Sweden was small enough for everyone in the horse world to know everyone else, or at least have very little difficulty getting information.

In due course, two horses were presented for John's consideration. Both were experienced campaigners. One was handsome and the other one not. Neither had qualified for high-powered shows like the two that Walter had ridden Inca in, but both had regularly placed high at smaller competitions. It could be assumed that if well ridden, either one could win hands down in the States. While John and the trainer were trying out both mounts, Hilary was explaining their tight schedule, which included visiting many famous stables in Germany. I interjected a note of warning about making horse decisions too quickly. "Don't worry," she said, "we'll look at a lot of horses and then John will decide. He claims he will know the right horse instinctively."

Watching John, I wondered if he could even find an animal that he could ride in the entire country. He sat like a champagne cork on top of each horse; it was obvious to me that neither of the two creatures had the slightest idea what John wished them to do. His signals and aids were unknown to them. Poor fellow. I sympathized with him, as I'd had the same experience myself. Riding a German horse when you've just come from America is like rapping on the front door when there's no one at home.

Meanwhile, Hilary was asking me why I was at Stall Tasdorf: "You came all this way to learn dressage?" I told her my story: my desire to be where dressage was practiced as a tradition; the invitation; my plan to train for a year. I tried to explain that most Americans had, as yet, no real concept of dressage, and that John should consider seeking education abroad, preferably in Germany. But other plans were milling through Hilary's mind. That very morning, she told me, as they were on their way to Stall Tasdorf, their trainer was impressing on John that when his new horse arrived home, he should plan on a good long season of local competition.

Did these people have blinders on? My sympathy for my countrymen came abruptly to an end. Suddenly, I was aware how my time at Walter's stable had influenced me. I felt more at home then I would ever have believed possible. At first, I wanted to blame the trainer for having inflated John to impossible ends. Then I wanted to blame John for thinking he could buy success and telescope the process of achievement. In the end, I blamed all three. Every one of them had eyes. Couldn't they see? Searching for some wisps of generosity within and not wanting to feel at odds with my own people, I decided that perhaps they had not as yet spent enough time on foreign soil to notice differences. It took time to leave the American scene, to cease being wrapped up in oneself, safe in one's own cocoon.

Pushed into deeper thoughts, I silently questioned whether the goal of riding always had to be competition. The American point of view frequently made this the case. Did I fall into this category myself? I wasn't sure; I needed more time to discover my answer. Later, I would seek Walter's wisdom. For now, my goal was clear— to learn as much as I could.

Breaking into my thoughts, Hilary asked if they were going to have a chance to see me ride? "Oh no!" I replied protectively, not yet ready to be judged by outsiders and certainly unwilling to take the chance that stories about my riding might reach home. "My lesson with Herr Christensen comes later." I hoped fervently that he would be too busy to spend time with me.

But I was wrong. John had finished riding. There had been a discussion in the ring when I noticed all three heads—Walter's, the trainer's, and John's—bobbing and nodding close together. Whatever they were saying didn't last long, as a real conversation was not truly possible. Then Hilary and John declared they wanted to stay on awhile and watch—and Walter ordered Inca to be brought into the ring.

Right up front, I told him that I couldn't ride just then.

"You mustn't let the Americans keep you from your work. Forget about everything else and ride," were his orders.

Walter set out to give me a lesson that allowed no spare thoughts. "Vorwärtz," (forward) he commanded. He had discovered that I needed urging to light my inner fire and that I rode best under pressure (when it was positive).

"Komm, komm, kein schlafen, komm," (come, come, no sleeping, get on with it). Like Inca, I had to be reminded, "You can do this," and then almost without fail, I could. In response to his directives, I began to ride as if I had been born in the saddle: I, free from fears and doubts, Inca, fresh and supple, the pair of us moving together through a program of Walter's creating. Nothing but my world of riding existed, and the power of the horse under me was glorious.

"Genug," (enough), he announced after about forty minutes, a little smile on his face.

A knowing eye might have realized what had not been included in the lesson. An educated rider might have questioned, "You don't practice this or train that?" We had avoided movements where unity between me and Inca fell apart. If the question of why this was so had come up, Walter would have met the challenge with, "We don't work on every single movement every day here."

I knew without any discussion that the lesson had been one of those times when everything falls into place and everything works.

However, it had been Walter's expertise that had made it happen. The weak points in my stage of development were never visible. The situation had helped me gain confidence, and had proven to me that a rider can ride through his feelings of doubt and insecurity and still perform. Seeing Walter's approval, I was ecstatic, wanting to spill out all the thrills that were dancing inside. But when I thanked him, he found a sugar for Inca, and ever the perfectionist, simply said to me, "Today is one day better than yesterday." I had heard Walter say this before and knew it was not meant to belittle the rider or the ride, but rather to give voice to his never-ending standard of quality. The measured way he accepted progress was another lesson for me.

Nevertheless, I purred like a barn cat on hearing John and Hilary's compliments to Inca and appreciation of our lesson. "I like the way you are being taught here," were John's words. The comment did show a certain degree of perception on his part, at least I hoped it did. I wished him successful hunting and really meant it. I hoped for Hilary and John's sake that their trip would make them wiser and that only the best would befall them.

A few Americans came and went that year, all searching for horses. Never again was there a pair as naive and childlike as the Californians. A few who tried out horses could ride rather well. That pleased me, because of course everyone in the stable who could, came to watch. I was proud of their American manner: their openness, friendliness, sense of fun and lack of guile, and I didn't see anyone do any of the foolish things that were said to be typical. More than anything else, these visits reconfirmed for me how fortunate I was to be at Tasdorf. My fellow countrymen didn't have to tell me (but of course, they did), that any one of them would be happy to be in my boots out there in the ring every day, learning.

As my time aboard Inca increased, the attitude at the Stall

toward training began to influence me and make me assess my role as a student. How was I doing? Physical changes were occurring; I could feel them clearly enough. I slipped in and out of new positions, new actions, and new feelings like a car with a loose gearshift. Nothing was reliable yet. When I reviewed the situation, I wasn't entirely pleased with what was going on in my head. During our lesson time I was asking Walter for EVERYTHING, acting as if my learning was all up to him. I'd put myself into his experienced hands, waited for him to mold me, direct me and make sure I rode correctly. At first, such an attitude seemed appropriate. However, as the days went by, I was bothered—something wasn't working, something was missing. Further thought convinced me I needed to assume a stronger role. It was time to cease waiting for help and firmly pick up the responsibility for my riding. This meant that I must think ahead, assert myself and take chances. In fact, when I came to ride I needed to say to myself, as if there were no other option, "I am a student, but in a sense, I am a trainer too." Perhaps this would turn out to be a progressive step.

So I acted on my new insights, becoming mentally more aggressive and therefore blatantly making more mistakes—which was hard. Walter, however, had been waiting for me to change my perspective. In a sense, I was giving him more to teach. I could see that he knew I was trying, and he welcomed the effort. I even believe he found me more teachable. For my part, because I was searching for the right way all the time, I clearly heard every word he said and acted on it more effectively.

Partnership

Of all the many changes that my year at Tasdorf brought to me, one of the most meaningful was the deepening of my relationship with my talented equine friend and dressage "dance" partner, Inca. My understanding of my horse began to take on new dimensions almost from the first moment I arrived at the stable, and to my amazement, continued to grow day by day throughout the entire year that I spent in Germany. Just as if we were two human friends taking a trip and faced with a new environment, Inca and I became involved in many ways that we'd never been before. I became attuned to him, more sensitive and more able to respond to his varying rhythms. We grew closer. I came to realize that we needed each other's company and it touched me deeply to find this large, impressive creature actually looking for me to put in an appearance. I was used to being "expected" by a member of the family, my dog, and my cat, but the repeated sight of a 1400-pound animal visibly waiting for me and plainly depending on me, was something I knew I would never forget.

Away from home, I saw Inca with fresh eyes and realized that there was much I could learn about him. I began to understand that the more knowledge I could gain about my horse, the better chance I would have of reaching the harmony, beauty, complexity and subtlety of the equestrian work I was witnessing at Tasdorf. Walter brought forth all of these qualities in Inca. He was not only a wonderful trainer but he had profound insight into the nature of horses—Walter and horses thoroughly understood one another. The depth of his connection to them inspired me, and in an effort to gain even a particle of his type of understanding, I decided to spend more time with Inca.

One bright morning at the beginning of my stay at Tasdorf, I marched purposefully down the aisle to his stall. Walter's regular session with him was planned for later in the day. Up until that moment, I had distanced myself from my horse: Walter and Inca were focused on competition, and I had tried to be the well-behaved owner who let them have their time together without interference. However, now that the shows were over, my reasons for staying away were replaced by the need I felt to be Inca's main person. Besides, I was lonely in this new country and I missed my horse deeply.

Inca lived two-thirds of the way down the stable to the right. I came upon him waiting like a kid at a window, pressed up against the front of his stall, intently peering through the bars. Clearly, he had been listening for my footsteps. His expression when he saw me seemed to ask, why didn't you come sooner?

I was touched by his eagerness, and more than a little surprised. Back home, Inca was apt to be casual: I passed by his stall so frequently that he would hardly turn around, unless, of course, I produced a carrot and called out, "See what I've got!" This time, his unusual response made me wonder if something was wrong.

It was plain to see that no carrot was needed: his mind was entirely concentrated on getting my attention, and it was very clear to me that in some way, he wanted my help. I was concerned. During the years I'd owned Inca, I had become increasingly aware that he was complex and unusual: while he was emotional, he was also capable of intense thought (not all horses are) and could hold back a great deal of feeling within himself. Although I assumed that I knew him quite well, I didn't always find him easy to read.

As I opened the stall door and entered, Inca stepped forward so close he was almost on top of me. In the intimate confinement of the stall, I could see the varied physical symptoms of his anxiety: tiny raised blood vessels, small knots, and lines of tightness. When I removed his blanket, I discovered more areas that were hard to the touch. Clearly, Inca was not having an easy time.

What could be causing these subtle indications of distress, I asked myself? His coat was so shiny that I had to believe that his physical condition was basically healthy. Might Inca's tension be mainly rooted in what was going on in his head? Could he, like me, be dreaming of home and missing it desperately? By taking Inca to Germany, I had changed his life: hauled him away from his home, his bed, his food, his pasture, his pals, his vet, his farrier, and his American schedule. He had every reason to be feeling troubled and anxious.

Perhaps life at Stall Tasdorf was taking more out of him than I'd supposed. Did the unusual regimen of daily training, which, when I considered it, must feel unbelievably strict and confining to him, leave him tense and unable to relax? Was he bothered that he lived and worked indoors and never even saw the natural world outside? Inca's discontent, I realized, might be rooted in something as simple as not being able to settle down. After all, Walter's establishment was not the cozy, seven-stall barn Inca was used to.

As I stood there ruminating, Inca suddenly brought me right back to the present moment, demanding the attention he felt was his due. He stamped his feet, butted me with his nose and almost pushed me off balance. "Don't just stand there," he was telling me, "come on, do the things you know I like," and he turned, presenting his neck for me to touch.

I took this as my signal to begin working on his body, and commenced massaging the areas that I knew so well. First, I looked for the places where the muscles were knotted, tight as peas. Using both thumbs, I spread the tiny fibers apart until the lumpiness gave way, allowing me to massage the surrounding flesh with the whole of my hand and to feel the rising warmth of blood returning to the trouble spots. Though I was not an equine therapist, I still knew what could bring Inca comfort. Combining a variety of touch and massage, I made my fingers ask Inca silent questions: where are you holding, where does it hurt, where don't you feel right?

In subtle but perceptive ways, Inca answered me, directing me to apply more pressure or less, to move to the left or to the right, or even to remain longer where he was still tight. When I reached the soft areas—his throat, arm pits, the under belly of his neck, and the inside of his haunches—I was struck, as I had been in the past, by how much Inca's flesh was like my own. As I held my hand completely still on one of these sensitive places, I became aware once again how the mere act of being with my horse made me feel totally alive and healthy down to the deepest level. Just at that instant, Inca's frame gave a shudder and he let out a long sigh. I saw that his eyes were closing. He'd given me a real response.

In order to continue this new kind of conversation, I planned to visit Inca every day, usually close to the hour he was to be ridden.

I wanted to assure him that he wasn't alone, that I was there for him and that he could count on time together as part of his routine.

Inca's anxiety disappeared quickly. Over a period of weeks, he stopped the insistent, goat-like nudging he would display whenever I entered his stall, and he became noticeably gentler. In turn, I approached him in a spontaneous frame of mind, varying my actions with every visit: I might braid strands of mane, or straighten the hairs of his tail one by one, play with his soft lips, or give him a total rubdown. Occasionally, I just sat in a corner of the stall and did absolutely nothing but enjoy the atmosphere. It seemed to me that each of us was learning that being peaceful together is an aspect of partnership.

Now and then, during these quiet moments, I would breathe in Inca's smell. I had loved this part of him from the day we met. Not all horses smell as good as he always did. When I inquired about this, an American veterinarian told me that breath reveals a lot about the state of a horse's health. From the time I was a child, I thought that horses smelled as wonderful as fresh earth, and I never understood why the adults around me said that horses stank. To me Inca's animal aroma was as pleasingly rich as the English pipe to-bacco my father used: the essence of both these odors seemed quin-tessentially natural.

Except when the smell of bleach or perfume clung to me, Inca in turn, appeared to like my human scent. During stall visits, he gave me close personal inspections. He'd smell my clothes up and down, nuzzle under my shirt collar, blow hot breaths down my back, mouth my ears, and taste my hair. He was funny about hair. He mouthed it tentatively, as if my hair might be like the mane of another horse. In the beginning, I was afraid he'd give a yank or have a chew. As it seemed important that I show him my trust, I never flinched or pulled away. Every time, to my relief, he let go gently and of his own accord. Was he humorously imitating my way of combing and fussing with his mane? After all, experience had shown me that horses can have a great sense of humor.

Yet while we had traits in common, in my efforts to draw close to Inca, I had to remember that he could respond with non-human behavior as well. One day, for instance, one of our peaceable stall visits together was interrupted by a situation that really frightened me. A truck drew up to the rear entrance of the stable to deliver feed. Without any warning, the roar of hundreds of pounds of fresh grain blowing into empty metal containers fractured the stillness. It was so loud that the back wall actually shook. Inca leapt in panic and whirled around in his confined space. Normally, he would never intentionally step on me, but in this fear-filled moment, he had forgotten that anyone was there with him. Luckily, I had my wits about me. I flattened myself against the cinder blocks, waited until the split second that Inca reached the opposite side, and then made a quick dash out to freedom, barely escaping his flailing legs. Gradually, he was able to tolerate the racket and quiet down. He gazed at me still wide-eyed, but listened to my reassuring voice coming to him from the aisle. As I spoke to him, my mind was filled with frightening thoughts of how close I had come to an accident!

I understood that in order to protect both of us—which is the role a person takes in partnership with a horse—I had to be constantly alert. Hadn't Inca reared and struck out playfully with a front leg one nippy morning? Hadn't I been frightened? Hadn't I cupped his nose affectionately in both hands only to have him bare his teeth and lay his ears back? Provoked, irritated or taken by surprise, Inca, like the rest of his kind, could be counted on to react instinctively, as if he were still in the wild. I tried to be careful never to overstep his boundaries or confuse his behavior with my own: we were two different cultures, equine and human. The way in which we experienced events and expressed ourselves was bound to be different. Mutual respect between us was a "must" in order to avoid misunderstanding.

When you love animals, it can become easy to anthropomorphize them, endowing them with human characteristics they don't necessarily possess. During the months that I was drawing closer to Inca, I often thought about this subject and how easy it is for people to fall into the trap of being overly sentimental about their animal friends. One such case, a rather sad one, occurred at Christmas time in Tasdorf. In spite of the festivities planned for everyone, a lonely young member of the stable crew spent her entire Christmas Eve in her horse's stall. Apparently, the creature was not happy to have her there and repeatedly tried to kick and bite her. When we asked her why she stayed in the stall under those conditions, the frailty of her explanation as well as her confused emotions made us wince. Refusing to pay attention to the messages her animal had given her, the girl explained that to her, Christmas Eve was the most important night of the year, and she couldn't bear to think of her best friend being alone. This unfortunate incident focused my desire to foster nothing but the clearest and most direct connection with Inca.

During my early months in Germany, I obsessed like an anxious mother about the changes, demands, and adjustments that occurred for Inca. The details of his care made me uneasy and probably got to me more than they did to him. On the day I saw Inca being fitted with new shoes, I could hardly breathe. As I watched the man in the leather apron strike his anvil with enormous power, I was filled with the fear that he couldn't possibly understand about my horse's particularly tender feet. The first time I saw the stable crew pull the hay wagon down the aisle, I was concerned: the hay looked markedly different in texture and color from what Inca had been accustomed to. Even if I allowed for foreign soil, weather and seed types, I wondered if there were sufficient nutrients in the grass to keep an American horse healthy.

Inca, on the other hand, had concerns of his own that were little, usually inexpensive, quite uncomplicated, and most often immediate: a treat, an opportunity to eat grass, a chance to roll in the dirt, a desire for more attention. A short list when one considers lists, but vital to him. As for gratification, it had to come *now*, as is true for all members of his species. And Inca always let me know that his "now" meant by the next breath.

Some people think animals can't talk. In my experience, that's simply not true. Lacking the spoken word, Inca had his own ways of talking. He communicated through his eyes, his facial expressions, his body language, and occasionally in other, unexpected ways.

Some of these ways were quite ingenious because Inca was unusually intelligent. In fact, from the first moment I met him, I thought, "Oh that's a college professor." This instant impression may have come from his long angular nose, serious eyes, refined body, intelligent face, and the knowledge that he had been trained to a high level. I came to him as a relatively new and humble student of dressage, full of respect, anticipating that he would teach me everything that he knew. I hadn't owned him very long before I discovered that he did indeed have a great deal to contribute to my life, not only as my instructor, but socially, as a friend.

It was in Germany, however, where I often felt socially isolated, that I began to really understand just how subtle and supportive Inca's friendship could be. On a day to day basis, I missed speaking English as much as I missed just plain speaking. It came as a huge relief when I realized that the lines of communication between Inca and me were always open and that he was the most patient and interested listener I could ask for. He'd stand as though teth-

Just a note...

by Manuela
Rüedi

ered, cock his ears forward, and gaze steadily at me with what seemed an air of approval. Some days, I would hear myself assure him in a chipper voice that our being together in Germany was not just my adventure but his, too. My faith in our future was inevitably bolstered by telling Inca that given time, patience, and the grit to see this through, we, as a pair, were bound to succeed. The instruction we were receiving was going to do that for us. Never once during my recitations did he fall asleep, wander away in the middle of a sentence, or turn his back. By the time I had reached the end of whatever it was I had to say, I had the distinct impression that we had helped each other to feel important.

Unlike me, out in public it was Inca who did most of the "talking." Mornings, when we began our lesson, he made a sound like a person continuously clearing his throat. This guttural rumble lasted sometimes as long as ten minutes. It wasn't phlegm, but a complaint about having to start work. Walter used to laugh. He knew a lot about stiffness and the sludge of early morning beginnings. "Is it as hard as all that, Old Boy?" he'd inquire as we passed by. Then, he'd say to me, "Give Inca a pat."

On good days, Inca taught me more than I could have imagined. At these times, riding was like an effortless dance: Inca would allow me into the soft hollow of his back, and then the miracle would begin. We would cross space in a manner that I had never before experienced. My horse would perform movements that I used to dream about back home, movements I had only recently seen executed by the best European riders. My horse was making me feel as though I was his Ginger Rogers and he, my Fred Astaire.

It wasn't as if we could do this on our own, Inca and I—it took three of us. We were dependent upon Walter's coaching to bring us together as a team: without him, the magic would not have happened. Back home in America, Inca's work had not been this good.

There had been glimpses of his ability, especially under professional riders, but nothing steady or concrete and certainly nothing that could stack up to standards abroad.

Walter's lessons demonstrated to me that once Inca's engines were started and he understood what was wanted, he could perform most of the classical movements quite correctly by himself. My job was to rev up those engines and then fine tune them down. I was given short and simple directions, like breathe, sit quietly, don't interfere, give him a bit more leg, stay soft. At the heart of Walter's skill was his subtle and precise sense of timing—he knew exactly when to do what and in what order.

Had I had the power to do so, I would have extended these moments of instruction into eternity. The work I did with Walter never felt like the work I had done with anyone else. The trouble was that the exercises went by very fast. Of course it wasn't really fast, it just felt that way to me because what we were doing was complicated and full of variety. On my own, and as a relative beginner in dressage, it was easy to get stuck and obsessive and continue practicing one movement a dozen times. However, under Walter I was not allowed to treat my horse like a machine that was capable of endless repetition. So, during my time in the ring, I asked every part of me down to the marrow in my bones to record the experience: the rhythm, the balance, the action, the gaits, the suspension, the crossover, the manner in which the outer leg supports and the inner leg reaches under. I wanted to store it all. Make a video tape just out of the feeling alone. When we took a break, Walter would ask eagerly, "Did you feel this? Did you feel that?" Hardly knowing what world I was living in, I'd shake my head, trying to find an inch of free space, and for at least twenty-five seconds I'd find myself unable to say a word. The truth was, my body had so much to remember, I needed time to sort it all out.

Walter, always the grateful one, would want me to reward Inca immediately. "Pat him," he'd say in a tone that clearly suggested I should be concentrating entirely on my horse, not on me, "Let him know what a fine fellow you think he is." Later, over cups of hot drink in the casino, he'd ask me for the umpteenth time if I *really* knew how lucky I was to own such a "giving horse."

Initially, my lessons in Germany were concentrated only on being the follower in a dressage dance duo. Then, step by step, without haste and with deepened understanding, I was asked to reverse roles; I was to become Astaire and Inca was to be Rogers. This, of course, came about only after Inca and I had worked out an agreement about how we worked best together, both physically and mentally. I discovered that creating a partnership with one's horse was an art in itself. Prior to seeing foreign competition, I thought that if a rider could ride well and was on a good horse, he could rise to the top and win anything. Moreover, after witnessing the artistry of international equestrian pairs, it became as clear to me as a drop of rain, that without a solid partnership, the "breath-taking" aspect of dressage could never come into being.

Inca was a fascinating partner. He had a mind of his own and his own agenda and personal preferences. Any exercise that was performed on a straight line charged his jets. He'd take off and I'd wonder if I had a seat on the Concorde. "Not so fast!" Walter would roar, and I'd be thanking God that the arena was contained within four high walls. However, as the months went by, Inca calmed down. I was encouraged by the progress we were making together; we understood each other much better and were working more effectively in many ways. I even began to see that eventually, I might learn how to harness Inca's propulsive forward energy and someday use it to our advantage in the show ring. There, our gait extensions would keep the rhythm and gain us points—certainly an

8, but maybe with luck a 9.

Then one day, at a point about four months into my year, Walter said, "take up the reins," in a tone that suggested I was about to move to a new level. "Think of yourself as Inca's trainer," he said— meaning it was time for me to take on full control. Noticing my uncertain look, he reminded me that when the time came to leave Tasdorf and go home, I really would be my own trainer. The change of mind-set had an immediate effect: I improved overnight. When I asked myself why this had happened, I realized that because of my change in thinking, I now started off my rides with a new approach.

"Let's try the exercise this way," I began to say to myself, or, "Why not begin here?" Thus, I tried to think creatively, to drop the old heavy, pedantic, "got to succeed" approach, and to offer varia- tions in our program that would make progress easier. Immediately, Inca gave me evidence that my efforts made a difference to him. Once my horse began to trust that this firm, positive but patient view would last, he became twice as willing as he'd ever been. In turn, I began to accept his "not so good days" with calm equanimity instead of my former reactive, "oh, damn" attitude. I thought to myself, didn't I have bad days, too?

Even my view of time underwent a change. Before knowing Walter, I was the sort of person who was casual about time. I rode six days a week for an hour, or maybe two. Walter, however, pre- sented me with a new concept: his concern was with the quality of time spent rather than the duration. Walter's lessons were intense as well as focused; they ran twenty or thirty minutes, seldom forty. There was no uniform length to a lesson, rather the time spent depended on the circumstances. On a Tuesday he might say to me, "We must go on until we work this question out." Then, the next day, he might surprise me with the announcement rather early on, "Today, we will stop." Once I got a feel for the effectiveness of

Walter's timing, I looked forward to the day when I might have learned enough to make decisions of this kind myself. I could see that these variations helped Inca maintain a fresh attitude toward his work, and that therefore it never became routine.

As soon as the instruction was over, I'd give my boy a slack rein. He was never so worn out that I didn't sense an immediate rebirth of energy, especially when he was cooled out enough to leave the ring. Invariably, Inca was in a hurry. Upon reaching the unsaddling area, he'd start searching my vest pocket for post-lesson-time sugar. Having satisfied himself that he'd found all that was there, he'd shake himself impatiently, move around, stamp his feet, and generally be a pain. We had been sparring on this issue of cooperation after his exercise for years—an on-going reminder to me of my fellow's deeply ingrained independent nature. A good brush down, a bracing rub on all four legs, and a careful once-over to check for rubs, nicks, or bruises took time, but was necessary for his well-being. Inca, however, had other ideas, which he wasn't about to change.

Whether he wore me down or won me over, I'll never know, but we ended up compromising. I developed the attitude that he was a kid freshly liberated from a day at school. Keeping this image in mind, I'd give him the minimum after-work check necessary so that we could head down the stable aisle fast. When he became utterly impossible, I'd give him a smart yank on the lead rope and pull out a phrase in German, the language of immediate control. "Höre mich an, Pferd!" (listen to me, horse), I'd growl. I'd brace my body like a backwoodsman and refuse to allow him to drag me down the aisle to his stall.

To me, Inca's stall was a cell; but that was clearly my view, not his. He would enter his quarters with delight and turn to munching his sun-toasted bedding before I'd even left. Eating was not the only way my friend and equine partner occupied himself in his off-hours, I was told. During the second month, the stable crew couldn't wait to inform me how often he fiddled with his automatic waterer, wiggling the "on" and "off" level with his lips and thereby flooding the place and causing extra work. Though the implication behind their reports was that these bad manners were my fault and the result of American training, the fact was that Inca had never seen a waterer before, and his inquisitive nature had simply taken over. We solved the problem by buying him a salt block he could lick like a lollipop. Two months later, to make sure that he didn't run out of entertainment, I went out and bought him a ball.

Horses like Inca, who are in intensive work, need three good meals a day. Not surprisingly, they appreciate having definite meal times. For Inca, just as for me, the stellar event after a long morning's work was lunch. Both of us could sense the noon hour approaching with the accuracy of a Swiss watch. Inca would express his impatience by bumping his feed tub as hard as he could. On the days that grain didn't appear as fast as he thought it should, he'd nicker for the feed gang, making any customer who was standing around in his area think, "Heavens, this poor fellow's half starved." In a big stable, this type of pain-in-the-neck behavior was considered downright annoying, especially when the culprit succeeded in riling all his neighbors. Inca had long ago discovered the fun he could derive from influencing others. I knew his game. Had I been on the grain duty any one of those times, I'd have looked him in the eye and called him a con artist, and a control freak. I'd have asked him why he had to play king.

Even though I understood the attitude of the stable crew, I had to allow my horse a game or two. After all, if it had been me standing in Inca's shoes during the bad weather months, having to live and work indoors without ever seeing the sky, I'd have gone plumb crazy. When I asked the Germans about the effects of indoor life on horses, I always received the same practical answer. Their animals, they told me, seemed perfectly able to deal with it. However, I was warned, "Come those early days of April, be especially alert on your first outings."

Wise advice! On the first warm, sunny day that the outdoor arena was open, Inca pranced out of the stable eager to take on the whole world. Unlike the other horses, who calmed down after an initial display of stored up energy, Inca was unable to settle down. For weeks he acted as if he had never seen a rock, a tree, or a patch of brown earth. Every time a cyclist or a hiker passed on the road behind the trees that bordered the ring, he'd bolt. Was he frightened? Impossible. I couldn't believe that he had forgotten the trucks, motorcycles and all the traffic that used to pass us on our weekly treks through the countryside back home in the States. Quite plainly, winter containment had taken its toll on his psyche; he was a horse who was used to freedom, fresh air, and the relaxation of regular hacks down a cart road.

During this entire period of early spring from April to June, we were considered hell raisers, and on certain days I saw our popularity sink almost out of sight. Inca managed to get us in everyone's way, and Walter was constantly growling at me, "Control him!" Could Walter really think I wasn't trying? The riders shot me looks I pretended not to see. On all sides, I heard riders warning one another, "Vorsiecht, Inca," (watch out for Inca).

It was, however, not the irritated riders, but the arrival of the Tasdorf town stork that drove me to consider buying two tickets for home. Almost immediately after my arrival in the town, I was shown something that meant a great deal to the villagers, a large stork's nest on the roof of a thatched cottage at the crossroads. I was told that the whole dorf (village) waited like one eager family for the birds' annual springtime return. The male stork came in advance of his lady friend, to check out his lodgings and perform necessary repairs. Then, once ensconced, the nesting pair was believed to bring peace, privilege, good luck, and prosperity to the village. I too, looked forward eagerly to the birds' arrival. My partiality for the species had begun in childhood, when these wondrous creatures had appeared as magical figures in tales told at bedtime. I could hardly wait to see them in real life.

No one had told me, however, that this much-esteemed fowl's favorite dining place was the grassy strip beside Walter's arena. One day the male stork flew in and made a landing for a late brunch. Inca and I were in the middle of an excellent lesson. I was feeling unusually good about the way we were working, so I gave myself the luxury of consciously breaking my focus and stealing a look at the stork. I knew that my four-footed friend was already familiar with cows, llamas, donkeys, ducks, chickens, crows and Canadian geese, so I didn't give Inca's possible reaction any special thought. He however, took one look at the unfamiliar bird and headed for the sky. We were instantly airborne, and I discovered just exactly how high and how far Inca could fly. When we descended, by some miracle I was still aboard, but the show was not yet over. In the equine repertoire of disruption, there are buckers, rearers, climbers, twisters, duckers, and crow hoppers. Inca had perfected his own combination of all six possibilities. Up and down we went, like a horse and rider on a park carousel, and I continued to hold on while all the other riders stared. Finally, I heard someone say, (and I think it was Walter), "Gut getan," (well done).

At last, when Inca had quieted down, Walter came over, like the true horseman that he was, and inspected each of Inca's four legs to see if our wild ride had done any damage. He ran his fingers up and down the long muscles and felt the bones. He lifted up my crea-

Halle, the Danish apprentice, atop one of Walter's horses in training.

Here I am—clearly something wonderful has happened while I was riding. I have probably just learned to keep my left elbow at my side.

Walter as "vorreiter" (test rider) on Inca in the Neumünster Dressage Show.

Walter Christensen on the bench, deceptively relaxed at his favorite post in the ring. From this position, Walter was able to teach while keeping his finger on the pulse of the stable activities.

I particularly love this picture because it shows Walter's masterly but "soft" rein. Inca's ears and expression tell me that he is truly "listening" to his rider.

Celebrating Walter's 50th birthday in the Stall Tasdorf indoor arena. In his honor, a "show number" has been put together and is being ridden by his students.

Cornelia Piening from Lübeck, one of Walter's long-time and very successful young riders, has just finished riding in the birthday program and is receiving his heartfelt thanks.

Normally a somewhat shy person in social situations, this day Walter stepped right up to the situation and outdid himself with obvious profound pleasure. He is presenting roses to Martina Lakomy. In the background is his assistant, Klaus Rat, with his mount.

Partying in the casino. To the left are the large windows through which guests could view the proceedings in the ring. These are the windows that caused me so much anxiety and made me feel as if I was always being watched whenever I rode.

Left to right: Kerstin Christensen, Frau Becher-Eggert, a dressage judge and daughter of Walter's early teacher, and Hermann Duckek, well-known expert on footing. Herr Duckek travels all over the world sharing his knowledge with show managers including those who organize the Olympics, and European and American championships.

Walter and Twiggy (Kerstin's fox terrier) inspecting the back barn. Photo: Foto Huck

Besides cats, dogs, and horses, Kerstin and Walter kept sheep for a while. Being "animal people," the entire Stall Tasdorf family fell in love with the baby lambs like this one here with Kerstin.

A picture of Christine Stückelberger and her horse Granat hung in the stable on the end wall of the dining room where the Christensens, the apprentices, and I took meals. The smile on Christine's face always warmed my heart—gave me courage—especially on the days my riding hadn't been so good. It was then that she made my lunch taste better!

An aerial view of Walter and Kerstin's little house right at the turn of the road in Tasdorf. The vegetable garden and rough pasture to the right belong to the farm next door.

Kerstin and Twiggy about to leave for Hamburg and a few hours of shopping on "their day off." If Kerstin returned with the trunk of her car full of packages, the outing was a true success.

The Tasdorf "ladies" on their way through town to pasture. Kerstin used to say to me, "They have their own special perfume, don't they?"

Frau Siever's house, the second place I lived during my yearlong stay. To me, the house and driveway always looked as though they had just been scrubbed—maybe they had been (while I was away riding).

ture's hoofs, discovered a stone no larger than a pea wedged under the shoe, and muttered, "A pebble like this could make a horse unsound." Then he slapped Inca on the rump, pronounced him hale and hearty, and we all took up our exercises again as though nothing had happened.

Isn't anyone going to ask me how *I* feel after such a ride, I wondered? Guess not! While thinking about this seemingly callous reaction on the part of my fellow riders, I came to a new insight: equestrians often focus on their horses to such an extent that they can appear to care more about the animals than they do about the riders. Though this attitude can seem to exclude the human and personal side of life, it is not mean-spirited at heart.

Inca's reaction to the stork turned out to be his grand finale to big-time bad behavior. After that, his traumas became noticeably less, and I sensed he was being influenced by the steady attitude of the German horses. He looked at rain puddles in the ring but no longer leapt aside, and when the north wind blew through the trees he merely wiggled his ears.

When our year was up and it was time to return home, I came to the poignant realization that both Inca and I had been changed forever. While he was still his strong-minded individualistic self, he had become more trusting, more caring, and infinitely more willing to listen to and obey me. All of his reactions were expressed with far greater refinement. As for me, the remarkable closeness and partnership I was able to develop with my equine friend gave me a vastly strengthened confidence and the ability to "talk" and work with other horses at levels I had not known existed previously. My new understanding, bequeathed to me by Walter and Inca, was a gift that would go on developing and never, never wear out.

~8

Grönwohld

E ven before I came to Germany, I was familiar with the name
and reputation of the phenomenally gifted young German
competitor and trainer, Herbert Rehbein. Back at home, I
would come across his name in the "World News" section of an
equestrian magazine, or I'd hear well-traveled dressage enthusiasts
sing his praises. He was renowned throughout Europe as an expert
in preparing riders for serious dressage competition.

Therefore, I was doubly excited to find that not only did this celebrated trainer teach at a center only an hour away from Tasdorf,
but his stable, Grönwohld, was considered to be one of the most
beautiful in all of Germany—a veritable "show place." Obviously, a
trip to see both Grönwohld and Herr Rehbein at work was a must!
Fired with enthusiasm, I asked Kerstin if she would join me, but
though she was usually eager for an adventure, this time she seemed
a bit reluctant. In fact, in discussing my idea her voice had a tight
sound that I couldn't interpret and she seemed bent on finding dif-

ficulties. She'd have to see whether she had time, find out when Herbert was there, perhaps one day would be better than another, she'd have to ask what hour the best horses were worked, check on which was their rest day, and make sure everyone wasn't away at a show. Finally, however she agreed, "Yes, you really must see the place. I'll take you," and opted for a Monday when our stable was closed. It was a trip, she told me, which we would make quietly on our own. I understood this to mean that I was to keep quiet about our plans. Quiet in front of whom? Walter? Surely not.

At shows I had been to, the two trainers would get together: Herbert would drink a Jagermeister while Walter would take tea and they'd have one of those head-together, low-voiced talks professionals indulge in when their clients aren't around. The two men had been friends since the days of their apprenticeship. Perhaps it was the customers to whom I was not to broadcast where we were going. I wondered whether there was a kind of hierarchy among dressage stables, an unspoken rivalry, which set up certain patterns of loyalty, competition, and even conflict as well as a demand for appropriately diplomatic behavior. Maybe I had innocently asked to visit the "other camp," and that was the reason for Kerstin's hesitation.

With these questions still buzzing in my mind, Kerstin and I set off, on the Monday following our conversation. She did not seem particularly tense and I wondered if I had drawn too many conclusions from her initial response to the trip. I decided a wait-and-see attitude was my best bet. We began our drive toward Schwarzenbek, taking a dozen short cuts out of Tasdorf. Hedgerows bordered roads so narrow that I held my breath at the sight of every oncoming tractor. The wheels of our Honda could easily have slipped into an irrigation gully, but Kerstin piloted us so expertly that we sped along with the ease of birds winging in the sky. In a matter of minutes, we came upon route 404 and joined the autobahn full of cars flying south.

In Germany, people drive very fast and I was often afraid when sitting in the passenger seat. The only way I could feel comfortable was to allow my hands and feet their involuntary expressions of terror while I would look off into the distance and pretend to be somewhere else. There was no point in saying, "Bitte, nicht so schnell" (not so fast, please) or in faulting any one of my drivers. To do so would have meant going against the culture of an entire country whose cars are built to be racing stock. Earlier in my stay, when I did comment on the lightening pace of traffic, I was told, "Cars don't drive the way they should unless you go at a certain speed," or "Speed forces you to stay alert, so you see, it's really quite safe. Don't worry." But of course I did!

As the miles sped by, we suddenly entered a different world. The hectares of flat fields surrounding Tasdorf had disappeared, replaced by a gently rolling landscape of successive low hills. Gone were the endless squares and rectangles of plowed earth, wire gates, and lines of fencing. Gone was a feeling of earnestness and daunting physical labor. There was still evidence of farming and agriculture, but it existed in such large, open, freeform spaces that it appeared casual in comparison with the north. The lay of the land seemed to speak for its owners, saying, "Land is valued and should be worked, but the lives of the owners have taken other directions." Then suddenly, in the midst of this peaceful, lulling landscape, a surprise came into view.

High on a knoll, I spied an ancient castle with four towers, high battlement walls, and a huge drawbridge. The structure hunkered down on its site like a slumbering guard dog and would have been easy to miss had I not been eagerly looking about. It seemed a conundrum to come upon a handsome fortification in a setting so pastoral, so utterly peaceful, with only a luscious green valley below needing protection. Here in real life was a fairy tale picture, exactly like those that had enchanted me in the books of my childhood. I had spent hours cutting towers out of cardboard with round-ended scissors, and the Christmas that I was given a castle to construct was one of the nicest ever.

Kerstin broke into my thoughts, "Walter and I were invited to a 'Fest' in that castle just last year."

"Someone lives there?" I was incredulous.

"Yes," she said, and went on to tell me that the castle had been completely restored and the descendants of the original owners, who were horsepeople, still lived there surrounded by this unimaginable beauty. The party that Kerstin had attended there had been a birthday celebration. The present owner had marked his sixtieth with an enormous gathering to which he had invited every one of his friends. Most of them were riders, and in fact, several were among the famous dressage riders in the country. As their birthday present to the castle owner (who obviously had every material thing that he needed in this lifetime) they offered a special program of riding. Keeping their preparations a secret, they created their own choreography, programmed it to music, and in the evening presented a stunning equine show on the lawn with the castle as a background behind them. Kerstin remembered two Pas de Deux, one Quadrille and a group ride with eight gray horses. A rumor that there would be another gala on the owner's sixty-fifth birthday had everyone wondering how the magic of that first evening could possibly be topped.

The social aspect of riding and its potential for fun and celebration was new and intriguing to me. Everyone, performers and spectators alike, appeared to have such a good time, and the enormous amount of organization required seemed to be something that people did quite willingly. I was to find out as time went on, that since such soirees and equestrian social events took place often and indeed were even an almost "expected" part of life in the German horse world, many riders acquired a certain performance know-how and could either be instantly creative or knew where to find someone to help them. I once heard Walter advise a successful student that if she were asked to perform with a certain group at a certain "show," she must do it without fail as the invitation alone was a tremendous compliment.

However, as we turned off the autobahn toward Herbert Rehbein's stable, it wasn't castles or performances that I wanted to think about, it was dressage training. I wondered if I would be so overcome by what I would see that I would wish in my heart that I was a student at Grönwohld instead of at Stall Tasdorf. Thinking this, I glanced guiltily at Kerstin. I must be careful. She was perceptive enough to notice if I were to have such a reaction. But no—I caught myself—it wasn't as if I had come here looking for something more than I had found at Tasdorf: I was more than satisfied there. In fact, I knew with complete certainty that there was no one who could teach me better or faster than Walter.

Learning had seasons, like weather. Changes could come fast or slow; they might be continuous or interrupted. Learning was a waiting game, and as I worked within the earnest circle of Tasdorf's riders, I had even begun to notice *how* I waited, during those times when nothing else seemed to be happening. The quality of mind with which I approached the work was important, perhaps in the end as important as the work itself. Finally, as we sped along the tree-bordered side road, my mind settled and I knew beyond a doubt that the visit to Rehbein's was right for me. I was simply satisfying exactly the kind of curiosity that was appropriate to further my education.

We arrived in Trittau, the small town that was the mailing address for Herbert Rehbein. In size, it was like any one of the villages around Tasdorf, offering a mixture of both old and new and the usual basic essentials. After several minutes of driving through "nothing special," I was quite unprepared, when we turned off the road, to wind up in a parking lot large enough for a half a dozen tour buses. The simplest of signs announced that we had reached our destination—Grönwohld.

We were the only vehicle in the lot that morning, so I couldn't help wondering who normally filled it. Perhaps the turn-around space was needed for the enormous vans that transport horses to the competitions, or was it that this man was so famous that he drew vast crowds of spectators? I felt small before I even stepped out of the car.

So, there it was—Grönwohld. I studied the complex of the riding hall and the adjoining stable, first in terms of construction and second in terms of design. The bones, muscle, and flesh, so to speak, were wood, glass, and brick. A hard finish of white paint gave off a distinct gleam of cleanliness and perfection. It was as if the building had reached the apex of being competition "fit." As for the layout of the establishment, it was so spread out that in order to get any true sense of the whole you would have to see it from above like a bird, or staying earthbound, explore the entire place on foot.

I had been told that the stable unit had been constructed a dozen years ago on the grounds of an old and beautiful estate, with a castle that was still standing and in beautiful repair. From where I was standing I could see a pond, an outdoor dressage ring, paddocks, cultivated fields, and finally, far in the distance, hectares of woodland. The pathways from the parking lot and the roadway were immaculately clean. No dead branches. No leaves. No piles of manure or remnants of straw. The place exuded an atmosphere of elegance and ancient quiet in a setting as cared for as a small private historic park that was, on occasion, open to the public. Set off to one side were several low, green, wooden farm buildings that housed the horses involved in the breeding program that was the passion of Grönwohld's owner, Herr Otto Schulte-Frohlinde. It was Herbert Rehbein's job to train these stallions, which he and his wife Karin then rode in almost every important dressage competition in the country.

Kerstin led the way into a new-looking building through a small green door. We walked past a secretarial office, through a second door and, wondering if I was entering a place of business rather than a stable, I was just about to ask, "What kind of a workplace is this?" when, opening another door, I found myself in a rotunda with a ceiling two stories high. Our heels clacked loudly with each step on the hard tile floor. This was not at all the way I wanted to make my entrance: I had the feeling that perhaps we should remove our shoes, but Kerstin, undisturbed, was explaining that on the other side of the rotunda was a casino for the customers and above it, the owner's luxurious apartment. The indoor ring was just beyond. Customers and friends could watch the riding through a wall of windows that looked out on the arena and the owner could look down anytime he chose and see Herbert working his horses.

Three aisles led from the rotunda into the stall areas. I could see horses standing out on cross-ties being groomed. As we entered one of the aisles, we heard a voice call out a rather mystifying order: "Don't let the rabbit out!" The first box on the left of the aisle farthest right belonged to Gassendi, Herbert Rehbein's top horse. I would have recognized that fellow anywhere. He had the kind of frame that could have supported a knight in full armor with ease. What a horse to ride! The breadth of his neck, the melding of work muscle and stallion conformation made the horse's crest more pronounced than any I had ever seen.

"You'll never believe this," Kerstin said, "look over here." I looked to where she was pointing under the feed tub, and saw the reason for the earlier warning—a rabbit the size of a Jack Russell Terrier was sound asleep in the straw, not a carrot's length away from Gassendi's front hoof.

Noticing our astonishment, one of the barn workers came over and explained to us that the stallion was high strung and nervous in his training, so Herbert had thought that giving him a companion might relax him. He presented Gassendi with a rabbit, and the friendship was instant. The horse never stepped on or harmed the rabbit in any way, and it was quite obvious that the two cared about each other.

For a few minutes the excitement of my visit to Grönwohld faded, as I thought of my own bunny back home and how much I missed him. My rabbit wasn't anyone's roommate, but he was every-one's friend. He and our cat acted like the proprietors of my barn, checking with all the people who came and went. My horses were comfortable with them, interacting with them in many interesting ways. Though none of my animals needed a "bonding pal," I did know of some instances in my neighborhood where a pony, a goat, or a dog became a special friend for a horse. There was a cat who spent his nights sleeping on his horse's back, a rooster who adopted a jumper, and a mouse who came to a stall for dinner and stayed to nest and produce a family.

Putting my thoughts of home behind me, I noticed that Gassendi's aisle was becoming suddenly more active. Kerstin had returned to the rotunda, but I hung back, curious to see more and get the feel of this famous place. A chestnut with a snippet of white on his forehead was being led back from the shower, his coat glis-tening the color of brick where the saddle had been. I saw he had eyes that looked anxious and frightened, and his attendant told me that he had just come in from an auction. When I was warned that he might kick, I flattened myself against the wall until he had passed.

A large-barreled gray was being attached to the cross-ties. His groom was wiping his face with a piece of white toweling and talking to him. This was obviously a ritual they both loved. Directly across from Gassendi, the stall door was open, and I looked in to see a groom on her knees earnestly trying to put leg wraps on a restless bay, while a helper simultaneously checked the fit of the bridle over the animal's large Roman nose. Every time she tightened the strap, the horse jerked his head upward, pulling the leather right out of her hand. The irritation this person was feeling made her oblivious to her animal's stamping feet. How much more helpful it would have been, I thought to myself, had she allowed the groom to finish her job before she had begun fussing with the tack.

From a distant box a voice called out, asking to borrow a string girth. Then the groom, a thin young girl with a worried face, came out to explain. The horse she was caring for had unexpectedly developed a small sore on his belly and the leather girth that was customarily used would surely irritate the tender spot. The horse was scheduled in the ring for training in five minutes—would someone, anyone, please help?

The someone who came to the rescue was an Englishman. I identified him as a visiting student because when he went to his equipment trunk, I saw a book on the effects of the German seat among a portfolio and a pile of official looking papers. Horses in the "big time" require passports as well as trunks of their own. Some of these containers can be impressive, with heavy brass edging, a sesame lock, designer stable stripes, and a large nameplate. Most tack trunks are the size of an old-fashioned steamer trunk and are models of organization, expert packing, and practical housekeeping. It was from a most conservative trunk, painted silver and sky blue and labeled "Hollow Tree Farm, England," that two string girths of different sizes were found and graciously offered. One fit.

The young groom pushed her stall door wide, her face bright with relief. "Eyes up!" she called out, and led her charge down the aisle with such care that he could have been made of blown glass. Sympathetic smiles followed her passage toward the ring. Everyone there knew about the urgency of lesson times.

Dressage is not only about horses. It's about clocks; a discipline that operates on a precise timetable. Competitions are scheduled to the second and the rules allow a rider only one minute to get into the ring once the judge has blown the whistle to announce that "it's time." If you arrive any later, you are eliminated from riding that particular test. The discipline of dressage teaches you to gauge the dimensions of time and its increments. What is a minute? Is it long? Short? Does it seem to stretch? In training work, the rules are individual rather than standard, and are certainly far less rigid than those of show time. However, trainer, rider, and groom are still expected to arrive in the ring precisely on time. Excuses are not acceptable.

I joined Kerstin in the ring in time to see what was obviously the owner of the young groom's horse prepare to mount her steed. The woman looked stunning and I was struck by the difference in the riding clothes of Americans and Germans. I was accustomed to a casual, comfortable, even sloppy look; I had even gone out to buy shirts, vests, and jackets that had been purposely made to appear worn. This woman looked elegant enough to lunch at a high-toned restaurant in Hamburg. Nattily dressed in matching gray pants and shirt, and just about the handsomest blue heather sweater I had ever seen, she jolted my sense of what was appropriate dress for daily riding and even made me wonder if I had made enough effort with my own appearance for this visit. "Who is that?" I asked, thinking she was too dressed up to be much of a rider. If I would have noticed at that moment rather than later that her boots were worn only on the inside of the calf, I'd have known that she rode well. Wear marks don't lie. They can tell you almost anything about a rider you might want to know.

The groom buckled the girth into the final hole and handed over the horse. The woman took up the reins, put a foot into the stirrup iron and swung aboard. It was obvious that she knew what she was doing and didn't have to think twice about it. Crop in hand, eyes focused on the direction she would take, jaw firm as a gavel, she was immediately "all business" and ready to be under Herbert's professional eye as soon as he dismounted from the chestnut he was riding.

I wasn't surprised when Kerstin informed me that this accomplished lady was one of Herbert's most long-term customers. He had found her the stallion she was riding and he regularly trained both horse and rider. The woman, Kerstin said, was an experienced "hobby rider," the term used in Germany to explain those who rode for the pleasure of it. How I disliked that term, "hobby rider." It undermined the art—suggested it could be a casual endeavor—and to me did not in any way describe or suggest the out-and-out hard work involved in learning to ride dressage well.

We joined a dozen and a half spectators on a long bench near the entrance door of the arena. I discovered that the observers came from many distant lands. Several had horses in Grönwohld for training, but most of them were friends or acquaintances of the riders, a kind of "in" group so totally focused on the activity in the ring that any needless conversation and the usual German-style introductions were unimportant and unfinished. We were a serious group of bench sitters that morning at Grönwohld—it was obvious that watching the work was the center of each person's world. I felt that my eyes were out on stalks trying to take in every combination of horse and rider and still concentrate on Herbert.

Apparently, he was about to finish working with the animal he was riding. There was just one small matter that they needed to iron out—a question of a transition—the one between the piaffe and the passage. The horse seemed to be having difficulty maintaining rhythm, collection, and suspension when going from the elevated, suspended steps of the piaffe done in place to the forward motion of the passage. He would lunge flat-backed into the first seconds of passage. I wondered if the horse was afraid of the movement, confused or perhaps a bit muscle sore. Herbert's face was impassive, but there was a kind of set quality to it that that I interpreted as "This kind of a performance can't continue." In spite of the creature's infraction, he was sitting as quietly on that horse's back as if he were a cat, unmoving, solid, never for one second out of balance. I thought, "Boy, this is Herbert. This is what he is so famous for, the quality that everyone talks about as 'unmatched' in today's world: his unparalleled ability to sit on a horse, to always be in the perfect place at all times." I had seen Rehbein before—had this amazing quality pointed out to me at competitions—but here was the perfect-seat-man up close. Here I was observing him right in his own home territory. What more would he have to show me?

Within minutes, Herbert brought the horse so thoroughly under the saddle, had him so well in control and listening with such attention that the flattening and lunging had entirely ceased. With an expression of surprise and utter compliance, the chestnut responded to Herbert's demands and stepped into picture-perfect transitions. "Do you see that?" said one woman to her neighbor. "That horse only arrived here yesterday. The owner should see this.

She won't believe what Herbert has done with her horse in the first day of training. She's been struggling with these transitions for two years. There was a sudden death in her family so I offered to bring her horse on ahead to Grönwohld. It was a good excuse for me to come—I've always wanted to see this place."

"You were smart to keep the commitment," Kerstin said to the lady, "Herbert is so popular it's not easy to get in here." Turning to me she commented, "Herbert can get things out of a horse that no one else can."

It seemed almost as if all he had to do was indicate to the horse in his way, "I'm ready, are you?" With another trainer this would have been a question; with Herbert, it was a statement that meant "no wasting of time." He was focused, efficient, almost businesslike, and went straight to the points that he wished to finely tune.

Dressage at this high level demands attention to the tiniest refinements. Where each hoof is placed, how much do the haunches lower, is the rhythm maintained, and does each stride flow—these are just a few of the concerns. To my "learning eye," every step Herbert and his horse took was exquisite, and in tune. I knew that I was just beginning to be able to see the corrections that he was making.

At one point, as he was working a second horse, a black stallion, a sound burst from the spectators sitting next to me, an "aaaah" of amazement. Herbert had begun the work with the piaffe. At first, it appeared that the horse was unsure about what he was supposed to do. He stiffened and became a classic picture of resistance. Herbert remained quiet and waited a few seconds. I wondered whether he was talking to the horse. It was hard to tell. The horse appeared confused by this waiting tactic. He became desperate to move on. But, Herbert continued to wait. When, at last, he did allow the horse to move, by some magic that I was unable to detect, the animal went right into the correct rhythm for the piaffe, gaining confidence with each second, the skin of his body growing tight with power and his legs lifting higher, achieving greater suspension. A slight smile crossed Herbert's face. He gave the black horse one quick pat on his sweaty neck and gave him a long rein. Obviously, that four-legged student's lesson was over for the day.

I was hot with excitement and wanted to applaud, but none of the other bench sitters had their hands out and ready, so I curbed my enthusiasm and decided that Herbert's work was regarded as simply "every day schooling" around here. It pleased me to recall that Walter and Herbert were good friends of long standing. They had, in fact, shared the same instructor and apprenticed in the same stable in Flensburg. "From the day Herbert arrived," Walter had told me, "that young boy's talent was obvious to everyone. He could sit on any horse and always bring out the best."

By the time Kerstin and I rose to leave, I realized that I had witnessed living proof of Walter's words. As we retraced our steps and returned to the stable's rotunda, I asked myself the question, "Do I wish I was training here?" "No," was my answer. After all, I could always visit Grönwohld. Herbert Rehbein and Walter Christensen need not be compared. They performed two quite different functions. It was evident that Grönwohld was a show stable, a kind of graduate school, a place for a rider who already had a great deal of experience to prepare himself and his horse for high-level competition. Tasdorf was a training stable, a teaching stable, and an institution in which to learn from the bottom up—certainly the right place for me. If I had accomplished only one thing in Germany, it was to gain an ever greater and deeper respect for the discipline, endurance, and endless patience required to perfect the art I had chosen. Falling in love with it over and over again as I had just done at Grönwohld helped to renew me, to give me hope, to see my struggles as inevitable, and to prevent me from getting so discouraged that I'd think about going home. My training was becoming more than just riding—it was a personal revelation, causing me to view myself with fresh eyes. Before Germany, I had thought of riding as separate from me, as something I "did." Now, at last, I was facing facts—riding *was* me.

As Kerstin and I drove home through the late afternoon shadows, I was attempting to thrust such thoughts into the background and come up with heartfelt words of appreciation for the welcome "ausflug" (day trip). I wanted to tell her that she had added yet another strand in the weaving of our growing friendship, but it was Kerstin herself who broke our companionable silence. "It's a treat to watch that man, isn't it?" she remarked. From the rosy color in her cheeks and the cheeriness of her mood, I could tell that she had reacted to the experience with her own brand of interest, excitement, and intensity. "Good!" I thought, "she's enjoyed this almost as much as I have." I had not forgotten the mixed messages with which she had greeted my initial suggestion of a visit to Grönwohld. Kerstin's response, I now surmised, had probably been a naturally protective reaction given the complexity of pressures all German horse professionals live with—nothing more.

In the twilight, we sped toward home, chatting happily, reviewing our Grönwohld stay and planning the dinner we would put together when we arrived at home.

Boot Camp

During my stay in Germany, I was always keenly aware of the pressure of time passing. In the beginning, there were weeks when I was plagued with the thought that I could just as well have been at home. Days, hours, even minutes went by without a sense of accomplishment. Finally, I had to face the fact that I wasn't going to have things as I wanted them. I was going to have them the way they were. Wasn't that why I had come to this foreign country in the first place?

I decided to become adept at the art of observation and to use my unaccustomed spare time to learn from the world around me. On weekday mornings, I would come to the stable early, arriving by eight o'clock. The stable's apprentices would be on their horses in the indoor ring that still contained small patches of fog. Condensation rose everywhere like steam from a cup of coffee. The overhead electric light was mournfully dim and the nip in the air kept everyone turned inward. Nobody had thought of switching on the radio; music to ride by would come later in the day. This was no doubt the quietest time at Tasdorf, although the staff was already hard at work.

Up in the casino, the stable cook would have begun her war against dirt. She commenced with the two lavatories off the entry hall. Working from top to bottom, she confronted every surface in reach with a scrub brush in the manner of one daring the world on her side of the ocean to be anything but shiny and clean. As a rule, customers weren't around at this hour, nor had the usual deliveries for the kitchen and the casino begun. Both front entrances to Stall Tasdorf remained locked. Only the small, wooden, metal-latched door that led directly from the parking lot into the main stable aisle was open. The outside world was not yet welcome.

I, however, was not the average customer, and my presence there expressed what was often foremost in my mind: believe me, I felt like saying, I'd be one of you if I were allowed. I know this is not my hour to ride but I want to watch so I don't miss anything.

It was in observing the apprentices (lehrlingers) during these early "pre-business" hours of the day that I began to realize how much their lives at Tasdorf intrigued me. They inhabited a world that I privately came to call "Walter's Boot Camp," a kind of preparatory training site for entrance into Germany's equestrian world. Walter ran his "camp" with the dedication, discipline, and precision of an excellent military leader (in time I was to discover that though I was not an apprentice, I was, to some degree, also perceived as a "rookie" here at Tasdorf.)

I found the well-known and much admired German equestrian apprenticeship program fascinating. We have nothing quite like it in America. Back home, young people wanting to follow a career involved with horses attend any one of a dozen colleges or universities offering a two year curriculum and a special diploma in horse mastership. Following this, they must find a way to further their equestrian education on their own. They may apply to a stable as a working student or if they are extremely lucky, they may find a job training directly under a teacher of their choice. The United States offers no formal, structured program of equestrian education on a national or even local basis.

In Europe, however, the concept of apprenticeship has been a tradition for centuries. Germany's National Equestrian Federation, which is based in Warendorf, establishes and maintains a hands-on, in depth, no frills, three-year equestrian apprenticeship program culminating in national certification.

This primary course requires full time commitment to an accredited stable. Apprentices are given training in every possible aspect of horsemanship. One day a week they must continue their general book education and attend a normal school. With typical German thoroughness, a recruit's progress is checked midway through the course, when he or she must go to Warendorf for three days of written and oral examinations. There, the student is tested in horse care, basic veterinary knowledge, equine theory, barn management and, of course, riding ability. At Tasdorf, I would hear the apprentices warn the newest among them that they could look forward to a grueling time in Warendorf.

At the completion of three years of commitment in a teaching stable, the lehrlinger returns once again to Warendorf for more examinations and several final weeks of training by some of the country's top professionals. At this time, the young person must meet specific qualification in jumping and dressage, must be able to train a young horse, and must demonstrate rudimentary skills as a riding instructor. He or she may even be asked to draw up plans to build a stable. Should he wish to pursue teaching, he must, according to German law, be certified as an instructor. Small wonder that while other countries struggle to make up one Olympic team to represent them every four years, Germany could easily field four or five, and all of them would be of the best quality.

The Stall Tasdorf apprenticeship program was accredited by the Federation and maintained an on-going student body of from four to six lehrlingers for the three-year commitment. I saw that while this certification brought in many hands to do the work, it simultaneously placed a day-to-day responsibility upon the Christensens, especially Walter. Fortunately, he took a great interest in the program, both from a professional point of view and in a personal sense. He had come to think of the students as his children (in a non-sentimental but dedicated way). I saw Walter exhibit real pride when he remarked to me that at testing time, the apprentices are given two grades, one for *how* the requirement is fulfilled and the other for *the manner* or *attitude* with which it is done. His lehrlingers had done very well in both areas. Hearing this, I began to understand much more about the atmosphere in the stable.

Was Stall Tasdorf a typical German stable? No, by general standards it was small. Thirty-five stalls are not many in a country where stables can consist of over a hundred stalls, several barns and two or three indoor rings. Moreover, Tasdorf was not quite in the center of the "horse industry" country. Further south, around Frankfurt, more money and intense competition surrounded everything to do with equestrian life. There, parents regularly buy horses for fifty to seventy-five thousand dollars to insure that their sons and daughters make them proud during the Junior Championships.

Tasdorf was some kilometers out of the way, tucked into an area known primarily for farming. The physical isolation of the stable allowed for a slower pace and less distraction. It was an ideal location for the kind of intensive apprenticeship program that Walter Christensen offered. Well-known for his strict adherence to basics, he trained both riders and horses at all levels and gave those who came to him not only ample opportunity to school young horses, but a sound grounding in horsemanship, horse care, and theory. From one point of view, you might say that Tasdorf served as a unique and personal kind of finishing school.

Walter's own commitment to his lehrlingers was an essential ingredient in the character, the atmosphere, and the scheduling of workday activities. As I lived alongside of and observed the apprenticeship program, I envied the trainees their opportunity. I often wondered if I could have coped with the long hours, the intense labor, and the almost totally mind-consuming focus. Could I have stood in an apprentice's shoes?

The responsibility of maintaining a training program wearied Walter, but there were times in the year when his life changed emphasis. I didn't know anything about those times until one morning when I saw him taking leave of his stable crew, sporting a business suit, a pair of glasses, and a briefcase. The look on his face said, "This is serious business." Everyone knew where he was going except me. I noticed their pride in him so I asked what was going on. Only then did I discover that this reticent and modest man was one of the judges for the Warendorf testing commission.

He returned three days later a different man, tired but exhilarated as if he'd heard the best news. Typically for him, he would not come right out and say "his boys" were doing very well and getting high marks. He would slip his news into the conversation only after he had dwelt on it a good while privately. At times, he might not even mention his apprentices' successes until he was home alone with his wife. It took a customer to tell me that the previous year one of the Stall's graduates had completed the Warendorf Reitlehrer class (the certified riding instructor course). Jurgen, I learned, had not only received the highest score in his class, but the best score in all of West Germany. He had even been summoned to the spotlight during the Neumünster Dressage Show to receive a special award and the applause of several thousand countrymen.

Early on an ordinary weekday morning in the stable, awards were certainly not on Walter Christensen's mind. I usually came upon him sitting on his bench just inside the ring. I suspected that he was preparing for the day, pondering over the work to be accomplished. Walter had a posture both mental and physical that I'd observed and loved in natural born woodsmen. There was an aura of easiness about him that was at once relaxed and fully alert. This ageless, timeless, essential way of his touched a deep chord within me, and seeing him quietly sitting on his bench, I would take the place next to him and silently watch the work going on in the ring.

This first hour of the riding day belonged to the apprentices: it was their special time to take out the more difficult or advanced horses to which they were assigned. When they rode under Herr Christensen's eyes, school was intensely in session as the principles of training and riding were hammered home. Although the lehr-lingers rode at other times of the day, it was for these moments of Herr Christensen's undivided attention that the apprentices waited with both nervousness and pleasure, each hoping to do the best he or she had done yet.

Part of Walter's work was to keep on top of everything and to anticipate what lay ahead. His ability to do this was both frightening and amazing to us all. I used to think of him as a frog on a lily pad, never even needing to turn his head, accumulating information in his own still way. Walter could tell me that the stable cat hadn't been seen for two days, that a most important client was angry when she came to ride although she was smiling, that the "new boy" was complaining about the treatment he received at Tasdorf, that the girl from Finland couldn't keep her eyes off Jurgen, that Dieter hadn't polished his boots all week, and that a certain other lehrlinger was ducking work.

Walter had straight and simple things to say about chores that didn't get done. From boyhood on, he had faced the need to work, and it was as much a part of life for him as breathing. For Walter, life and work were one and the same thing, and he expected his apprentices to live by this principle as well. Lazy young people, like lazy horses, were seldom allowed to stay in the stable long, and although it wasn't used as a threat, it was common knowledge that there was sizable waiting list to apprentice at Stall Tasdorf.

In Germany, the learning process is approached with a critical attitude that demands perfection and separates "good" form from "bad" with razor-sharp keenness—one possible reason why the apprenticeship program is so successful. At first, this approach set me back on my heels. I had not expected the horse world of my dreams to be a place of such rigid distinctions between right and wrong, where good and bad are absolutes; however, I soon discovered that I had entered a world with no gray areas and no room for personal observations. Once the school bell rang, my state of mind and my opinions were of no interest—considered instead as the kind of fluffery that could be aired later or perhaps not at all.

At Tasdorf, I saw this attitude applied to youngsters and customers alike. It didn't matter an oat's worth whether the client had a title, was a "Von" something-or-other, or a newly arrived American like me. Excuses were not countenanced while you were in the stable. You did whatever you were doing in ways that were considered correct or you didn't do it at all. I believe that Germans accept this philosophy easily. Americans have a harder time: they have personal opinions.

One day, after an especially trying morning, I was feeling as if I was the most inept recruit in the entire establishment. Looking for sympathy, I sought out a German member of the working crew with whom I felt a certain kinship. I stood in front of her, dropped a bitter remark and waited. She surprised me by saying, in a tone of voice worthy of a pulpit, "Now you know why riders here are good. You have to keep trying with everything you've got. One day perhaps, you may catch on." If she had added that riding could be a kind of religion and that working at it day after day was as fulfilling for her as daily bread, I'd have said, "Now, I'm beginning to understand."

When I first began taking my own hour of instruction with Walter, I had trouble adjusting to what I saw as his "boot-camp" mentality. "How rigid this man is," I thought, wishing that he could occasionally be satisfied with the way I rode, or at least accept my work as "near right." I wanted him to note the sweat on my brow, consider that my muscles were straining, and be satisfied with my efforts. Wasn't all that worth something? No, it was not. The way I was riding wasn't right. Later, so slowly and gradually that for a long time I did not perceive the change in me, I grew to rejoice in this manner of instruction. I wrote home that my lessons were to the point, clear, and wonderfully clean. Except, of course, for those moments when everything seemed to fall apart.

And certainly, there were those moments. In the ring, you never knew what events might bring about an upsurge of adrenaline that would destroy your carefully laid plans. For instance, there were mornings in February and early March when snow slid off the roof, making a sound not unlike that of an approaching train, causing immediate wide-eyed terror amongst the horses. Then later, in spring, at a certain hour the sun would enter from the roof ridge high above us and lie in one single yellow ribbon across the floor from one end of the ring to the other. I never knew who among the horses would cross it and who had no intention of doing so. Or again, the cat, who Walter jokingly threatened to name "Priscilla," might appear out of nowhere, walk along the side rail like a sailor on a plank, and then jump into the ring, causing every horse in the place to bolt.

Inca was an old hand at snow, sun, cats and all of that, but he was a sly fellow as well as being a Thoroughbred stoked with hot blood. In addition, he had his own brand of humor. On occasion, he liked to remind me never to think of him as an old man!

Some of the male apprentices thought a certain amount of bucking and jumping around was fun. "It's like a rodeo today," one of them would say gleefully, reminding me how much the Germans love our wild west. I noticed when the boys got going, the female apprentices cleared right out of the way and stayed quiet.

"Do you like this?" I'd ask them?

"Oh, a few bucks are nothing to worry about," might be the answer, yet I never saw a single girl join in.

Without much feedback on their fears from the other riders at Stall Tasdorf, I began to wonder if I thought more about it than they did. The people who came daily to ride appeared cool and impressively professional, and after a time, I too was calmer, reassured by Walter's presence and the fact that his swift intervention prevented many a mishap.

In the presence of fear, Walter would take control. Without even rising to his feet, he could make himself felt over in the farthest corner. Anticipating the uncertainty inherent in such a moment, Walter's voice would become immediately loud and commanding. I understood he was trying to break through the rider's fear in order to get him to respond properly.

For me, one of the most frightening equine experiences is to be on the back of a horse that is rearing up, straight as a palm tree. Not only is it a terrible feeling, it can also be a dangerous moment.

Instead of sitting on top of the beast, you are gripping on to his sides, probably more than likely holding on for dear life, wondering whether you are both going to topple over. You're so nervous you don't even know what you're doing to those reins. "Let go of your reins!" Walter would shout. "You're pulling him over backward!"

To someone looking on, rearing may look as if it's happening in slow motion, but to the rider it feels very fast indeed. You must react swiftly, catch the precise second when the animal comes back down on all fours and then send him forward. You must make him use all parts of himself on terra firma before he can think of rearing back up again.

It was at these moments that Walter would bring out his cannon voice and boom, "Vorwärtz!" making you more frightened of him than you were of the horse. Hearing the shouted command, you would find yourself giving over both to the horse rearing and to Walter's instruction. "If it kills me, I'll do what the man's saying," you'd say to yourself.

Whatever the level of fear, it is an aspect of riding that confronts all riders from beginners to apprentices to Olympic competitors. Most experienced riders are comfortable about admitting to fear, for they have become familiar with it over the years. Unlike the young German Tasdorf crew for whom the subject (at least in front of me) seemed taboo, Olympic riders will discuss fear and point out that, at times, it is positive and beneficial. Fear can help you stay alert and be especially careful, and it can give you an instant shot of energy.

It is helpful also to realize that human fear has its counterpart in animals for whom it can be equally as paralyzing. Horses, for instance, are generous and trusting by nature, more so even than children. However, sometimes, through bad handling, they can lose that trust and develop fears that can change and distort their natural responses. It is wise to bear this in mind.

It didn't take many weeks to discover that fear was only one of the challenges that confronted the young apprentices at Tasdorf, and I came to appreciate what a hard career these committed lehrlingers had chosen. They faced never-ending work and in addition lived with the anxiety that at the end of their apprenticeship there might not be a job open to them in the big "out there." To establish a professional career centering on horses appears easier to people who are not pursuing it. They imagine that anyone with coordination and love of horses can become good enough to enter the field.

Even the lehrlingers' visiting parents sitting in the casino over beer or coffee and proudly watching their offspring often had little understanding of their sons' and daughters' worries. Frequently, I would overhear these young riders questioning each other about their futures. They did it endlessly, even obsessively. How did they look? Did they show talent? Would there be a job open for them? What would they end up being: riders, trainers, instructors, breeders? Each had his or her preference. In most cases, the desired goal was to become one of Germany's most famous and recognized riders, the equivalent of a successful performing artist. In their country, these young contenders faced more competition than they would have met in America or even in any other European country. Their concern for the future was like a hunk of gristle to be continuously chewed on.

Once in a while, I had trouble with what seemed the harsh treatment meted out to my young apprentice friends. I'd have to shake my head to vent my feelings, and I wondered whether young Americans would have been equally able to handle the military-style rules and discipline. When I imagined one of my children in such a situation, I realized, I wanted niceties. Weren't niceties important? We were accustomed not only to politeness, but to having our opinions asked for, or at least heard. We expected our emotional and physical needs to be noted and perhaps even accommodated. Had all of us back home been coddled and spoiled? These were the questions that arose for me, but at the same time, I also wondered if I was asking for too much from a work situation that dealt primarily with physical action that very often brooked no delay.

The apprentices themselves did not seem to share my concerns. "It's very good here at Tasdorf, it's the best," I was assured. These post-adolescent young people appeared to grasp the concept of wholehearted commitment and accept the roughness of their hard life in a way that I could not. Dissonant moments were met with an appearance of toughness, a shrug of the shoulders or a slap on the back. "Let it pass," or words to that effect might be said as one passed another on the way to do chores.

It appeared to me that the apprentice's most trying time came with his or her arrival as a "new" boy or girl. The newcomer had to figure out, learn and remember the individual details relating to each of thirty-five horses. This eager soul was expected to watch, question, fumble, and pray. Nothing mattered as long as he got the facts right. "Please" and "Thank you" did not exist. There were only more and more demands and sometimes the query, "Why wasn't this done sooner?"

When the new lehrlinger tacked up a horse for Walter's assistant, his work would be carefully checked. Had the student put the right equipment on the horse and had he done it correctly? Details were important.

For instance, there is one correct place on a horse's back to put the saddle, and it's easy to make a mistake. If the saddle is placed too far forward—the way I did until Walter's assistant (bereiter) pointed this out—the movement of the horse's shoulders may be restricted. If it is placed too far back, the rider's weight sits uncomfortably close to the animal's kidneys. I was warned never, NEVER, to girth up a horse so there is a wrinkle in his skin. Because I had made these mistakes myself when I first arrived, I sympathized with—no, more than that—I empathized with whoever faced "learning how" at Stall Tasdorf.

In his or her first days, a new apprentice was hardly ever seen. The first lessons were out back: feeding horses at 6 AM, cleaning stalls and tack, and sweeping the stable aisle. If he was lucky—no horse returning from the vet, and no unexpected, unexplained, late hour occurrence—his day ended at 6 PM. Unless of course it was his turn to do night check.

For the newcomer, recognition came when he was ordered to put down the pitchfork and "cool out" a horse. "Cooling out" took no talent. All that was required was that someone climb up in the saddle and walk the horse dry. If the apprentice was wise, he would keep a sharp eye out and not get in anyone's way. Only the unenlightened considered this a moment to rest. If he had his wits about him, he'd sit tall, hold the reins correctly and notice everything happening around him.

There appeared to be no rule as to how many days should pass before the novice would be assigned a horse of his own. The deciding factor was the number of horses needing to be ridden. The apprentice's first mount would probably be unschooled, or "recently backed" and perhaps not so easy. It was considered ill-advised to give a horse well along in his training to someone who didn't know how to ride well because the rider's inexperience might confuse the animal and cause him to regress in his work. The novice had to learn the basics first: that way, horse and rider could "come along" together. The night following his "promotion" to riding his own horse, the new lehrlinger would no doubt telephone his parents to tell them he had taken the first step in his career. Walter, on the other hand, considered the moment when an apprentice first took a pitchfork in hand as his true beginning.

How long the newcomer remained "new" had to do with many factors: talent, ability to learn and, on occasion, other specific bits of knowledge he might have brought to the job. If he had been lucky enough to grow up on a breeding farm, he'd already have expertise with young stock. If his older brother had been a mechanic or his father a plumber and he had worked with them, his know-how might make him more instantly essential and thereby integrate him into the crew faster. A unique skill was an asset not to be thrown away. Running a stable like Tasdorf was an endless and varied task. People's ingenuity as well as experience were being continuously tested.

As I learned more about the apprenticeship program at Tasdorf, I became intrigued with the question of how Walter chose his lehrlingers. What was the process? What were the criteria? And from the viewpoint of the young people, how did they even know where they might wish to train or with whom? Upon discreet inquiry, I learned that settling on the stable of one's choice was a matter of investigation. In short, one asked around. Better still, one visited. Although Walter was not famous in Germany in the sense certain riders or a few top instructors could be, his reputation in the profession was rock solid and well known. Once having chosen a stable like Tasdorf, would you need an interview, I wondered? Or would a letter with references and a request suffice? If an interview was required, did an applicant have to take a test ride? What if you hardly knew how to ride, could you still be considered?

In the early months of my stay, I didn't have the chance to observe the recruitment process and see my questions answered first hand. There were few changes in Walter's stable among the trainees and therefore few interviews. Then, on a sunny April morning, a young man arrived. I was told of the visit because the fellow was said to speak English. Walter used to inform me when someone who spoke my language was due to arrive, just in case I might wish to be present and have a chat. Usually, I found myself face to face with a somewhat startled German, who upon being told to "say something in English," couldn't remember any words at all—not an easy situation for the poor victim.

However, on that particular spring day, the blond young man who greeted me was surprisingly fluent in my native tongue. His name was Volker Brommann and apparently he had grown up in the same town as Jurgen, Walter's bereiter. It was Jurgen who had told Volker he should apprentice at Stall Tasdorf and highly recommended his young friend to Herr Christensen. When Volker and I shook hands in the casino and exchanged smatterings of conversation, I could not have foreseen that his better-than-average knowledge of English, his desire to teach, and his ability as a horseman would ultimately bring him to my land to live and finally to my farm as an instructor.

After our initial chat, I sat down at a respectful distance away, and kept an eye on the meeting between Volker and Walter. Observing the procedure made me think of Walter Christensen as a theater director, and I wondered if the interview was like casting a play. I knew that to take someone into his program meant that Walter had to consider many factors. The most important quality of all in an applicant, he claimed, was teachability. A student who knew practically nothing and was almost a total beginner would be preferable to one who thought he was experienced, felt he knew it all, and had set ideas. That kind, Walter had learned over the years, was the hardest to train.

Walter's requirements were basic and offered little variation. Did the boy or girl appear to have a comfortable way with horses? Such a quality was helpful. Did he show a natural talent for the job? Walter always hoped for at least some. Was he intelligent? Here, Walter defined a difference between intelligence in life and intelligence in school. When he first began taking apprentices, he had not thought that the latter was necessarily important. Then he changed his mind and looked for both. Would the young person be a good worker? Had he or she truly thought through working with horses as a lifetime career? Would the applicant fit in with the others?

In addition to these considerations was the fact that Walter had to take into account the size and shape of the horses that needed backing and training. A candidate's size, height, and build could therefore influence acceptance. Did Walter need a tall or a short rider? The applicant needed to physically fit the horses available at that moment.

Cleanliness and personal grooming were also factors, although this was not mentioned at the time of the interview. (Walter actually looked at people's hands.) Volker obviously had no problems in this area: he had the scrubbed look of a most appealing young man.

Though Volker's references must have suggested that he was an open, intelligent, hardworking candidate, anyone could have perceived these values just by looking at his face. He was in his late teens, a graduate of Germany's equivalent of our high school and eager to begin his "beruf" (career). The bright blue sweater that he wore outlined a boy's body that had yet to develop and a pair of shoulders that sloped like a pear. I remember thinking, "this fellow's just a kid." Later, Walter told me that Volker came from an earnest, careful family that didn't waste a thing, the sort who, as he put it, "broke the penny in two and thereby got double."

Walter claimed that, in general, he preferred taking on boys rather than girls. Stacking hay and shoveling snow were heavy work, and in the summer the special sand in the outdoor ring had to be turned over by hand. It was easier to find boys who could drive tractors, fix machinery, paint, wash horse trailers, stack hay and maneuver trucks into tight places. Too, they were more likely to be handymen of all kinds, good at carpentry and plumbing. In spite of this preference, Walter did include two or three girls in his group. One of the main reasons was to have lightweight riders for the young stock. A three-year-old's back is tender, without much flesh or protective muscle. However, once Herr Christensen accepted a girl, she was expected to do the same work as the boys.

Acceptance into the Tasdorf crew involved practical considerations as well, such as where the young people would live. These managerial decisions fell to Kerstin Christensen. The stable had three bedrooms, and at the time Volker appeared, they were filled. To handle overflow, the Christensens rented rooms from a local farmer down the street. When no space was available, an applicant might have to wait six months to a year. Luckily for Volker, Kerstin was able to put him up in the farmhouse.

After initial moments spent in conversation with Walter, Volker was taken down to the ring where he was given a horse named Vidette. The young man's long legs hung down nicely, and most importantly, his body remained relaxed and still. From my observation spot at the entrance to the ring, I heard Walter ask Volker when he could begin. May first, Volker told him. "Gut," said Walter.

Later, Volker remarked to me that he would always remember both how excited and how horrified he was that morning: committing himself to three years felt as though he was relinquishing a whole lifetime. Yet, halfway through his time at Tasdorf, he suffered moments of near panic when he realized that there was still so very much to learn and that he would not have Herr Christensen around very much longer.

The day that Volker began his Tasdorf training, it was his bit of luck to be given a horse to work with immediately. Without any preamble, while Volker peeled the shell off his breakfast egg, Herr Christensen gave the young man his first mounted assignment: Ajax was to become his responsibility. No reasons were given for this move. No explanation was made. Marin, Ajax's former rider, suddenly had one less horse to ride.

I discovered the explanation for this decision quite by chance. Kerstin told me that a young man from southern Germany would be appearing the following weekend in search of a horse to buy. Several would be shown to the visitor, but Ajax, being young and sizeable and well along in his basic work, seemed the most appropriate candidate. She also told me that it was Walter's habit whenever possible (if he or his assistant didn't sit on the prospective sale horses themselves), to have his boys work the horses that might be tried out by male buyers, and his girls ride the horses to be tried by women. Walter believed that men and women rode differently, that perhaps without realizing it, men used more strength and women more intuition. So, Ajax had been transferred over to the "new boy" whose build was similar to the buyer's.

Changes happened in the stable frequently. The reasons for them were open to all kinds of interpretations among the apprentices, but both Volker and Marin had learned to accept the boss's reassignment of the horses they would ride with no thought of asking why. After all, their daily existence was no longer in their own hands and they knew not to question what they were told to do. However, Ajax's former rider was unhappy; apprentices measured their worth by the horses that they were assigned, and Marin now felt herself to be in as low a place as Volker was high. When she heard that her Ajax was to be taken away, she immediately assumed she'd done a bad job. "What else should I think?" she asked when we spoke in the aisle. Her lips were drawn as tight as two reins, and two misty, sad eyes informed me that she no longer believed in herself.

Such disappointment was painful to see in one so inexperienced, vulnerable, and young. My motherly instincts rose to the surface. "Why," I asked myself, "at a period when life is hard enough anyway, can't the existence of these apprentices be made as easy as possible? If Walter had explained his reason for changing riders, how would it have hurt anyone?" The answer came to me almost as quickly as the questions: in Germany, any aspect of business is a very private matter (more private even than in America).

Nevertheless, I still found it very difficult to accept that these young people were not involved in at least some of the plans and decisions affecting their lives. Wouldn't allowing them some degree of input be one more way for them to grow? These were some of the questions I struggled with in my position as observer, but I kept my thoughts to myself, reminding myself that I was not a German native, that I didn't run a stable, and that I was not in charge of anything but myself and my riding. Furthermore, I understood that if I wanted to reach out to anyone around me, being judgmental wouldn't help. In the end, I wound up simply trying to offer a listening ear and an attitude of quiet support.

Among the crew in the stable, moments of irritation, anger, jealousy, hurt, and desperate feelings were certainly not uncommon. Invariably, they hid their moods from the customers and remained poker-faced in Herr Christensen's presence. Of course, not all of their gray hours were his fault; much was inherent in the job. Dawn to dark, the lehrlingers' lives were necessarily scheduled and confined. Evenings offered television, card games, reading, or writing letters, and little outside diversion. These young adults seldom got away from their work or even left the compound of the stable. Every second week, when they had a day and a half off, most of them went home. Monthly remuneration was the equivalent of merely a few hundred dollars, so that forays into Neumünster were rare and were anticipated as very special occasions. Pizza, junk food, soda pop, movies, or discos were expensive, even for the German apprentices' pocketbook. Yet, in spite of these limitations, the atmosphere in the stable was positive, primarily because every person was totally absorbed by and committed to this stage of their life's work. They focused upon the riding above everything else, discussing the training endlessly and in the most minute detail. Actually, the subject of horses—and every aspect concerning horses—was one they never appeared to exhaust, for they truly loved the animals deeply.

When the apprentices weren't cleaning stalls, brushing horses, holding them for the vet or the farrier, riding, feeding, or watching a lesson, they could be found in Stall Tasdorf's tack room. This was where a good portion of their lives was centered. They went there primarily to complete their duties, as well as to grab a few moments just to hang out. Observing that it was a gathering place, I headed there whenever I could, wanting to join them.

Like the casino, where the customers gathered, the tack room could be full of people one minute and empty the next. I liked it both ways and used its emptiness or its fullness to my advantage. Standing inside, I was just on the fringe of the mainstream comings and goings, but right at the heart of the stable. I could observe what was going on and not be obtrusive or in anyone's way. Best of all, I could be of help to the apprentices by cleaning tack. It was hard for me to find any sort of work to do. The chores were assigned only to the apprentices, so that I often felt excluded from the kind of stable duties that I was used to. Here was one place I could happily work away.

The room was half the size of Inca's stall, with a sign on the door that read "Sattelkammer" (saddle room). Housing all the horse equipment used on a daily basis, it was locked when Walter or the apprentices weren't around. Inside, the darkish space was a bit chilly and basically uninviting, but neither drawback bothered us. I'd go up close to the radiator under the one small window, clean tack and listen to what was being said. During the course of exchanging sponges, borrowing a towel, and passing the saddle soap, the customers, and especially the young people, began to say more to me than "Wie geht es?" (how's it going?) and "Bis morgen" (see you tomorrow).

When the moment came, as it so often did, that customers said they were late and rushed out the door to head home, I'd envy them. Home! Two or three of them said they envied *me* with time on my hands and the chance to remain in the stable. Then I'd think, no, you don't realize what it's like to be so far from home. I'd have to concentrate on a piece of leather until the pictures of home that flooded my mind flowed away. When the images were too strong and hung around for a while, I'd get tough the way the young people did, tell myself I was the real thing, an apprentice with a job on my hands, take on the whole pile of tack and scrub my way back into quietness of mind.

The Stall's tack room was a revelation. One side wall of the Sattelkammer was lined with three racks of saddles, the other wall with two tiers of bridles: the double bridles above and the snaffle bridles below. Every rack and each hook carried the name of the horse to whom it belonged. Such attention to personalized equipment, exact fittings and specific training requirements impressed me. At home, I'd known stables where one saddle fit several horses and a single bridle was simply enlarged or made small. One of the boys told me that shortcuts went on in Germany as well, especially on the farms, but never in the larger and recognized riding establishments, whether they specialized in dressage, jumping or any other aspect of equestrian sport.

Tasdorf's tack room was small, so we'd often have to jockey for space. Every rider, even a customer, was supposed to clean and store his or her own bits of equipment. On the busiest days, tack used on the horses sent in for sale or training piled up faster than it could be cleaned and put away. Saddles accumulated on the back of the wooden horse like a pile of German pancakes, and the whole mess looked as if it would topple over. The bridles were hung on a post with three metal hooks; when you went to pick one up you often grabbed something someone else was working on. That made for apology and sudden laughter.

I hoped for conversation. The stable had become the largest part of my new world and I wasn't content to stay on the outside rim. Without intruding, I wanted to be as involved as possible; that meant trying to get to know the young workers. What exactly was the length and breadth of their world? What went on inside those heads? This would have been an easy task back home. But here, I was faced with barriers: age, culture, language, and my position as a customer and theirs as workers. So I took my time. The very nature of the room forced people to feel easy. When someone came rushing in, "high" after a good ride or "low" after a bad go, we muttered "Uh-huh" or "Oh-oh" as one single community. We saw suffering or rejoicing every day and we all knew those feelings. Such moments hardly needed words.

One treacherous Saturday morning, when the fog was so dense no one on the outside dared drive and the stable remained unusually quiet, I got to know Marin, who, like one of my daughters, was in her early twenties. I sensed that life was not easy for her and that it might never be. However, the hours she devoted to the care of horses seemed to move her deeply. I suspected that horses, even more than human beings, touched her soul.

Marin needed someone with time to listen, and that morning we found ourselves alone in the intimacy of the tack room. With very little urging, she told me the cause of her unhappiness: the best riders should have long legs to wrap around the bellies of their horses—hers were short. She had, of course, lived with this all of her life, but since her apprenticeship was almost complete, reality was waiting at her front door. In a short while there would be no Herr Christensen to help. Would she be able to make it out in the world riding horses on her own? She was as near tears as she would allow herself when she said, "All I want to do is spend my life around horses. My father says it's no life for a woman and I should train for something else." Her words were more a plea than a statement, perhaps a hope that my foreign wisdom or my parental status might support her choice.

"You ride so well," was all I could say to her. Generally, her rides appeared fluent and pleasing in spite of her size. However, on several occasions, I had watched her carefully and noted that although she handled her body well, her anxieties were expressed in the taut cords of her neck.

"No, not well enough," she stated with the magisterial firmness that was typical of her when she thought about herself.

"Didn't you hear what Herr Christensen was saying to you in the ring just this morning?" I responded. Marin's desire to be a good rider worked against her. Her low self-esteem mixed with her burning desire to excel influenced how she interpreted Walter and how she actually heard what he said. When Walter said "Ja-a, ja-a" to her, she never took it as praise for herself, but rather as an impersonal recognition of correctness. Wanting to help her, I gently pointed this out.

While we were sharing the saddle soap, she took a long breath and said to me, "I'd like to frame one of those times Herr Christensen says 'Gut' to me, hang it up in my bedroom, not ride for a week, and live with the feeling that for once I got it right. Maybe then I could believe it."

I knew that Marin spent most of her non-working hours watching the riding at Tasdorf and studying every horse book she could get her hands on. Not much seemed to interest her besides horses, which was why her pockets always bulged with sugar and snippets of carrot. She would never have treated a horse the way she treated herself. It wouldn't have occurred to her to say to an animal, "You're not good enough." She saw every creature as offering something unique and special. Yet, when life didn't go well for her, the solemnity in her eyes seemed to say, "This is my lot. I can endure it."

If life was hard for the regular German apprentices, it was also difficult for the steady trickle of young foreigners who came during school vacations to train and who, by individual arrangements, became informal apprentices or short-term working students. Those that came from somewhat privileged homes arrived with a list of their own expectations; sometimes they had ingrained habits of eating or not eating certain food, and sometimes they had a hard time understanding how work related to the discipline of riding and the maintenance of a stable like Tasdorf. Many of the part-time workers were Swedish girls possessing that special, dawn-fresh loveliness that Scandinavia bestows upon its female young. I welcomed their arrival with the same feeling with which I welcomed spring flowers. Besides, the talents they often brought to the stable, like the ability to sing and play the guitar, caught many of us up in their fun. While the rigid attitude that ruled the real apprentices took time for these young girls to fathom, they were serious about being part of the home team. They fell in love with Tasdorf and acted as if it was a second home or at least a favorite camp. When the moment came for them to leave, everyone hugged everyone in sight and the girls left with tears in their eyes. They were seldom gone for long: over my year, I found the same young women returning time after time.

Sometimes these part time apprentices learned more than riding and stable management. One morning, I overheard one of them crusading for "justice" with the teen-age passion of a Joan of Arc. The previous evening, the group had gone together to a local bar and dance hall in Neumünster. One of the boys had drunk too much and had a bad hangover. The girl was furious because even though it was clear that the boy felt ill, he had been assigned more work than usual. Furthermore, he was expected to ride every one of his horses. She could not believe the stable's attitude. Why had Herr Christensen not let him off? Couldn't he see that the fellow was having a hard time? It wasn't fair! She canvassed as many of her peers as she could, looking for agreement.

Marin's accepting German attitude countered the young foreigner's tirade with the reminder, "Wait a minute, aren't we here to do the work and to ride?" After these words, the young Swede's audience vanished and everyone went about their daily chores. Several weeks later, when the group went to town, the young man was more careful.

Another time, a story about a newly arrived, messy apprentice came my way, first from the customers up high in the casino and later from the young people down below in the tack room. The two groups reacted with opposite points of view. From the casino came a judgment delivered in few words: the case clearly showed the need for discipline and training. The opinion of those in the tack room was expressed in angry adjectives that my German lessons with Frau Kunze had not prepared me to decipher. However, it wasn't hard to gather that the apprentices were resentful of the treatment meted out to the guilty one.

The story: a certain young lady had been repeatedly reprimanded for her lack of personal grooming. Even I had noticed that the girl's clothes were never tidy, her riding sweater was dirty and worn out. Buttons were missing from her shirt cuff and neither of the Christensens considered safety pins to be proper replacements. It was discovered that the girl took her midday naps under the bedcovers fully dressed in her riding clothes; Walter was unable to tolerate such a thought. One morning when everyone was out in the ring riding, he marched straight into the girl's room. Finding her belongings scattered helter-skelter and the place a mess, he pulled out every single one of her bureau drawers and dumped their disorderly contents into a pile in the middle of the floor. Returning to the ring, he pronounced her grounded for several days—no riding until the ban was lifted. No punishment could have been felt more severely.

Tempers flared in hidden corners, people whispered where they couldn't be seen. The horses heard more talk than they ever had, while their stalls got forked over lightly rather than properly cleaned. Human juices boiled thick as the kids banged the heavy stall doors into their metal closures until the aisle echoed like a jail corridor. The crew had bonded behind one great cause—themselves. Herr Christensen had gone too far this time! Who did he think he was? What right had he to enter one of their rooms, encroach on their space, invade their possessions? After all, weren't they adults? Old enough to be called into the army? What kind of an apprenticeship program was this anyway?

This last question was the crux of the whole matter: Herr Christensen saw dressage as total training, total human development. He went about teaching in many ways. You might wonder at his method, at these stories, but everyone knew he would carry the emotional load of ten men before he got riled. When he chose to act, he was direct and straight to the point. His methods usually had the shock of clean justice, even a kind of superhuman wisdom;

they felt right in this black and white land where there was no gray. As with any strong action, however, a few souls would always see events differently and need to criticize. Whatever the controversy, it was quite clear that while you were at Stall Tasdorf there was one boss—and that was Walter.

In a matter of hours, the rebellion grew weaker and weaker and finally extinguished itself when there was no one left to fan it. The reprimanded girl wore an injured air, but that too disappeared when it was ignored.

I never knew quite what to think when I happened in on someone's tale or encountered the aftermath of an incident. Fortunately, even though the mother in me sometimes rose up, I was not in a position to judge. Gradually, as I saw Walter's system work, I grew to accept and even admire it. On the whole, the young lehrlingers at Tasdorf had won my interest, my sympathy, and my approval. The lessons of "boot camp" had become my lessons too, giving me a new perspective on discipline, sharpening me and making me look at myself. I had begun my stay at Tasdorf by observing the world around me. By the end of my year, I realized that I had become part of that world.

10

Watching the Big Time

Walter Christensen firmly believed that watching others ride was the greatest aid to anyone wishing to learn. Within twenty-four hours of my arrival at Tasdorf, he had already stated his conviction that "You can never watch too much good riding." Emphasizing his viewpoint with a nod and a raised eyebrow, he looked directly at me and I could imagine the unspoken words behind his eyes, "Pay careful attention to what I have told you."

From the first day, it was clear to me that Walter was never too busy to notice which of his lehrlingers took time to watch the lessons, the training of horses, and the riding in the ring. He appreciated the seriousness of their intent, especially if the person watching wasn't also chatting with someone. In Walter's view, watching while socializing was useless; people could go elsewhere to talk.

And talk we did: at the stable everyone was constantly comparing notes. Overhearing the young people discussing what they had noticed about horses and their riders, I realized that there was much more to watching than I had previously thought. Not only were the apprentices picking up many more details than I could at just a single glance, but each person perceived the same scene differently. I began to understand that the ability to watch constructively was a talent we are not all given equally, and that it was certainly an area in which I could learn or at least improve.

My own perceptions those first weeks in Germany were primarily those of an admirer. I was filled with wide-eyed wonder that all the horses and their riders looked so beautiful—in fact to my eye, they seemed close to perfect. Six weeks later, when my lessons on Inca began, I found that I was concentrating almost entirely on watching riders. Walter had been continuously correcting my position so that I was intensely focused on myself. My observation, therefore, had become quite basic and self-involved, narrowing down to whatever I could relate to my own problems.

When a member of the stable crew asked, "Did you see how Frau so-and-so made her young horse improve his trot today?" I had to say, no, I hadn't. I had, in fact, been exclusively interested in observing how expertly the woman sat, how she never lost the alignment of her shoulders, hips, and ankles the way I did. Whatever exercise she rode, she remained flexible even in her wrists—keeping her thumbs upright and her fists closed in the way that Walter was teaching me. However, by limiting myself to noticing only the rider's technique, I was eliminating the other half of the picture; I needed to encompass the horse as well as the rider.

I knew I was catching on to the real business of watching—the kind of watching Walter Christensen had been talking about—when my perception widened. With time and daily practice, I began to see the horse and rider as a pair, a whole. I could pick up small details without losing any of the larger picture.

For a time, I made written notes about what I saw, thinking that by keeping a riding journal I would formalize my education. I recorded warm-ups, patterns, and programs (even to the point of counting circles going left or going right) until I saw that with each rider the process was different and dependent on the way the horse felt. Finally, I decided that I was spending too much time staring down at the white page when my eyes could be much better employed taking in all the experience they could register.

I had plenty of role models to observe at Stall Tasdorf. Everyone there, including the horses, was making progress of some kind. Certainly, no one was riding just to pass the time of day or to get exercise. I found that watching moments in the instruction of others helped me to remember my own concepts of what was correct. Very soon, the lessons of other people became my own. Instead of enjoying the higher-level lessons as a pleasant spectacle, I focused my gaze and asked myself classroom questions. Was the movement well ridden? Could it have been better? Was I able to pick up a mistake myself or did I have to wait for Walter's observations to find out what was happening? I paid attention to precisely what it was about the student's technique that made Walter speak out strongly—I tried to see what he saw. Then, I observed whether the rider made the necessary correction. As my questions became more astute, my watching gained in energy and visual mileage. I changed from being a passive spectator to an active one—I became the rider I was watching and made the corrections that needed to be made internally. No question about it, involvement was an essential part of "good watching!"

One day, I discovered that there could be even more to observation than "meets the eye." I was sitting on the bench watching the activity in the ring and worrying about my lack of visual memory. While I understood what I was observing in the moment, I had trouble recalling the information later for my own use. Just as I was wishing I could find some way around the problem, a piece of music by Scott Joplin came over the German airways. Its familiarity caught my attention and I found myself humming the tune. Soon, I was instinctively viewing the horses in terms of music. I was seeing episodes of training as themes: original themes, bits of themes, repetitions, and variations on themes. The phases of work done by the riders became one long melodic line with a beginning, a middle and an end. That evening, because I had used the concept of melodic line and rhythmic theme as memory aids, I was actually able to mentally replay a lesson, or a segment of a lesson. I could bring up different pictures in my mind's eye and discover details that had previously gone unnoticed.

This kind of "instant replay" was an art well understood by a few of the old "regulars" who came to the casino every week, ordered a pot of coffee and then settled down seriously to watch the horses at work. How I admired them, though since they were instructors and judges, I found their presence somewhat formidable. When they talked to one another, their eyes seldom left the ring: it was as if they were at work. Each could draw on a personal memory bank of phenomenal moments, and, like Walter, could keep in mind all sorts of details about the progress of individual horses. One of them might tell you that a particular horse in the stable was using his back more correctly than he had been last Friday, or that the newest fellow to arrive for training was becoming more balanced in his gaits and maintaining a far greater degree of self-carriage on his own.

These ever-faithful visitors even remembered tests they had watched or perhaps judged months or years earlier. I heard one of them ask the other, "Do you remember the piaffe Granat did in the Grand Prix test at the Dortmund show? It was unbelievable. Such elevation. Such regularity. Not one step was uneven as he made his transitions into the piaffe and then back out of it." The other responded, " I remember the test you are talking about. Didn't you think the second piaffe in the test was the best of the three?" They then began an in-depth discussion of every movement, neither one of them having any difficulty recalling them. I found such explicit recall amazing in view of the fact that the Grand Prix they were speaking about had occurred a year earlier. Not only that, but there are thirty-three movements in this test, and more than likely there had been just as many contestants. I made an inward bow to the skill of the judging profession and rededicated myself to an all-out effort to become an "educated spectator."

Several months later, as if in answer to my vow, I was given a supreme opportunity to practice the art and pleasure of informed spectatorship. The Tasdorf crew (and I) had just finished eating lunch, watching in silence as one of the boys hurried through his second helping of mashed potatoes. Walter cleared his throat and made an announcement: he had secured tickets for all of us to attend the big show night Holsteiner Horse Auction which was to take place within two weeks at the Neumünster Holstenhalle, a few miles from the stable. The "Auction" was actually a long weekend event that combined a noted horse auction with varying demonstrations of the superior talent of this breed in all equine fields.

Europeans, and Germans in particular, are especially good at staging colorful annual equestrian events that draw large crowds of both amateur and professional horse enthusiasts, and everyone at Tasdorf looked forward with excitement to attending these grand occasions. Kerstin smiled at our eager response and held up the tickets.

Then Walter, with an unexpected flair for drama, topped this announcement with an even more powerful piece of news— Christine Stückelberger, one of the greatest international dressage champions in the world, her renowned trainer and companion Georg Wahl, and her extraordinary stallion Granat, had been asked to create a special show number to perform at the Holsteiner Show. They would be traveling from their native Switzerland, and prior to the event, they would be visiting at Stall Tasdorf to rest and to practice their program.

To watch this celebrated threesome at work would gain us a behind-the-scenes look at dressage riding. I would never be in a more intimate setting to witness top level dressage than this. Even if the three of them did no more than walk around the ring, given who they were, they'd have to be spectacular. I was sure I'd learn something new just from watching.

Orders were for the stable to continue functioning exactly as if nothing unusual was about to happen. Walter made it quite clear that only he should inform the customers and whatever outsiders he himself chose. He emphasized these pronouncements with a long look at every one at the table.

Of course, we could hardly contain ourselves, and hard as he might try to hide his feelings, I could see from Walter's face that he too was full of anticipation. I knew that some people found him overly secretive, but I saw him more as a self-contained, thinking man, even a bit of a hermit, who longed for more hours to himself. Walter was simply not one to talk a great deal, but he had already told us enough to make me absolutely sure that I wanted to be in the stable when the stars arrived. I hoped that perhaps I would even be allowed to watch an entire practice session in the ring.

Walter's reluctance to provide the details of the forthcoming "celebrity visit" caused some grumbles, but there was more to his reticence than just his customary reserve. He knew, as exactly as he knew when the straw in the surrounding fields should be cut, that acquaintances he hadn't seen in a long time would suddenly decide that the days Stückelberger and Co. stayed at Stall Tasdorf would be just the perfect time to renew old friendship. In addition, all the nearby judges, show organizers, and important functionaries of the Schleswig-Holstein Pferd Verband and the Holstein Horsebreeders Association would turn up bursting with curiosity and officialdom and a sense of their neighborly right to appear. They would take over the tables in the casino, greet Kerstin with overly familiar smiles, and suggest that she pass on word of their arrival to her husband. While each would profess to understand if Walter didn't have time to leave the ring, Walter knew that men like this did in fact expect him to sit down with them for a chat. Of course after that, they would want to watch Frau Christine Stückelberger ride and then they probably wouldn't go directly home. Between seven and eight o'clock the question of supper would come up, and Stückelberger and Wahl would be pressed into joining the group. It was almost a foregone conclusion that the evening would continue until well past midnight.

Most of the time, Walter made huge efforts to accommodate customers and friends. He clearly gave a lot of thought to how he could include people in the ordinary routine of work. But this visit was special and he wanted to set aside the time for himself. He wanted to be in the ring when his famous guests rode their practice sessions, free to sit on the bench, stand in the doorway, smoke a cigarette, perhaps talk to Georg Wahl and above all, watch them in action with every fiber of his being.

Walter was insatiably curious about training horses. Harsh methods involving the use of force in training did not interest him. When a training technique failed to produce a result with an animal, he'd try another approach—and then another. He looked for how he could obtain willingness; he searched out fresh ways to solve problems. Walter was not just a trainer or a rider; he also remained a student of horses all his life.

In this context, he looked forward to what he might learn from watching Wahl and Stückelberger. Of particular interest to him was the fact that they had made champions of more than one horse. This was the true test of a trainer's ability. Also, unlike most world class competitors, these two could not afford the high prices of young animals with proven bloodlines, horses who would reveal an exceptional talent early, who had gorgeous bodies and receptive minds. Instead, they bought animals that had been rejected by other riders and trainers, or horses with unknown potential but a glimmer of promise.

Granat, the stallion who Christine would bring to ride at the Holsteiner Show, was a case in point, and a tribute to the couple's particular gift. There were endless tales being told about what a rogue Granat had been when they bought him, how he had been difficult to train and even dangerous to ride. It had taken years for these two people to bring him into willing obedience—and even now he wasn't totally reliable. He could still revert to adolescent behavior. I remember sitting in the audience of the international competition in Holte, Denmark when the thundering of many thousands of people at the end of his test startled him and sent all four feet off the ground like a skyrocket. The clapping stopped in less than a wink of time, and we watched in dead silence, hoping Christine would be able to stay in the saddle. Her face was as white as the stock around her neck, but she left the ring that day, in every way the winner. It was precisely this spark, this craziness, this kind of equine temperament, which when harnessed and focused for work, set Granat far above other horses. It was his genius.

At last the eagerly awaited day arrived. The September weather was crisp as a fresh apple. Christine and Georg drove in under the big Tasdorf sign, and I thought of that day, a lifetime of changes ago, when I had first passed under it myself. Plans were made; the famous trio would practice their show number in the late afternoon when the ring would be empty. Had they brought a tape, Walter asked, or did they want background music of some kind? No, Wahl said, this was to be a simple, preliminary practice, he just wanted to "move" the horse and get any stiffness out.

At 5 PM, as I walked toward the ring, I thought that Stall Tasdorf had never seemed so quiet. The horses boxed near the front door looked out at me through their stall bars when I came in. The others farther down the aisle were so still I thought they must have been fast asleep. The place had the peace of a day off.

I found Walter, Kerstin and the lehrlingers standing in the doorway to the ring. They had the serious demeanor of people in church. Every eye was concentrated on Christine, who had begun her warm-up: walk, trot and canter, changing directions, making transitions within the gaits, using circles and half-circles and straight lines. I felt as though I was dreaming—Christine Stückelberger, European Champion, World Champion, 1976 Olympic Gold Medalist riding in the same ring I was training in, Granat's hooves turning over the very turf Inca worked in, and myself a privileged spectator at a private showing.

Where does a woman find the sheer strength to control a large stallion when she is chic, lithe, and stylish, and stands only a few inches over five feet in her boots? Yet, even in the first few minutes of observing Christine, I could see that she had amazing strength, a strong, deep current of it, rooted in a calm and quietude that I knew Walter would particularly appreciate. She revealed very little outward sign of effort. I saw no pulling on the reins, no jabbing of spurs or cracks with the peitsche (riding whip)—and since obedience is an important part of equine training in dressage, I had to assume that her effectiveness lay in the fact that she knew precisely

171

when to use her power and make her commands known.

Christine's strength was understated—even her face belied her chosen role. She wore her blonde hair pulled back in a kind of chignon that gave her a refined, even non-physical, ladylike look. She seemed more like someone who played a musical instrument than someone who rode dressage. Yet, anyone could tell that horses were Christine's passion. Her fine, chiseled features carried the glow of a person engaged in what she most wanted to be doing, even though it was downright hard work.

If Christine's face had expression, so did Granat's. Like all horses who have years of close contact with humans, Granat's face was alive and showed what he was thinking. I saw in it not only his no-one-can-compare-with-me attitude, but his respect for Georg Wahl. Just as Granat knew where he placed his own four feet every minute, he knew precisely where his trainer was standing. The horse's awareness of his rider was equally apparent, making itself visible in tiny movements of the small muscles of his face, especially around his eyes. His ears also expressed his response to her, moving deep in their sockets, saying, "Now I'm listening, now I'm not." I couldn't help but remark to myself, "Boy, is that fellow doing a lot of thinking!"

Georg Wahl was walking around the ring behind Christine, holding a dressage whip in his hand. He had the intense look of a ferret, which is not to say cruel, but as if nothing in the world would escape his gaze. He talked to her in grunts and short words. At first, I could only make out that he wanted more from her. More. And more.

Warm-ups are intriguing. The ability to get started varies from person to person, from horse to horse, and from day to day. How the practice begins reveals a great deal about the partnership: just who helps whom, when, and how? As Christine loosened Granat's body and called forth his energy, I could see she knew his body as well as she knew her own. I wondered if, as an athlete in top condition, she suffered stiffness or lethargy at the start. To my eyes, she was immediately and comfortably in charge. Granat, however, surprised me. He did not seem such an extraordinary creature after all. Where was my "giant?" My star? Seeing him at the beginning of work that particular afternoon revealed that he needed to come into the dynamic self that everyone talked about. During the next hour, we were the delighted witnesses of just such a metamorphosis.

I was lost in watching Granat and Christine when suddenly I heard Georg Wahl give a growl like an anguished bear, "Christine, when are you really going to start riding?" he asked her!

I wondered whether I had heard right. That was one of the criticisms I was always getting. How could Wahl find anything wrong with what Christine was doing?

Her face tightened. In answer to her trainer's voice, she thrust her body deeper into the horse's back and took an altogether stronger hold of Granat, insisting that she, not he, make the demands.

Practicing her entry for the night of the show, she rode down centerline at the canter, halted at the midpoint, X, and made a salute. As I watched horse and rider, I thought of the ocean liner *Queen Elizabeth* coming straight as a die into dock. Perfect! But, I was wrong: Granat's right hind foot was perhaps two inches out of line with the left. A trained dressage horse must stand absolutely four square.

Next, Stückelberger came to the end of the ring, turned right, rounded the first corner with a soft bend, and then took her horse on the diagonal with a canter extension that had so much verve, so much energy, it looked as if the two of them might be heading off to war. All of sudden, the Tasdorf ring seemed too small for them.

"Ja, gut!" Georg Wahl said, giving them his rare approval. I wanted to shout, "yes! yes!" a hundred times.

Granat's reputation boasted three outstanding gaits: the walk, the trot, and the canter. Each was pure, imbued with natural rhythm, elasticity, and impulsion. Such rare talent must be cared for and not lost in the tension and tightness that can creep into the performance of the most difficult exercises. Horses can be compared to singers in this regard: when their talent is forced, strained, or overworked, the ability that they were born with becomes impaired, ruined, even lost. Dressage riders consider the walk as the most precious of all three gaits—when it goes it can seldom be brought back. Such a tragedy could never happen under Georg Wahl. Ever present at the center of action, he would not allow any kind of damaging restriction to rear its ugly head.

One of Georg Wahl's most remarkable assets was his background, unique by all standards in both depth and variety, which I suspected truly intrigued Walter Christensen. Georg had worked as a young man with the Circus Knie in Switzerland, known for its amazing feats with trained animals, especially with horses. This family circus represented the best in the art of performance all over Europe. Then years of apprenticeship in the Spanish Riding School in Vienna exposed Georg Wahl to the tradition of classical dressage known as "Haute Ecole." As the name implies, this is the highest level of dressage and includes the amazing "airs above the ground," exercises in which the animals leap into the air, all four feet off the ground in a prescribed fashion, upon command. The work is performed only by Lipizzaner horses, whose small compact bodies make these specialized movements possible, leaving an audience to wonder whether these creatures are athletes, dancers, or perhaps both.

Wahl was not a big man, but he stood on his podium of demands like a towering giant. Flicking his dressage whip on the ground against his shoe, he was the conductor. He orchestrated magnificence bit by bit: demanding, imposing, requesting, even pleading in order to duplicate the image he held in mind. He called forth every possible equine variation and then tested the extremes, always—always—pushing the limits.

"The transition again, please. And again! Ja, gut. Now how does that feel?" A trainer may take control, but he never keeps it, knowing this role belongs to the rider. His repeated task is primarily to reflect, to be critical, to be the rider's "eyes" from the ground. He knows that the rider must ride the horse into the movements in the best way she can, and subsequently, the horse must perform them. Since the rider cannot always be sure of what details have escaped her, the trainer is there to tell her. In this way, dressage is a creative interaction between trainer, rider, and horse. To achieve the ultimate goal of beauty and perfection of movement, the three must braid their efforts together.

Wahl had sharp criticisms for Christine. "Don't look down," he said, reprimanding her for not keeping her eyes straight ahead. Then he pointed out that her left hand was higher than her right. This was an old habit, he accused her despairingly, why was it still going uncorrected? In the next sentence his voice cracked with intensity, "Why are you making the tempo so hectic?" He called for vigor without rush. I heard directives like, "Keep it going. Bring him together. Ask for more elevation. Be alive." I, myself, could see none of these imperfections, or very few of them, and what I did see that was incorrect seemed infinitesimal. To my eyes, Christine Stückelberger rode like an empress. Standing there ringside, I was having the best time I'd had since my arrival in Germany. I was daydreaming that I was riding Granat like Christine.

Dressage riders sculpt space. Air is invisible, but riding a truly straight line can feel as difficult as driving a wedge with a sledgehammer. Of course, rather than the hardness of the air, it is the resistance of the horse that defies you. In time, you learn that wisdom helps more than strength. When nothing worked right, which is what happened to me sometimes, I cursed this granite-like quality the air seemed to have. Christine had moved beyond such difficulties and was able to conquer air, resistance, and whatever other obstacle presented itself. She rode her straight lines as if there were no other option, as if she were precision itself.

Precision is another of the intrinsic requirements of the dressage art. Christine rode circles as if she were drawing a perfect full moon. No matter what size she wanted them to be—four, ten, or twenty meters large—she executed them with an exactness of movement that flowed like liquid. I couldn't help but compare my own efforts: why was it, I asked myself, that my attempts at circles wouldn't let me circle? Instead my circles seemed to want to be square.

I marveled too, at the perfection of Christine's serpentines. A serpentine is a looping snake design, patterned to fill the entire arena. Most of us probably have childhood memories of making these designs in the sands of the beach or the sandbox. It's certainly a familiar motif, and therefore it should be very easy to ride. Not so for most riders. Christine, however, was a genius with the form. I watched breathlessly as she constructed her serpentines with many loops, always winding, always bending, dividing space precisely, molding each turn after the one before, remembering to reposition her horse on the centerline every time she crossed it. At the end of the movement, Christine was at the opposite end of the ring, facing the precise spot where she had set out. I was awestruck. Once again, she had made her ride seem so effortless that it was hard to figure out why I couldn't do the same.

I thought about the last time I practiced the serpentine. I remembered that I'd lacked concentration. I rode a succession of loops and forgot where I was going and where I'd been. I wondered if Christine had ever faced similar sorts of moments? Watching her in the ring that day, I found it hard to believe that she had ever been a beginner like me.

As for Granat, with the warm-up work behind him, he now epitomized the performer to such a degree that it was hard to believe there had ever been a moment when he didn't know it all. He moved in such a way that he hardly seemed to need the ground. His stride appeared to carry him just above the earth's surface so that when Christine asked for the next movement, the half-pass, he fairly floated. He crossed the diagonal of the entire ring, keeping his body parallel to the long sides, his front and rear outer legs crossing obliquely in front of the inside pair. The effect was of a large sweeping motion going sideways as well as forward. Although there was no change of rhythm because of his huge crossover steps, I had the sense Granat was going slower. A sudden comparison flashed through my head—"Good heavens," I thought, "he's begun the tango!"

Wahl, apparently liking what he saw, gave a grunt of affirmation. Then, continuing to direct the flow of the program, he called out, "Traversale, links und rechts" (half-pass, left and right). This time Granat began on the centerline and took three steps in half-pass to the left and three to the right, repeating the pattern four times. All the while his body bent like a soft wide ribbon, first left and then right, as he made the precise changes in direction. What a horse!

"Continue! Continue!" Wahl urged his student. She turned toward the center of the ring once again, and I saw her lightly check Granat as if to tell him "Something special is coming up." Riding a small circle, she asked for a pirouette. It came out to perfection: eight tiny canter steps done almost in place and the two of them had turned around 180 degrees. Nothing to it, the body language of the pair seemed to say. But I wasn't fooled—that kind of pirouette requires perfect balance. No dancer, to my way of thinking, could have done better.

Using the dynamics of high energy and collection gained from the pirouette, Christine rode lines of flying changes. At first, she asked for changes every third stride, then every second stride, and finally every other stride. Changes seem difficult when you don't know how to ask for them, simple when you do. The horse must respond within the canter stride by thrusting his leading hind leg distinctly forward followed by the front leg on the same side. Granat responded to being asked to perform the exercise like a kid with a skip rope, telling the world this was a lot of fun. Suddenly we were all smiling, even Wahl. Yet, in spite of the creature's eagerness, I noted—as Christine's trainer did—that the flying changes were begun at the moment they were asked for and ceased when his rider said, "enough!"

Then came the finale. Granat returned to his previous enormous trot, gathered himself up, and took off in an extended trot down the far long side. Here was a true super horse, cutting space like a power-driven cleaver. I was transfixed.

"Noch einmal," came the command from the one who was never satisfied. The trot extension we had just witnessed must be ridden once again. I held my breath. It was hard to imagine how this second try could have surpassed the first, but it did. Certainly, it would have gained Granat one more judge's point—a ten—perfection.

Wahl let out a long, deep exhalation as though he had performed the trot himself. Then he put down his stick, his signal that the practice was over.

"Just a light work out," Christine said to the group of us standing at the door. "Tomorrow we'll do more," she promised.

We, however, needed no promises of more: our senses were filled to the brim. Each of us felt capable of single-handedly raising the roof with applause. Christine laid her reins on the horse's neck and patted him. Wahl uttered "gut" once again, and I wasn't sure whether he was speaking to the horse, the student, or simply saying that it was a "good" thing they were finished.

Trainers like Walter and Georg have the kind of vision that drives people ever onward. They seek the perfection that they can clearly see with the mind's eye but that is seldom achieved. They are forever reaching for their dream, hoping the day will come when dream and reality are one. It was obvious to me that Wahl wasn't one hundred per cent pleased with the afternoon's work. Actually, pleased might be too passive a word. Perhaps "accepting" would be more accurate.

I, however, as an average spectator, had no such demanding dreams and could simply react to what I liked. It was appropriate for me to call the ride "magnificent," and to say that I found dressage at this level magnetic. If I had seen this caliber of performance at a show, I'd have joined the audience and stamped, shouted, hooted, and ridden the waves of applause. I'd have told Granat in no uncertain terms that he had as large a following as any rock star. I'd have expressed to Frau Stückelberger that her riding had earned my unbounded admiration.

In less than an hour, I had a received a year's worth of education. I saw how champions work, and for the first time, I noticed how winners present themselves. Every exercise had been created as if it were a small piece of art—no movement was wasted, no movement thrown away. Granat and Christine made me want to look at them; they drew my eyes. I think this was due to their presence, their stature, and their state of mind. Exactly how, as a rider, I would make use of this past hour was hard to say, but I knew that by having had the chance to see Christine and Granat, I had stood on a mountain peak where the view was spectacular.

That evening, I met Wahl and Stückelberger as ordinary people. We sat down in the casino to coffee, tea, and the doughnuts that Kerstin had promised Herr Wahl. The two couples talked like old friends. I heard Christine say she loved strawberries and that Georg made her cross every time he took a wurst (sausage) snack to bed with him. I marveled that this woman's smile was so incredibly gentle, and noticed that when she raised her coffee cup, she did it so delicately that she could have been lifting a small bird. The four of them discussed the competitions they had attended and the ones that were yet to come. The conversation centered around who had been judging and which of Europe's top horses had entered. As I listened, I realized there is a game plan to competitions that is not unlike a military campaign. The object for the present champion is to remain unassailable while the other competitors try to "unseat" him or her. I had assumed that like Inca and me, riders who competed signed up for all the competitions they could in order to win ribbons and gain mileage. Georg and Christine, however, picked their shows carefully, considering the dates, the length of travel to get there, the rating of the show, the scheduling of competition, and its effect on Granat. Had I not been there, they would probably have discussed all of the factors involved in much greater detail. I did, however, hear them say that in general, they preferred to enter international shows rather than the more national German ones.

One of the major elements that Georg and Christine considered when deciding to enter a show was the matter of who would be judging. Dressage judging is a highly respected vocation all over the world. For some people, it's a hobby. In America, judges are given both a fee and their expenses, while in Europe they receive only their expenses. One of the rewards for judges on both sides of the Atlantic, besides the pleasure of looking at horses, is that judging is often the way for the best of them to become leaders in the organi-

*Louise Nathhorst.
A happy moment in
competition. Photo:
Cappy Jackson*

*Basically, it seemed
Walter's work was never
done when he was in
Germany—weekdays
teaching and overseeing
stable matters, weekends
looking at horses to buy,
attending competitions,
and again, more teach-
ing. Here, Walter and
Klaus Rat are involved
in a serious moment.*

Nothing escapes
Walter's keen eye . . .

. . . or for that matter, Louise's critical eye. Although she was Walter's student and always turned to him for masterful advice, there were times when they would work together as fellow trainers.

One of my favorite pictures of Walter, taken while he was at a local show in America. Photo: Carole MacDonald

A winter day at The Ark, my farm in Harvard, Massachusetts. True to the promise Walter made to me on my last morning in Tasdorf, he began coming on a regular basis—at least twice a year—to America.

The indoor ring at The Ark. Walter is brought flowers from a grateful spectator, Betsy Hestnes. The smiling person behind her is me. Riders and spectators alike showed their appreciation in a continuous outpouring of presents such as homemade goodies, photographs, artwork, books on America, and maple syrup (which he adored).

When the weather allowed it, we rode outdoors. Walter is riding Demian, a handsome Danish Warmblood that he found for me. Photo: Carole MacDonald

We welcome Volker Brommann on his arrival in America. Volker had been an apprentice at Stall Tasdorf and came to carry on the teaching and training at The Ark during the months that Walter could not be there. To the far right is our neighbor and clinic participant, Karen Webster, in whose home Volker would live for many months. Standing next to Volker is Walter.

Sitting next to Walter in the indoor ring, Volker translates as Walter gives a lesson.

Here I am riding Philotrix, a Swedish Warmblood found for me by Louise Nathhorst and Walter. Philotrix was of international quality and eventually I loaned him to Louise when she needed a second horse to try out for the Swedish Dressage Team.

Inca and I in competition at the annual West Chester Fairfield Dressage Show in Connecticut. Photo: Reiner Niewisch

Walter always reminded us when we got too serious that riding should be fun. Here he is having the time of his life aboard Mountain Dancer, our neighbor Karen Webster's horse. Chuck Grant, one of America's early dressage teachers and competitors, had taught the horse his tricks. Notice how Walter keeps his body balanced throughout.

Broom in hand, Walter happily winds down his clinic day by bringing my stable floor up to his standards. At the same time, he fulfills that voice in the corner of his German soul that urges him onward saying, "sweep the floor and then you can rest."

Walter on wheels!

zational aspect of the horse world. In short, they become part of the equestrian elite. One might wonder how anyone could feel elite doing a job that requires you to start work on a weekend morning at 6 AM and breakfast on "brotchen" (rolls) and coffee in a judging booth. And that's the least of it. The days are long and a judge is expected to be impartial, unbiased, and so knowledgeable that the comments his or her scribe records on the test sheet will be helpful to the competitor. Of course, true impartiality is hard to achieve in life. As in every competitive activity, all sorts of outside and subjective elements can enter into both the performance of the competitor and the opinion of the judge.

Judges are kings at a competition. Every score they give is important to someone. Judges hope that their marks come reasonably close to one another. Nothing enrages a competitor more than big differences of opinions. Wide variations affect an audience as well as the entire atmosphere of the show. Questions flow: Which judge is right? How can the same movement be judged so differently? Is there no standard? Are politics involved?

How a judge scores can be subtly influenced by a number of things other than accomplishment. He or she may be responding to national prejudice, politics, personal preference, or some other human emotion. Also, judges must score performance the minute each dressage move is completed, leaving no time for reflection. To mitigate these drawbacks, the rules assert that five qualified judges must adjudicate every major test in a recognized competition. In general, the judging system works reasonably well. Certainly it's important, since everyone knows that a point or two given or withheld can change sport history.

Most of the other critical factors that Georg and Christine considered were practical. In one show, for instance, the footing had been too deep due to the numerous jumping classes that had taken place between the dressage classes. Every minute that they were at that show they had worried that Granat might step in a hole and pull a muscle. At another show, the flapping of the decorative international flags had so distracted Granat that he had almost lost his mind and they might as well have withdrawn and gone home. Aside from footing and outside disturbances, not the least of the problems to consider was stabling. This can be either the best or the worst. Usually, it falls somewhere in between. At one venue Wahl told us about, the stalls were so unprotected that Granat nearly froze. At the next, the stalls were confining and the air so warm and badly circulated that both riders and horses found it almost impossible to breathe.

There was no sign in our conversation of the glamour that I had imagined surrounded the lives of champions. Instead, I listened to tales of long seasons of travel, endless miles of driving, and nights in different hotels. Not that Christine and Georg were complaining— it was more that they were simply trying to keep the details of their lives in perspective. I sensed that as they headed off into the grueling competitive part of their lives, they needed to emphasize the grounding love they felt for their house and garden back home in Switzerland.

Perhaps life at the top was exciting enough to warrant everything the three of them had to put up with. As to receiving awards, ribbons, show money, sponsor's gifts, and the winner's victory gallop past the stadium, how much time did those magical moments take? I wager about as long as it takes to eat a crispy doughnut.

I reveled in the days of that visit. Inspiration beamed over all of us at Stall Tasdorf like the sun and gave our world an unpredictable boost. Everyone rode better than they ever had before. We all hoped that Christine's talent was catching and that our horses were having midnight pep talks with Granat. Smiles appeared on faces that seldom smiled. Walter and Wahl huddled like two trainers during the ninth inning of a baseball game with only seconds to go. As for me, Christine Stückelberger opened my eyes not only to the beauty of all that I was trying to learn but also to the beauty in the effort of learning it. I ceased thinking about riding as just hard work.

11

In School

At Tasdorf, there were times when I felt like an army recruit and times when I felt like a fifty-year-old exchange student, but common to every day's experience was an overwhelming focus on learning—learning of all kinds—personal, spiritual, and equestrian. Slowly, as my year progressed and Stall Tasdorf's environment and teachings became my whole world, I began to view the stable as a kind of "university-at-large," a school where the subjects, educational style, and learning curve were different from anything I had ever encountered.

The challenges were many. The most difficult involved my training; others were personal and cultural. In respect to my training, I had no idea that the pursuit of learning dressage involved more than riding, and soon realized how unrealistic I had been. I had viewed dressage primarily as a physical sport in which I could be taught specific movements. I had anticipated that in a short amount of time, a great master could tell me exactly what to do.

Nothing of the kind happened. As for the personal and cultural challenges, I repeatedly stumbled into social attitudes that I had never encountered before and ways of thinking that were hard to fathom. Clearly, Germany was not like America.

Even before I left home, I had been warned that American riders have a difficult time in Germany. However, at the time I didn't think this cautionary advice applied to me. I believed myself to be unique and thought that because I wanted to be a good dressage rider almost as much as I wanted to breathe, I'd have no trouble being a beginner. As I was older and thus more experienced in life than most other new arrivals to the German equestrian scene, I reasoned that I could survive almost anything for a period of time. Once I got to Germany, however, the truth behind all the words of warning came home to me both personally and as an American.

Americans consider themselves capable dressage riders on their own turf. Therefore it comes as a shock when they discover that in foreign eyes they are viewed as downright beginners. Almost immediately, they realize not only how much *they* have to learn but also how much *there is* to learn. And, of course, it's impossible to say how long such learning will take.

German riders grow up with a tradition of dressage. They know just how much patience it requires. In contrast, the sport is relatively new to most Americans and though they arrive prepared to learn, they do so with a timetable for success and a premature return ticket. Then suddenly they find themselves confronted with a return to basics and a demanding attitude toward training that is totally foreign to them. To make matters even more difficult, Americans are used to constant encouragement, which to the Germans is not only unnecessary, it's inappropriate: "get on with the work," thinks the German. Thus the American equestrian student in Germany must change her expectations as well as accept the fact she is no longer ahead, but far behind anyone else. Can she catch up? The eagerness with which she initially approached training slips into depression. Unless she can view the learning experience as one of the great challenges of her life, she may well ask herself, why stay? Not all American riders stick it out. A few return home bleak and unhappy. Some never want to look at a horse again.

A despair of this magnitude was never a part of my experience, but as an American in Germany, I found myself continuously forced to reexamine my identity both as a rider and as a person.

In a country preoccupied with its own categories, divisions, qualifications, and details, my presence at Stall Tasdorf seemed to defy classification. Certainly, during the first months, when a new face or even someone who hadn't been around the stable for awhile turned up in the casino, I would often be introduced with the words, "Meet the American." Then I'd hear "oh?" in a tone that nudged for explanation. Germans seemed more confronting than the average American, causing me to wonder if I was expected to offer credentials, give an international password, or explain myself. If I was silent, which I often was, I'd be met with silence. Then after a certain amount of staring, there'd be specific questions which I often found difficult to answer, such as why had I come to Tasdorf. The questions would continue: was it true that Americans were just beginning to ride dressage? Were our Thoroughbred horses any good for the purpose? Was I a professional or an amateur? Would I please state my goals?

I found these questions about American riders and American horses to be frequently demeaning and disrespectful. I was angry. Why should fledgling efforts (which included mine) be denigrated? After all, I thought, German riders don't own the sport! Perhaps this was too strong a reaction, but I don't think so.

Sometimes the queries would veer from the equestrian to the

personal. One question clearly intrigued Deutsche folk, particularly the men, more than any other. "You say you're married?" a man would ask. I'd nod. Obviously, this was a loaded question. At the time of my visit in 1979, old-fashioned marital ideals still prevailed in many German homes. The husband, especially if he was of the older generation, was the decision-maker, the head of the household, and the prime mover and shaker. To put it plainly, he wanted to be assured that his wife would always be on hand to get him his supper.

"Your husband *allows* you to do this?" The inquirer's voice would now have risen half an octave.

"He does," I would answer forthrightly, "My husband truly wants me to ride well. He knows how much riding means to me and supports my being here completely."

These conversations totally altered my natural responses. When facial expressions froze and queries were not posed gently, explanations about myself stuck in my throat. I used to wonder if my audience was aware that they were shaking their heads back and forth as if to say, "I can't believe what I am hearing."

Some of the regular riders made efforts to be friendly, but even though they invited me to join them for coffee, there was a wall between us that never came down during my entire stay at Tasdorf, an I-don't-know-you formality that kept me from feeling comfortable. "Is it me?" I kept asking myself. "Am I the distant one?" Part of the difficulty, I'm sure, was language. I did learn that when I spoke German, fast was better than slow. Talking with my hands helped, too. When I wanted to add real spark to my flat and uninteresting, textbook sentences, I even resorted to some big, Wagnerian style operatic gestures.

Germany, I discovered, is not a country where a person makes friends overnight. I had to learn to be respectful, to cool my impatience and wait. The easy American way, the casual, "Hello, Joe." or "Hi Mary, come on over for a potluck supper and we'll get to know one another," could hardly happen here. Toward foreigners, such immediacy seemed not only inappropriately casual but unbelievably speeded up.

In spite of these cross-cultural awkwardnesses, I frequented the casino a good deal. During the cold weather, the viewing room offered the warmest spot in the entire establishment. On damp days, I warmed my toes under the radiators and my gloves on top. I was content to combine looking through the window at the horses working in the ring with listening to the people chatting. What did it matter if I only put in two words or even none at all? I was beginning to "read" and "see" the world around me as though I had acquired new glasses. The need to belong became less important.

Whenever Kerstin appeared, she assumed the job of explaining me to others just as she explained the others to me. She also helped me understand that my search for personal excellence was a path the younger generations of German women were also beginning to explore. She added that she had more personal freedom than a majority of German women because, luckily for her, Walter's mother had been Danish. Her influence had prevented him from thinking and behaving with the machismo of most German men of the older generation. To me, the Christensens seemed like an American couple, each allowing the other to express a quite opposite self.

Walter or Kerstin's presence instantly transformed the casino into a welcome place. Whenever I was urged to talk about home, I'd take snapshots of my family, the farm, and all the animals from my handbag. Here was an easy link to illustrate the facts that I couldn't verbalize and prove that I wasn't the enigma I appeared to be. Invariably, Walter took these occasions to let it be known that he liked being reminded of America. He'd butt right in when I was passing my pictures around and describe my farm as "a dream place." Americans, he would say, make you feel as if you've known them all your life even if you are being introduced for the first time. And the riders he had worked with were so grateful and eager to learn that he had loved teaching them. Even though his visit had been a working clinic, the time spent at my farm had seemed like a vacation.

In spite of their friendliness, it was hard to determine exactly where I stood with the Christensens. I hoped that because I had crossed the ocean to be at Tasdorf and because I was not German, they would, with time, consider me more of a personal friend than a "client." Then one evening in their home, we had a long discussion about American informality. They confided to me that a few of their American clients and certain of our customs were hard for them to understand. Right then, in the intimacy of that moment, I knew that I must have won the beginnings of trust and acceptance.

After three months at Tasdorf, my attitude toward life at "school" took a significant turn. Oddly enough, this was brought about by an American I was never to encounter. One morning, Kerstin invited me into the "büro," the Christensens' office. It was a closet of a room. One wall was decorated with a collection of bits and spurs, another with file cabinets above which hung black and white photographs of both Kerstin and Walter riding in competition. With the exception of Kerstin's sack of apples and her box of sugar, everything bespoke work. At the stable, the closed door of the büro was viewed with the same respect as that of a school principal. Its metal exterior was uninviting and I'd noticed that few knocked without an urgent reason. I had seen Walter head there when I suspected he had enough of his customers and wanted a quiet retreat. Until that day, I had only entered this inner sanctum for about five minutes at the end of each month to pay my bills.

Therefore I was surprised at Kerstin's invitation until she showed me a letter to her husband mailed from the States. The handwriting was illegible to her, and she had postponed answering it, but deciphering the American scrawl proved to be no problem for me. The letter turned out to be a request to study dressage with Herr Christensen. As I read it to her, I pictured the writer, a college-age fellow, looking anxiously in his mailbox for a reply. Kerstin half expected me to know him until I explained that Minnesota was far away from Massachusetts. The young man asked whether he could come immediately for two months of private instruction on Herr Christensen's trained horses. He wanted help in preparing for a local championship and ended by saying that he'd buy his ticket as soon as the Christensens acknowledged his letter.

It was hard for the Christensens to understand the letter and even to take it seriously. I, on the other hand, felt the writer was totally in earnest, merely uninformed about what he was asking and unaware of German punctiliousness. Walter shook his head at the young man's assumption that he could just appear at any time. He was appalled that a sense of hurry could be connected with learning dressage. Furthermore, not every instructor had trained horses for hire, and why would those who did give a promise to a total stranger that he could take lessons on these precious creatures for two months? In any case, Walter replied by claiming he didn't have the time.

Although on this occasion things did not work out for the American, his letter did wonders for me. This was the first time I had been asked for help or information by anybody since I had arrived in Germany. How good it felt to be offering an explanation and to be trusted for advice! Suddenly, I realized how badly I missed being needed. Until that very moment, I had been the person needing help, asking questions, and having to learn even the simplest thing. As I sat in a chair far too low for my long legs, trying to make the Atlantic a smaller ocean and the letter writer a credible person, I secretly thanked this young man for our connection even though he would never know of it.

After several months in Germany, social life at the stable was becoming less daunting and incomprehensible to me—except for Sundays. On that day, I had to deal with both the social and the equestrian challenges of the Tasdorf "campus" at the same time, a situation that often made me feel overwhelmed and lonely.

The Sabbath at Stall Tasdorf was anything but a day of rest. The stable closed for the day at 1 PM, but this didn't seem to deter the hordes of neighbors who considered Tasdorf the perfect destination for a Sunday outing. Germans young and old, male and female, like to watch horses the way Americans like to watch football, and Sunday at Tasdorf provided the irresistible combination of hospitality, horse-viewing, and horse riding. All morning long a steady stream of riders would arrive, along with their families, dogs, friends, and any other interested parties. In the casino, every chair would be taken and endless cups of coffee would be consumed. Sometimes conditions would become so crowded that people would ooze out of the room and block the entry to the ring.

The casino was not the only place where crowding became a problem. The entire horse population of the stable had to be brought out and worked in the ring before one o'clock when it was closed down. This meant that all the customers rode together during the same morning hours. One or two of them rode their animals as if they were driving Mercedes cars. Although there are definite rules for behavior and right-of-way in the ring, these particular owners acted as though those who didn't get out of their way and move to the side were sheer dust. Once I even had to stop dead in my tracks to avoid a collision. A woman rider glared at me with eyes of fire.

How dare I, they flamed, couldn't I see where she was headed? Rules be damned! She was the important one on that diagonal!

The spectator aspect of the casino also bothered me. When I was riding it was as if the ring had eyes; eyes that invaded my space. If I turned my head, which of course I wasn't suppose to do, I could look up and see a person's face behind the window glass, pick up an expression, note that the man on the left was bored, the woman on the right was deep in conversation. I knew the sort of sharp criticism and unkind remarks that observers were capable of, and I felt far too vulnerable with my mistakes on view out there in the ring for all to see.

After several of these unnerving Sunday mornings, I announced to Walter that I'd like to skip riding on that day. "Aber warum?" (but why), he asked me. I told him that I found it difficult to ride in the ring when it was so crowded with horses, and that I had a hard time concentrating on my lessons with so many witnesses. Walter's expression revealed that he felt more comfortable and patient dealing with complicated horses than he did coping with complicated females, but he let it pass and quickly launched into the main issue, my equestrian education.

What was I going to do when I got back to America and went into competition, he asked? Did I think for one minute that I'd have a warm-up ring to myself? Show arena conditions are always difficult, far worse than anything I was experiencing here at the stable. And as for riding in front of people, there was no time like the present to get beyond such a problem. Because Walter was kindly, he added that of course he would help me with my Sunday problems, but I also had to work with them myself. He emphasized the word "work" as if he had invented it.

Walter was right. I had been spoiled by riding in my own ring at home. Self-consciousness was an issue many riders have to deal with; Walter and I both knew it would only go away with time and practice. So I concentrated on my lessons and tried to dismiss everything but my teacher and my horse from my mind.

In spite of my best efforts, however, Sundays in the ring during those initial months were often disappointing in terms of expected improvement. In theory, the end of each week should have been a good day for us. Once upon a time, I had anticipated that I would see progress weekly if not daily, that my ability to improve would be visible and concrete. It never crossed my mind that I might have little to show for time spent. My progress felt not only slow but uneven. We might be at our best on a Thursday or Friday, our third or fourth work day. Too, when we did arrive at a new plateau or a notably good day, a period of regression would invariably follow. Accepting regression and not allowing it to get in the way and represent a low point took getting used to. I needed to believe in my lessons and in my own capacity always to be going forward.

Certainly, my "work weekdays," Tuesdays through Saturdays, were easier than my "trial by fire" on Sundays. The stable, the casino, the ring, the horses, the riders, and the atmosphere were quieter; I was able to notice details, feel differences, and remain concentrated. As the weeks passed, I noticed that I was starting to sit tall in the saddle, drop my shoulders, and keep my elbows by my side without continuous reminders. Since I had begun riding with Walter, my legs were dropping down to such a degree I had to lengthen my stirrup leathers two holes, and to my immense relief, the stirrup irons no longer slipped off my feet. These changes, along with others, told me that my riding position was beginning to change.

With each week I faced some fresh facet of the art of good riding. One of the hardest and most important skills for me to understand was "feel." My American instruction had focused more on "doing" than "feeling." Initially, during Walter's lessons, I often tried so intensely to change old habits, adopt new ones, and follow directions that I'd forget about the horse. Whenever Walter noticed this, he'd interrupt to ask, "Tell me, how does Inca feel?"

"Good heavens," I would think, "I have no idea."

Walter's approach made me notice that a good deal of my riding was going on primarily in my head. Other trainers who had taught me in the past had allowed this, or perhaps were not aware of it. The subject of feel had most certainly been covered by them, but apparently not in sufficient depth to leave an impression on me. For Walter, however, "feel" was central. Every day his insistent words rang in my ears: "You MUST FEEL your horse!"

For months, the question plagued me—"How does Inca feel?" My struggle to grasp the answer frightened me, awakening deep misgivings: perhaps I lacked the basic ability to feel and thus would never progress further. I noticed that feel would come and then it would go. The concept was subtle and hard to define; easily blocked or lost by any absence of focus. "Oh God," I'd mutter, "I'm working so hard, how am I ever going to feel anything but myself?" I had no idea what to answer Walter, so I'd grunt to let him know that at the very least, I'd heard him. The challenge he'd put before me hung so heavily in my mind that when I was taking a bath late nights before bed, I'd hear Walter's voice pop his question, "Tell me, how does Inca feel?" I'd lie in the hot water longer than I'd intended and search for the right words to answer.

The sense of feel informs the rider of everything about his horse. Walter must have hoped that by having me identify my sensations, I would gradually connect body and mind. When I looked around at the riders at Tasdorf, it was obvious that people were endowed with varying degrees of feel. Some had a lot, others less. The distinction between the two was easy to see: lacking feel, riders worked their horses without harmony or beauty and always gave an appearance of separateness from their mounts. Walter assured me that this ability could be developed. I wanted with all my heart to believe him.

He tried hard to open up for me the world of feel as he knew it. What actually helped the most was for him to warm up my horse for me. He'd make Inca supple, get him finely tuned and ready for me. Then I'd climb aboard expectantly and find that he had brought Inca to a point where sitting on him was like putting a spoon into warm honey. At those times, riding was exhilarating. It was not like work at all, but more as if Inca was hearing my thoughts and responding to them. It was at such moments that I began to be able to explore the dimensions of feel. To say it in riding terms, my horse had accepted the bit, was moving evenly forward, had given me his back and was listening to me. I felt Inca's stride in a totally fresh way, knew when he took long steps or short ones, which of his four legs preceded the others, whether the hind ones were sufficiently under him or if one or the other tended to drag. I had begun the process of kinesthetically reading my horse, with information traveling from my muscles to my mind. I began to consider and even to prepare myself for Walter's queries.

At last the day came when I was able to answer Walter's question, "How is Inca in the mouth?" with the response, "Light and even in the hand." At that moment, if my leather reins had suddenly turned to thread, I'd still have had no problem. However, Walter's concept of feel was more than just the rider's connection to the horse through the reins. It involved a sensitive "knowing" of the entire animal. Walter's queries to me concerned every part of Inca, including the horse's stride and how I physically perceived where the work we were doing was taking us. Since he never let up on this aspect of instruction, ever so slowly, my ability to feel my horse came alive. At first, my understanding was shy, tentative, and elusive as a whisper. It came in moments, and I would want to report to Walter that I was getting the feel, but then I'd be afraid to speak too soon for fear that in another second I'd lose it. At times, when I really lost my feel and couldn't find it again, Walter would say, "Let me get on Inca for you."

Most good trainers can make a horse right for themselves but few can make a horse right for *someone else.* Walter's outstanding talent was that he could prepare horses for all different kinds of riders. I always wondered how he could do this. He must have been able to assess the weaknesses and the strengths of both horse and rider and then known intuitively exactly how to prepare the creature accordingly. I used to think about this in terms of sculpture: Inca and me as the clay, and Walter as the sculptor who patiently, knowledgeably and creatively molded the two of us into one.

What were Walter's secrets? I didn't think he had secrets. He never pretended he did, he never seemed mysterious in any way. This was a man who knew about horses and the way to make any horse work well. I often watched him as he worked his gift with Inca, getting rid of tension, stiffness and resistance just by training in the walk. He would compact Inca's body and fully round it out, bring energy to one millimeter less than explosion and maintain it. Then, finally, at the right second, he'd push my equine friend one step further: Inca would move into an alternating, cadenced dance step, weightless enough to be walking on glass. This was the piaffe—one of the most difficult movements in dressage, one that is included in the Olympic test. Walter found that using the piaffe briefly in his warm-up was beneficial. He explained that a few judicious steps with certain tight horses like mine helped to supple the hindquarters and to establish a definite rhythm.

Sometimes Walter used exaggeration to instruct me. He'd ride up on another horse right next to me and demonstrate what I was doing wrong, only he would make it ten times worse so I'd be sure to get the message. Then he'd laugh in a way that clearly said he was not intending to be demeaning but merely mirroring me. He must have realized that I was a visual learner and that pictures in my mind were my best aides.

This coming together of teacher, horse, and student were the times I lived for at Tasdorf. They made me feel wonderfully confirmed, in myself, in my horse, and in Walter—in his steadfast belief in the correct process of learning the art. During these moments nothing outside the three of us mattered. When I walked away I was sure that the struggle to do things right was like a holy crusade, and whatever it took to get ahead was worthwhile.

In those early "school days," I learned that "whatever it took," to help the cause included the acquisition of special clothing and equipment. One day, a customer of Walter's told me, "I think you'd sit deeper in your saddle if you were to buy a pair of German riding pants like mine." I had already noticed that she wore a special type of pants that were leather-covered wherever the rider's body made contact with the horse, and I could hardly get to the equestrian store fast enough. When I asked for the pants with leather, the salesman knew precisely which kind I meant. "You want the ones the top German riders wear," he commented, and then added authoritatively, "they all say the leather keeps you right in the saddle."

"Exactly," I said, "I'll take two pair." I hadn't even asked the price.

Shortly afterward, Walter recommended that I try out a new saddle, the Swiss Roosli. It had a shape that would tilt my pelvis forward and hold my calf in a better position than my own saddle did. Christine Stückelberger had introduced him to the Roosli, and he was impressed enough to persuade others to buy it. In fact, few other brands were ever used in the stable. Within six weeks, my old saddle was retired to Inca's steamer trunk and his rack in the tack room supported a Roosli too.

Riding equipment was a subject of constant conversation and of vital interest to everyone at Tasdorf. Everything from gloves to horses' leg wraps was discussed and whenever possible examined, compared, and assessed. At the time, I was fascinated to learn that Germany made special stirrups that were set at an angle for riders who could not flex their ankles, rubber pads to insert in stirrup irons to help keep them on one's feet, and incredibly enough, a kind of glue to insure that a rider sat tight (now all available here in the United States). Walter's response to the purchase of such artificial aids was an emphatic "Nein!" On the affirmative side, he was equally emphatic on the importance of owning the proper riding boots.

Boots are made with a firmer, heavier leather in Germany than in America and, Walter informed me, give the rider more control over her leg. He recommended that I purchase the all-purpose, somewhat less handsome but more durable brand worn by the Stall's apprentices. Afraid I might be doing my riding an injustice if I didn't act upon this sage advice, I bought a pair.

As I became more immersed in the details of my new craft, other small changes took place one by one. Some of these fell outside of the requirements of the sport. The German women who appeared at Stall Tasdorf to ride always arrived coifed, with nail polish and make-up applied flawlessly enough to go to a ball. My surprise over these dressy and somewhat citified details puzzled Kerstin. "But such refinements make you feel elegant," was her comment. "Hm-m-m-m," I thought, "perhaps I'm being a country mouse," and so, succumbing to a buried desire for elegance, I joined in the "fashion parade."

Appearance, I learned, counted for a great deal here, in and out of the ring, and body image was a matter of no small importance. Thin was definitely in. Everyone, including the men, talked about being thin. If they weren't fashion conscious, at least they liked to think of themselves as fit. Most of the clients as well as the stable crew were thin, one or two of them even pencil thin. Everyone worried about how they looked in riding pants, aware that the cut of those tight pants was flattering only when covering straight lines.

From the very first day, I felt fat. I drank lots of coffee and tried to get along with less and less on my plate. I was grateful when I was given more horses to ride; knowing that I was not only improving my skills, I was also burning calories. To the same end, I supplemented riding with longer and more energetic afternoon walks. When hunger came calling, I'd try to ignore it, helped by a mental picture of myself already looking better on a horse. At the close of my year at the stable, I had dropped down two sizes and wondered how even at 5 feet 10 inches, I could ever have allowed myself to be an American size 16. But then, perhaps we Americans tolerate huskiness a bit more than do Europeans. Back home, I had noticed that visiting foreign dressage clinicians repeatedly remarked on the heftiness of some of our thick-thighed riders. It wasn't until I was on foreign soil myself and took note of the fit looking riders, that I could see how these sports-minded experts might have a point.

Thin or fat, short or tall, the way we ride reveals who we are as people; nothing is hidden. Small wonder that my innate, speedy style and tempo attracted notice. At every lesson, I heard Walter call out, "Priscilla, nicht so schnell," (not so fast). Finding the correct rhythm to ride dressage is of paramount importance and Walter claimed that I raced. He even showed me how it was that I raced, so that when I didn't change, his continuing reproofs were not surprising. Eventually, he began commenting as well on my rapid manner in the casino. I'd jump up to get napkins, or sugar, or to go home, and the disturbed look on his face sometimes said even more than his words. I would be instantly sorry. How right the man was! I had to admit that I walked quickly, ate fast, made decisions rapidly and in general took life at the run. I had always defended my speedy ways as being quite simply "me," but here at Tasdorf I finally understood that there was nothing to defend.

My time in Germany was filled with change: I was busy reinventing myself on many levels. I didn't try to judge whether these changes were superficial or necessary. Instead, I discovered that the important thing was the willingness to change in itself—to change in any way that would help me achieve my goal of becoming a better rider. In the end, while I did improve my riding, I did not return home having made the dramatic progress that I had dreamed of at the start of my journey. This was not a subject I wanted to bring up with Walter—at first because it was too painful, and later because I knew what he would say. He would look at me with those steady blue eyes of his and calmly tell me to, "go on, just go on." And so I did . . . and so, I do . . . knowing that the big lesson was, is, and always will be to welcome growth and change.

12

After School

Horses do best when they have a routine—and so do humans. There is something comforting about repeating acts and having customary courses of procedure; it helps us to avoid constant questioning, quiet the soul, and free the mind. The day-to-day rhythms of routine create a sense of gathering familiarity that nurtures friendship. The structure of routine creates a way to order one's experience of the world—and let it ripen. Back home in Massachusetts, routines supported me like a vital lifeline threading together my days, but here in Germany even routines were something I had to discover.

Certainly, when it came to daily life at Stall Tasdorf, the routines were beautifully clear. Almost from my first days, the predictability of the weekly schedule gave me a solid base from which to weather the uncertainties of the learning process. It was during my time off away from "campus" that I felt at first like a small, rudderless boat adrift at sea. Then, pressed by need and loneliness, I began to find all sorts of ways to organize my time—small ways, little rituals that put me directly in touch with the wonderful potential of my situation.

Daytime, Tuesday through Sunday morning, was totally dedicated to lessons at Tasdorf. The problem was, what to do with Sunday afternoon and Monday (rest day), and the long, silent evenings.

On Sundays around one-thirty, right after lunch with the Christensens and the apprentices, I would leave the barn and drive home in a rush of traffic. Most of northern Germany was out on the road at this hour: on foot, aboard a bike, or in a car. They were heading home for a nap. Unaccustomed to this midday habit, I found it impossible to think of sleep. Thus, I faced seemingly endless hours as my solitary afternoon stretched on into evening.

At first, I tried to fill these idle Sunday hours by reading a book, only to find that I couldn't sit still. "Let's get going," my body kept telling me. I couldn't even remain quiet enough to listen to music. Sometimes letter writing worked, but it couldn't be counted on to absorb me as it often did in the evenings. Not knowing what else to do with myself, I once went for a drive in the car, only to discover myself constantly eyeing the clock, wishing to be back in the apartment. I was overwhelmed with the burden of so many hours in which to do anything I wanted—anything at all. I knew that I should have been thrilled, but in actual fact those endless units of sixty minutes weighed me down as if they were cement bricks.

Clearly, I needed to organize my free time on Mondays: establish tasks and routines. I began making lists of things to do. Instantly, I noted that list making helped clear away the haze of confusion. Mostly my lists noted simple tasks: water flowers, do laundry, write letters, buy food, check tires, make hair appointment, deposit check, take a walk, visit museum. In the interest of variety, I offered myself options: do stay at home things (cozy and safe), or go right out and take care of the business of living. The latter made me feel best. After an outing, I could give myself a pat on the back and feel that I'd really earned the right to go back home.

By the second month, I knew which items on my list gave me the most input. Taking care of my car offered me the least—although it was practical, it was too impersonal. Going to the bank, the cleaners, the post office and the "friseur" (hairdresser), was a different story—it put me in touch with my new world. I looked upon these necessary trips as opportunities; they provided me with direct contact with people as well as the chance to inquire, "Wie geht es?" (How are you?), and the hope that I'd be asked a simple question or two, or even three in return. My most reliable talkers were the two elderly ladies in the cleaning establishment. They were as warm and friendly as the moist air that pervaded the place. The oldest of the pair frequently talked with pins in her mouth and I used to worry that because she was a little dithery she'd swallow them. Going to the textile museum by myself was a lonely affair, but I could listen to the tourists chat among themselves—speculating about nationalities was more fun than studying fabrics.

I found that watering flowers was amazing. At first, the watering stood for "something that had to be done," but then to my surprise it became a much-looked-forward-to commitment. I couldn't believe how intimately I got to know my plants, learning things I'd never known before. During my growing up years, my father had a greenhouse but I had ignored everything in it, only discovering flowers for myself after I had crossed the ocean. Aside from offering me pleasure, comfort, and scent, they filled my space with their gentle, sweet presence. I told my flowers they were beautiful many times a day, and whenever I spied a fresh shipment at the florist, I bought more.

There was never a question about what I should do or where I should be every Tuesday through Saturday morning between 8:30 and 9:00. It was then that the postman drove up to Stall Tasdorf in a small car, yellow and cheerful as the sun. Next to the time I spent on the back of a horse, I found his appearance to be the best part of the day. Trim in his uniform, he marched into the main aisle with a happy young man's energy, shouting "Post!" loud enough for us all to hear. He took the utmost care of every single person, accepting money instead of stamps, taking our letters and postcards away in his pouch, returning with exact change on the following day, and best of all, presenting the incoming package of mail as though it was his personal offering.

Often, it was Kerstin who had the privilege of sorting the mail while the rest of us would look eagerly over her shoulder. As a group, we were inordinately curious and hungry for diversion. We liked talking and thinking about far away places. Postcards with pictures reminded people of places they'd dreamt about or stories they'd heard, all of which we discussed with gusto over lunch. Next to the Christensens, I received more mail than the others, so it was a gray morning when there was nothing for me.

On the good days, there'd be several letters, as many as three, four, and even five. What a new experience it was to receive home in an envelope. I reached for every piece with greed and couldn't wait to see who had written. Usually I'd know at a glance, though every now and then, I'd get a surprise. Someone I hadn't been thinking about wanted to say "hello" or was planning to be in the vicinity. Could they stop by to see the horses and perhaps have a visit? I had assumed letter writing had gone out of fashion along with garter belts and girdles. The members of my family had never been letter writers before; we were accustomed to picking up the telephone and having long chats whenever we thought of it. But now, staying in touch had become an entirely different experience for us.

I made a practice of carrying my letters around unread for hours, playing a game, prolonging a rite, knowing that when I finally said to myself, "now is the right time," I'd be giving myself lovely warm moments. I spent time thinking about each writer before I tore open an envelope, loving him or her more than ever (or perhaps even for the first time) for having thought of me and taken so much precious time to sit down and actually write a letter.

Of course, the news I received was comparatively old, delayed ten days, sometimes two weeks. No one could explain why mail took so long. The Germans claimed the fault was with the American postal system; the Americans said, "no question, the hold up was due to the Germans." To me, the delay seldom mattered. The news I received was fresh enough.

Writing letters was a new activity for me. But, in no time, I grew to love sitting down with pen in hand and choosing to whom I would talk. Writing out my thoughts and feelings became a way of keeping isolation at bay and the fact that the conversation was one-sided never mattered. As the mass of correspondence grew, I noticed that letters, especially between myself and the family, got longer and appeared less quickly written. We seemed to have deeper things to say, becoming more trusting of one another. In a sense, we were exploring a new language. Years later, I heard my oldest daughter, Katrina say, "Mom, remember those letters we wrote back and forth when you were in Germany? That part of your being away, I loved."

Knowing that a trip to Europe to learn to ride held an aura of glamour to anyone who didn't know any better, I tried to share my adventures as fully as I could without admitting that my riding hopes had been folded into new shapes. Mainly, I didn't want anyone to worry about me, I was doing enough of that myself. Too, I was building up such an enormous new respect and love for the art I had chosen that I hadn't as yet found words to express my expanding horizons. How could I expect others to comprehend ideas that were not yet clear to me? When questions were asked like, "How are you doing?" or "What are your future plans?" I was vague. Writing about my riding lessons had limitations and could seem boring and repetitive when set down on white paper. So instead, I described the difficulties and pressures of going back to a school with a system as stringent as that of the Germans, a subject with which I thought almost any American could identify.

At times, letter writing put me in a bind. I was quite sure that both family and friends expected glowing reports like, "My riding's going splendidly, Walter's thrilled, every day there's improvement," but it wasn't in me to present a picture that wasn't true. I was experiencing so much within myself, emptiness versus overload, hope versus despair, that it was difficult to know what to say. One minute, I'd be ready to take on life as an adventure, the next I'd be filled with a sudden fear of making any move at all, to the point that even filling my car with gas became a trial. There were nights I went to sleep with my hands clenched into fists as if I were in battle. When I found something to laugh at, I often cried.

Part of me longed to speak out openly about how I honestly felt. My efforts to circumvent describing my situation until I could either come to terms with it or improve it became creative—even fun. In my free hours while out doing errands, I scoured the news stores in the towns around Neumünster, searching for old-fashioned black and white photographic postcards. West Germany appeared to have lots of them. I would take these cards home and use them as a circuitous way to illustrate how I was feeling.

One day, when I was searching for some way to send a hint of my German experience to two old friends back home, I found just the right card in a rack in Neumünster. The cards on display were the kind that told stories and in almost every case made me giggle. The prize of the bunch was one card depicting a middle aged circus lady sitting astride a galloping white horse. She was outfitted in a tutu and white leather boots and wrapped around her neck was an ostrich feather boa. The man depicted as Master of Ceremonies had obviously just thrown his long circus whip on the ground in complete exasperation. I wrote that this was a photograph of me taking a lesson at Stall Tasdorf. The M.C. (Walter Christensen, of course) was tearing his hair out because he couldn't understand why this frilly American lady couldn't ride any better nor why she wept as she sat there on her horse. Bursting into tears while riding at Stall Tasdorf had not as yet actually happened. It had crossed my mind more than once. Horrified at the thought, I prayed such an occurrence would never come to pass and vowed to avoid tears at all cost.

Many months later when I had returned home, I saw the card affixed to my friend's refrigerator. They said they appreciated the humor and the fact that it made them smile whenever they looked at it. By then, I was far removed from the European scene, but could not forget the complexity of those days. It crossed my mind that few of the people I knew had ever divined the depth of my anguish.

As much as writing letters served to alleviate my homesickness, as soon as the letters were back in their envelopes, I was once again back in my "new world." How best to explore that world and to lose the sense of being a "stranger in a strange land?" Shopping. Shopping is after all, international. When I wasn't at the stable and the shops had reopened after their midday closure, I frequently went out to buy food. In fact, I probably spent more hours involved in this activity than any other. By American standards, my icebox and my cooking facilities were small; storage space simply did not exist. If I wanted fresh fruit and vegetables for myself or carrots and apples for Inca, I walked ten minutes into town. Preparation for these forays often had to begin with the help of Frau Kunze, my German teacher. I wanted to learn the correct words for things like liquid and solid measurements, one half a dozen, a slice, the full container, as well as coarse, medium, or fine. My vocabulary grew straight out of need and expanded rapidly. During my lessons, Frau Kunze insisted on the importance of knowing the correct gender of each noun. She ceaselessly urged me toward high speaking standards—anything less was not to be tolerated. Dropping my voice in shyness or fudging syllables, verb endings, or pronouns was not acceptable.

I found shopping in Germany different from shopping back home. The freshest fruits and vegetables were to be found in a tiny market right on a main street that led northward toward Kiel. Two blocks further along main street on the right corner, came the bakery with breads, tarts, cookies, and assorted pastries freshly baked every morning. Directly across from that entrance, in a shop no bigger than a closet, was the lady who sold milk, cheese, eggs, and fresh yogurt. Then came the butcher, who displayed an amazing array of meats and birds both domestic and wild, as well as an intriguing variety of homemade sausage. I could have eaten the "grob leberwurst" (coarse liverwurst) seven days a week. Cold cuts in this land were a mouth-watering experience.

Sometimes, when these small shops were crowded, shopping became a trial. Women carrying huge baskets lined up with the docility of cows, but their appearance was deceptive. When these ladies drew closer to the counter, their eyes took on the look of hardened steel. They made it obvious that I was supposed to know exactly what I wished to buy the instant my turn came. There was to be no time for sightseeing through the counter glass. If I forgot the name of the bread, roll, or tart of my choice and was reduced to pantomime, the ladies lost patience. I found it hard to stay calm. When the sales lady added up my bill, I learned to watch the figures on the register, thus avoiding the problem of spoken German numbers. The way they were reversed caught me every time: for example, 29 pfennig was spoken as nine and twenty pfennig. To speed up the procedure, I whipped out large bills, thus putting the blame for being slow on the storekeeper. "Haven't you anything smaller?" I'd be asked, having handed out the equivalent of twenty dollars for a purchase of about two fifty. I knew she would have preferred exact change. Determined to look innocent to the baker lady, I'd shake my head "No, I have nothing smaller." By then the women in line would be shuffling their feet noisily on the floor, indicating there was not a moment more to waste.

Most of all, I looked forward to my visits to the fresh produce stand. There, the aproned proprietor put aside apples for Inca. "Don't pay for them," she'd say, "I have a few extra." She wondered if I also kept rabbits. "No," I assured her. "You eat all that lettuce and greens yourself?" she inquired. My nod confirmed that I was different. To this cheery soul, being different was interesting; so naturally I bought more than I needed. She'd ask, "How was your ride today?" and then really listen to my answer. When I bought green grapes (a luxury imported from Israel at that time of year) especially for Inca, she was surprised at my extravagance but immediately concurred that an animal could mean a lot to a person. She had once had a dog who went everywhere with her. They had understood each other as if they were two human beings. "He died a year ago," she confided. "I was with him when he went. Have you got a minute to wait? I have to run out back. My freshest grapes just came in a few minutes ago. I'll unpack them."

While out on my shopping expeditions, I was curious about the tasks and routines of others, and noticed with interest women in their aprons out on the stoop with buckets of sudsy water and scrub

211

brushes. I had not been in Tasdorf long before I discovered that "putzen" and "waschen" (cleaning and washing), was a huge part of many German women's daily routine. Early in the morning, all the windows of the houses along the road to the stable would be wide open. Often I'd spy bedclothes being shaken as well as mops, or someone might be leaning halfway out sudsing windowpanes. In the afternoons, as I walked around town doing errands, I saw women endlessly scrubbing down their front steps. One householder washed her truck-size macadam driveway on what appeared to be a regular basis.

This concentration on cleanliness appeared to be constant. On my drives to and from the stable, I'd been struck as well by the quantity of laundry lines I saw on the way. When it wasn't raining, the family's laundry would be hung out long before the birds were up. German women pinned their clothes with precision, lining the garments up as if the family itself was out on parade. What amazed me as well was that not an inch of space was ever wasted; every line was full. How unafraid of physical labor these people seemed to be. I couldn't help but wonder what hour their day began and when it finished. These German women went about their labors as if work was a national sport.

Curious to compare my observations with a fellow foreigner, I questioned Kerstin, who, as I mentioned earlier, was Swedish, about women and work and it turned out that she too had noticed these habits when she first arrived. The work ethic, she claimed, applied to men as well as to women. "Perhaps you are not aware that people from other countries say that Germans don't work to live; they live to work. I think they LOVE it," she added.

True. Where labor was involved, I saw no questioning, no be-grudging, no attitude shunning work. Discipline, determination, and the willingness to work seemed to be bred into the German mind. Getting a job done the right way was meant to be its own reward.

Because my days allowed me hours of time for long ruminations, I thought a great deal about the person I wished to be and about what I could learn from my surroundings. I even wondered if I might not incorporate cleaning into my life in a more central way; explore the focus, the rhythm, the motion, or the sense of purpose involved in some particular act. So, one late midday, when I came home and noticed an accumulation of dirt in my front hallway, my mind returned like a barn swallow to the aproned ladies. That afternoon, I got down on hands and knees and washed all my floors. Washing floors was of course not new to me, but this was the first time I did it with the true German fervor I'd seen here. I washed everything in sight.

Using the scrub brush gave me the feeling that I was accomplishing something necessary and important. The look of the water shining on the cold hard surfaces pleased me; the fresh smell of the place was like a reward. Best of all, my rooms began to feel more like mine than they ever had.

Admiration of my floors led me to the use of all sorts of different cleaning agents, not always with the results intended. The rapidly deteriorating color of my underclothes was causing me concern. They had long since forgotten they were ever white and had taken on the color of my recently purchased navy blue riding breeches. I might have endured the situation but for an incident that occurred at Neumünster's nicest clothing store. I was in the changing room casually undressing when the head of the department, a chic, immaculately put together sort of person, appeared in the doorway with an armload of garments. Noticing the state of my panties, she stared with such horror that I wished I could vanish. This, I thought, will never happen again.

With Dudens German-English dictionary in hand, I set out for the market to look for a new soap. One container appealed to me more than the others, not so much for what it said, but because of the picture. On both sides of the bottle, there was a large pearl. Yes! This was what I needed, a soap to make my clothes, particularly my underpants, pearl white!

So I washed my underthings in the milky substance, though every time I squeezed out a dollop from the bottle something about its thick consistency puzzled me. Never mind, I thought, things are bound to be different in Germany. After a rinse, I would hang my clothes over the radiator and the sides of the bathtub to dry. On the following morning, I noticed that my clothes had taken on the consistency of dried tree bark, but because I was thinking about my upcoming lesson, I simply got dressed and walked out into the new day.

One day, however, the situation became literally too uncomfortable to ignore. I couldn't sit on Inca! I couldn't sit on anything, even a chair! How had my clothes gotten into such a state? Then I remembered the soap. That afternoon, I took my deluxe-size-money-saving box with its decorative white pearl to Kerstin. "What have I got here?" I asked.

"Starch," was her reply. "The best starch that I know of. Is that what you want? Why did you buy such a large box?"

I told her my story, "I can't believe it!" she said, and we laughed so hard tears flowed down both our faces.

Kerstin and I were two people who could laugh easily together. Both of us possess the kind of energy that bursts out to release tensions. And we both did have tensions: hers caused by the many problems that surrounded the stable business, and mine by the effort of living in a totally new environment. As our daily common schedule increasingly brought us together, our friendship began to flourish. It was not that we discussed her problems or mine—that would

214

have been out of character for both of us and certainly not in accordance with European custom. Laughter was our best language of communication, and we soon began to egg each other on.

The first time she invited me for an outing was on a Monday in March. I could hardly say "yes" quickly enough. We barely knew each other at all then. She must have been thinking of me as "the American" as well as a customer, because she announced that she wished to take me on a sightseeing tour.

It was a cold, damp day. Snowflakes the size of children's mittens were coming down thick and fast. Visibility was very questionable but, undaunted, we sped off for an afternoon in and around Hamburg, about an hour's drive from Stall Tasdorf. We cruised through the streets going toward the harbor, along the Alster river, past the cathedral, the hotels, the restaurants, and to the stores where, she informed me, I could find fashions to dream about. I didn't understand how she could drive so effortlessly when I couldn't make out a single outline, not even a building, let alone a cathedral, a ship, or a shop. Bits of information flowed from her with an enthusiasm that was infectious. She kept waving her hand, indicating that somewhere beyond the falling white veil, what she was describing actually existed. I still didn't know why, but somehow my sightless-seeing tour seemed totally satisfactory.

Not content to allow Kerstin merely the role of caretaker, I pushed for closer friendship, convinced we would discover that we had much in common. By the time I had been at Tasdorf four or five months, spending evenings as well as occasional afternoons in each other's company was quite natural. In fact, I almost thought of it as routine.

During the hours that I spent in Kerstin's house, I watched her sew, iron, cut drapes, repair pillows, and perform all manner of home jobs. I was struck by her willing and meticulous attention to details.

"I like to iron," she said, holding up a complicated blouse she had just pressed in a thoroughly professional manner. I couldn't help but notice that these tasks seemed to slow her inner pace, bring her a sense of accomplishment, and put her in touch with an essential part of herself. The face that I glimpsed during these moments carried an expression of peace that I seldom saw. I need to find an experience like this for myself, I thought, and began looking.

My opportunity came soon. When Walter advised me that German riding boots offered a firmness around the calf and an upright stiffness that would keep my leg steady on the horse and probably help my riding. Kerstin took me to the riding store and supervised the purchase of new boots.

After the purchase, Kerstin shared her ideas about boot care. I listened carefully and bought the polish she suggested. I was already thinking that aside from using them to ride, I was going to take special care of these boots.

During the time that I had been at Walter's stable, I had heard him remind his crew that riding boots *must* be cleaned daily. Was boot cleaning going to become a chore to be completed, I wondered, or would it become the answer to my search for a tranquil task? Might I consider putting time aside for this task at the end of each day, as regularly as if I were saying my prayers? In a way, by turning the cleaning of the boots into a deep and quiet act I *would* be saying my prayers! Shortly thereafter, every night before bedtime, I was polishing away.

In learning this form of meditation, I discovered some good rules: find a place to sit firmly, balanced and upright with your rag, polish, and brush close at hand. When you begin to apply the polish, do so lightly. Don't be in a hurry or overly ambitious. Keep your thoughts focused. Try not to use the time to solve problems or make decisions. Lay every bit of mental work down and just be there with your boots. Notice when you come to the top so that you don't go over the edge. No need to get black polish where it shouldn't be. When you are finished, take up the brush. Feel the size of it and the weight of it in your hand. Hold the brush softly but firmly against the boot and brush. Now brush . . . and brush . . . and brush.

When I followed these steps after each day's riding, boot cleaning did become a source of profound tranquility. I soon realized that I needed quiet as much as I needed daily food. On certain days, I continued brushing until my boots became black mirrors. Sometimes I had no wish to stop.

I began watching the faces of people cleaning their boots in the stable, which was where many riders took care of the job. For some it was a perfunctory act. For others, it had a special point. Walter, for example, could stand right in the middle of the stable aisle and still be in his own peaceful place, all the while applying the thinnest film of paste. When he took up the brush, his arm echoed the rhythm of a horse's tail swishing, back and forth, back and forth, back and forth.

Shortly after I had began my polishing "practice," I chanced upon a verse from an ancient text and thought these words could have been written for me. I copied them out and taped them to the wall where I sat with my boots so that I could drink in their wisdom and make it mine.

> There is no need to run outside
> For better seeing.
> Nor to peer from a window. Rather abide
> At the center of your being;
> For the more you leave it, the less you learn.
> Search your heart and see
> If he is wise who takes each turn:
> The way to do is to be."
> —*The Way of Life*, Lao Tzu,
> Translated by Witter Bynner

I had been in Germany almost half a year and was beginning to believe that I had almost worked out the routines of my existence, when the scene changed. I was informed by my landlord that, unexpectedly, he needed my apartment for a member of his family. I had to find another place.

Luckily, Kerstin was able to relocate me. I went to live in one large room in the home of Frau and Herr Sievers and their two children, right on the same street as the stable. My room was furnished with a bed, a night table, a coffee table, a sofa, and an armchair—but no desk. Cooking facilities were not included in the rental, but I was told that I could use the kitchen occasionally, the washing facilities regularly, the clothesline in the warm cellar whenever I wished, and that I would share the upstairs bathroom with the four of them. I had instant hopes for a degree of intimate contact with a German family, but that never quite came about. What did happen were some interesting switches and additions to the routines of life.

In my first apartment, I'd had space that had offered me the "revelations" of cleaning; in my new room, while I no longer cleaned but merely tidied, I got cakes! Whenever Frau Sievers had a family gathering, she came into my room after the briefest knock (she was a lady of maximum speed and efficiency) to present me with hot coffee and whatever else she was offering her guests. And then because I saw that she did it, I took up knitting: day or night, Frau Sievers was always ready to help me with it. She knew how to refashion my sweaters into garments made for humans, not long-armed gorillas. Plainly, she liked setting things right.

I had noticed Frau Siever's house when I'd first come to Stall Tasdorf because part of the building had been turned into a small store. Neat as could be, it was a rabbit warren kind of shop that held a little bit of everything and featured hot breakfast "brotchen" (rolls) baked daily. Apparently the store provided more work than money, and so, suddenly, it was shut down. Married to a sweet man who fought ill health, Frau Sievers was a resourceful woman; she immediately turned to renting out rooms. She accordioned her family into a few of the rooms and offered living space to the Christensens who had a constant overflow of stable visitors. When I inquired about the rent for my stay, I found out that I cost less to house than Inca.

Living at the Sievers made me aware that Germans like to live behind closed doors. Wherever I stood in their house, I found everything shut tight. It took time to get used to the lack of flow or space in a home. Closed doors felt unfriendly and claustrophobic even though I learned that the practice had begun as a practical measure adopted during World War II in order to save heat. With only the downstairs and the upstairs hallways to look at, I was curious to know exactly where the family Sievers lived. One Sunday when the house was vacant, I took a peek. At that time, there were eight of us living there: two young Swedes who worked in the stable, another single boarder, the four Sievers, and me. Quarters were closer for the family than I could have imagined. The children had been packed into a dormer bedroom like two little cupcakes. To me, the marvel of the arrangement was that I never heard any noise: no bickering, no pushing or shoving, no hollering. What was Frau Siever's secret?

After I settled in, it soon became apparent that Frau Sievers was as curious about her American guest as I was about my host family. I first noticed her interest when she repeatedly complimented me on my progress with my German lessons. Obviously, she kept track of what I read and wrote, so that it was quite natural one afternoon to have a discussion concerning the German use of the subjunctive. Details interested her. Details like what did this bottle of perfume smell like and why did I have so much make up? When she came upon the chocolate bars in my drawer, she let it be known that she did not think that bed was the place, nor night the proper time, for anyone to eat candy. My books, my letters, occasional purchases of new clothes, and my what-I-should-do lists were part of her domain. But because I liked the woman, even admired her, I seldom resented what might have been regarded as intrusion. Answering her cheery questions gave me the opportunity to converse with Frau Sievers in her language. With her, I dared to experiment with inflection, practice new words, take chances, try to speak faster, and even pretend talking German took no effort at all. All the while, she'd smile like a mother, nod her head, and say "Gut. Gut." When I ran out of steam I'd be proud of myself and go off feeling the two of us had had a really great talk.

Though this second home did not involve living intimately with a German family, it did bring me more in contact with the neighborhood of Tasdorf. My two large windows offered me a close-up view of the doings on main street and looked directly across at a farm. Observing the life patterns of the little village helped me to establish my own rhythms and on occasion influenced my routines.

At dawn, I often woke to the predictably regular, daily sounds of the street. Cows with udders that bumped almost on the ground ambled by on their way to be milked. Lowing softly, they left behind a pleasant, rich, fertile scent that remained all day throughout the warmer weather. Sometimes, they made me feel I was living inside a cow barn instead of some hundreds of yards away from one. In good weather, farmer Sievers (a relative of my Sievers) across the way, put his Holsteiner stallion to paddock early. Every day, regardless of the weather, his son (who was so handsome he made the Stall Tasdorf girls giggle whenever he came around) chased pigs the size of his father's horses out to their pen. When I first heard the pigs scream, I was sure the building opposite me was a slaughterhouse. Thank goodness, I was wrong! I was informed that the pigs were only screaming in their eagerness to get to the food trough.

Weekdays, I watched cars leaving for work and town children walking down the street to the bus. Wednesdays belonged to the trash collector, and on Fridays the fishman hawked his fresh wares, announcing his presence in front of each home with a bell. Saturdays were quiet for an extra hour in the morning, then the women and often the entire family went off to town with their baskets to go shopping. In about one month, I could tell time by the sounds on the street without even getting up to look outside.

Once, when there was a sudden late frost and I had to scrape the ice from my car window, I found a small object affixed to one wiper —a box with a note wrapped around it. The box held a game, the small wooden kind that one takes along in the car to amuse children. The paper was half-frozen, and the writing was in pencil and hard to read. I had no idea what it said: there were words and spellings I'd never seen.

Walter was sitting in the doorway of the ring when I arrived, and was not so concentrated on the horses that I was afraid to bother him.

"What's this?" He had to put on his glasses to read the note. "You have a secret admirer," he told me with a twinkle in his eyes.

"Oh, who?" I asked in amazement.

"Hard to say," was his response, "there's no name on this note."

It was signed, "Ein Freund," (a friend). From the sense that Walter made of it, the writer had apparently been watching me closely for some time. Finally, he had written to me. Each short sentence ended with a "Ja." Perhaps, my admirer said, I would like this small present, "Ja?" If I brought the game with me to the Kneipe (bar), at the end of the street some night, he would teach me to play it, "Ja." He was sure we would have a nice time. "Ja."

The game and the note were carried up to the casino, read and reread over coffee with the ladies. There was laughter and questions like, "What do you do with your evenings when we aren't around?" I had achieved a bit of mystery in these women's eyes, and I was glad for it in this strong, tightly knit group.

I thought about the author of the note, the donor of the game. Which one of the early morning tractors did he drive? Was he the apple-faced fellow with the green rubber boots? The serious figure in the military cap, or one of those men who sat barely visible behind mud-splattered, plastic cab-protectors? Perhaps he wasn't a farmer at all but went off to work elsewhere? I wished I knew.

In the mornings, when I walked the several hundred yards down the street to the stable, I began regularly saying, "Moyn, moyn," the local dialect for "Good morning," to everyone I saw. Occasionally, I'd be tossed a wave as casual as a sparrow hawk's flight. The recognition warmed me and I'd catch myself thinking, "I'm beginning to feel at home here."

≈13

Master Teacher

Fine dressage teachers are rare—as rare as top artists and Olympic competitors—but they are seldom as widely known. Like great teachers in any field, they are deep and multi-level beings. They offer their teaching so generously, earnestly, and profoundly, that the essence of their work can never be forgotten nor can they. Their philosophy, their influence and, on occasion, even their exact words continue on with their students with new and important meaning.

Because I think of my life as one long lesson, I like to reflect on the high points—the places where learning was an experience of great intensity, fired by the inspirational passion of a unique teacher. Each of these gifted teachers exerted such a strong influence over my life that I enjoy bringing them back to mind, savoring each of their individual personalities and wondering what it is they have in common, what it is that lies behind their power to transmit knowledge. Why does the work we did and the time together stand out as among the most rewarding, intense, exciting, and glowing hours of my life? Why do I never forget these masters?

I took my first piano lesson before my feet could reach the floor from my seat on the piano stool. I was formally introduced to a mild, gentle, gray haired, and almost saintly man. Before our first hour was over, I felt drawn to him; when he sat down next to me at the piano, he seemed to light up from within. By the time I had committed my beginner's two-line piece to memory, I could see that my teacher loved music above all else in the world and that his nature was such that he especially enjoyed sharing that love. He surrounded me with this passion so completely that I was caught up in it with him. Instantly, I too, became committed. He used to hum along when I played for him, but I didn't mind, even when his humming would grow so loud that it became a song. Sheer joy in the sounds the two of us were making enveloped me in his world, as week after week, he pushed me toward perfection.

Every now and then, under conditions that I could not have repeated on my own, I offered this teacher my all and outplayed myself. My fingers sped over the keyboard without hitting wrong notes and I heard playing that no longer sounded halting and childlike. I felt lifted to a higher level, transformed, given vision. When I was finished with my lesson, my teacher would beam at me. He acted as if he'd known all along I could play like that. Typically, he would push aside his part in this leap of progress, and say something like, "That's what playing great music does for you." I'd go home warm and proud and think, "Maybe I'll become a musician."

However, in my youthful head, I knew the real truth. My *teacher* had brought about these moments. *He* had made it happen. I had just played as best I could and he had inspired me. At the time, I assumed that this special gift went with the teaching trade, but when I hoped for such moments under other instructors, there were none. It was years before I was to find someone of similar caliber again.

The next exceptional teacher announced on the first day of my junior year of high school that teaching Shakespeare to our class was the sabbatical gift she was giving to herself. My peers and I wondered at her taste in gifts. How could that ancient, wordy bard be so important to someone who seemed normal and nice? Ignoring the atmosphere of disinterest and sleepiness that pervaded the room, she began the hour with an impassioned reading. Listening to her, I decided that perhaps I had misjudged the subject and that Shakespeare might have something to say to me. Under our instructor's encouragement, I began to read diligently. Soon, Macbeth became more important to me than the upcoming school Thanksgiving holiday—what a tragedy, I was going to miss class. By the time Christmas came along, I had almost become Hamlet, I had grown to know him so well. At home for the holidays, I was devastated to discover that my father did not care to share Hamlet's speeches, which came so trippingly to my tongue.

Before the school year was out, my English literature marks were higher than they had ever been, and I was praised by my learned instructor for my good work. What work, I asked myself? This inspired woman had given me so much reason to study that the effort had become no effort, but rather my reason for being. Years later, at Tasdorf, when my heart was singing and my muscles aching after a hard lesson with Walter, I thought of her.

Being inspired to work is not hard with instructors of this sort. They exude a very special kind of energy that is as definite a part of them as the color of their hair. Whether they have a particular "aura" or send off elements of electricity, I can't tell. Like my piano teacher, Walter's energy radiated from within, and beyond question could be sensed by both students and horses. He could alter the entire atmosphere of the ring simply by appearing. Six or seven of us might be riding, training, focusing as hard as we could on ourselves and our horses, doing work on our own. When Walter turned up, an almost imperceptible change would take place. Inca's neck muscles would tighten and his ears turn and he'd try to steal a glance toward the doorway. The air seemed to hold a subtle charge. It brought us even more sharply to attention and asked us specifically to define to ourselves our individual courses of action.

During the first minutes, Walter seldom spoke to anyone in particular other than to utter a general "Guten morgen" (good morning). Then, he'd watch for a bit, making his own assessment of how we were doing. This bothered me since I suspected that he was capable of reading my mind at that moment, and that he might discover that I was often preoccupied with wondering how I looked to him when he appeared rather than concentrating on the work I was suppose to be accomplishing. Fixing his thoughts upon us, Walter could tell more than some of us cared for him to know. Walter understood riders the way he understood horses, by instinct and from the inside out. Was this an invasion? From his point of view, it wasn't meant to be. It was simply that while we were under Walter's roof and on horseback, we were in a sense "his," and answerable to the same high standards he asked of himself. Bad horsemanship was not only offensive to him, it was unacceptable. As for laziness in either man or beast, that too was not to be tolerated.

Naturally, thoughts about how I was doing were not confined to the ring. From the first moment I opened my eyes in the morning, I was mentally heading for my lesson. At a certain level, my riding, or at least my thinking about riding, never ceased but continued on from lesson to lesson, an endless preoccupation. Yet thoughts were only half of the picture: with each new day, I also woke to a brand new array of complex feelings. I wondered if my emotions had slept and renewed themselves while my mind had raced endlessly on. Whether anticipation, anxiety, determination, hope, or inspiration were predominant depended upon what had happened with Walter and Inca during our session the day before. I could dwell for hours on past difficulties, ruminate about things that I had recently been introduced to and was struggling to learn, and conjecture about what was yet to come. Daily, I promised myself to change old habits, not repeat the same old mistakes, and surprise Walter with the progress I'd made overnight.

When I drove to the stable, I would turn on the car radio and dial past the world news, seeking music that might buoy me up, melodies and themes that would suggest to me that I needn't be anxious, that the hours ahead were all going to be good. I would ride well.

What was it about Walter's lessons that was so special, why had they become so profoundly important to me? In asking myself this question, I realized that the answer lay in the man himself, in his years of experience and the intuitive way in which he combined what he knew, what he saw and what he wanted to have happen. His freshness and spontaneity were always astonishing me—no two lessons that I could remember had ever been the same. They varied in length, in approach, in intensity or lack of it and in the program itself. I'd never known a teacher to make so much use of the horse's mood, his attitudes, and the bursts of energy that would suddenly emerge, thus keeping the work fresh and alive. Walter made each lesson such a fully meaningful experience that I never left the ring as the same rider who had entered.

Strange as it may seem, the beginning moments of these lessons were not easy for me. Even though I took enough time getting ready, the preliminary moments aboard Inca were never as simple for me as they seemed to be for other riders. My mind seemed to race while my body was slow to respond and function—too slow for the reactions that I knew I needed for the job ahead. Walter, who on most days would be standing by waiting, would periodically say, "Priscilla, atmen!" (Priscilla, breathe). This might be followed a bit later by, "Bitte, lächeln" (please, smile). The first time or two he asked for a smile, I thought that I had misheard: was my trainer after the "Pepsodent" look or one of those Hollywood smiles seen in advertisements? Finally, I realized that all Walter was asking was that I relax the muscles in my face. Without knowing it, I must have been wearing a grimace. When I tried to explain, Walter stopped me with, "You can't expect to ride well when you set your jaws and clench your teeth."

Little did I know that I was to spend an entire year "working" on being relaxed and that proper relaxation didn't stop with my face. Walter insisted that there should be no tension anywhere. He asked me to concentrate on each of the areas of my body: head, neck, shoulders, back, seat, arms, legs, wrists, and ankles so that I would take in both the specific tensions that he picked up as well as the totality of the concept. Anxiety over my customary awkward, stiff, beginning moments probably served to prolong them, but I was seldom able to find a satisfactory way out of the dilemma. Looking back, I think it would have been more productive had I simply climbed on my horse and casually said to myself, "Let's go for a ride."

I had another habit that attested to the road blocks I laid in my own way—one that Walter politely took in stride until he could no longer bear it. Procrastination. In my effort to put off the inevitable, I would pull off the track just after I'd started and remove layers of clothing, rearrange my hair, tighten Inca's girth, roll up my sleeves, take a look around, and do anything else that I could drum up. Sooner than I wished, I'd be given the command to "Aufnehmen deinen zügeln," (take up your reins) and I'd notice how uneven my reins were and wonder why during the time that I had been trotting around this hadn't come to my attention. "You're the sort of rider who needs a push to get started," Walter once told me. "Keep in mind that a trained horse like Inca doesn't need to waste his energy mindlessly going around and around. Get down to your work."

Centering his attention on me, Walter would give me a crisp "wake-up" call with instructions to "Trab sitzen," (trot sitting). Minutes later, I'd hear, "Energie!" (energy) called out in no uncertain terms, followed by the inevitable command to *"SITzen!"* (sit). Walter could be impatient at the onset and he had a right to be. I should have been able to start up both my engine and Inca's without depending on him. As for the corrections of my seat, they continued regularly for at least six months until my body finally discovered how to sit "deep." Gradually, I heard "SITzen!" called out less.

There was reason enough for Walter to fixate on "sitzen." In dressage, the rider's seat is the central office of her ability to communicate. It is more influential even than the reins, the rider's legs, her spurs or a stick. There are varying (even opposing) schools of thought on how the rider affects the horse by the way he sits. Walter's way was to get his riders to "sit *in*" to the horse, and make themselves so "at one" with the stride of the horse that effective and subtle control of the movement flowed naturally. The ability to sit correctly in the saddle is elusive. To those who by nature are able to sit deeply, quietly, immovably, and effectively the way Walter could, sitting seems totally normal, thus hard to explain.

Aware of the seat's importance, I was determined to perfect Walter's "German seat." When I was aboard Inca, I continuously pondered the plain act of sitting. When I finished riding, I practiced "sitting" on a chair. Whenever possible, I studied horses and riders in action in the ring, and at night lying in bed with closed eyes, I envisioned them again; only in these visions, I included myself, sitting postage stamp perfect. Every now and then, I'd give myself a little gift and imagine Walter looking on and saying, "Ist gut," (it's good).

In real life, he had a way of uttering the word "sitzen" that I'll never forget. The first syllable was high, the second syllable three notes lower. "SIT zen." It welled up from his depths, perhaps even from his soul, expressing a kind of teacher's despair, even a sadness that I, his rider, did not simply sit on the horse in the manner he had shown me. He knew, of course, that I had to work on solving the problem myself, and that he could only give me reminders and little bits of help like touching my lower back, my knee, my thigh, or the length of my leg. Then, for a few moments, the knowledge in his hands would adjust my sitting and make me "feel" my position. By putting his fingers on exact spots, Walter was showing me exactly what areas of my body were "holding" or locked into unconscious tension when I rode. Small wonder, I thought, as I became aware of these tensions, that I couldn't "hinsitzen," truly "sit *in*."

In all of his lessons, Walter was not only focusing on me, he was working with Inca as well. In each lesson, he adhered to a certain structure, certain basic steps of dressage training that were like commandments to him. "Training is an act of building," he would say, "one step must be completed before the next step is taken." Although he was not a fierce man, he stuck to his process fiercely. Walter always made it clear that "There are no short cuts in the correct training for dressage. A horse is an athlete and must be treated that way in mind and body."

At each lesson, by the time I had ridden around the ring a time or two, Walter expected me to know how Inca was feeling. What was the horse's mood? Was he full of energy? Ready to work? These were some of the questions Walter might ask me. The answers that I gave him would be reflected in the rate of progression and the level of difficulty of our work.

The first step was the warm-up—a time to gymnasticize the horse, grow limber myself, and find ways to get in sync with my partner. For perhaps twenty minutes we would concentrate on the simplest exercises and movements in the dressage repertory; suppling, elasticizing, balancing ourselves alternately in walk, trot, and canter. Walter never allowed me to stay in one mode for too long. He believed in variation and change. "Don't get stuck," he'd say in German, "be creative. Think ahead. Try something new."

At a certain moment, Walter would decide that the warm-up was over and the time had come to continue to the heart of the lesson. There was no real defining boundary line between these stages, except that the work would become progressively more difficult and more demanding, and the exercises would follow one another more swiftly. Walter's corrections were often continuous, his instructions coming out in a rider's Morse Code, short, quick, and as the months passed more familiar, the complexity of their meaning becoming more understandable.

His directions to me were about my hips, my hands, the position of my foot, the length of my leg, where I was sitting, in what direction I was looking, how I was thrusting out my chin—the corrections were endless. For Inca, too, the list was long: adjustments in the carriage of the neck, the feel of his back, the engagement of the quarters, the straightness of the body, the fullness and forwardness of every single stride. I'd wonder how Walter could see so much and have so many things to say. It was as though Inca and I were separate elements of a puzzle that he was able to put together piece by piece.

Through this process of correcting and refining, Inca and I would come "into collection." Inca's ears gave me the first hint we were there. They'd be pressing eagerly forward like antennae, giving me the message that a world of excitement lay straight ahead of us. I'd feel tension and then the thrust of power in motion underneath me.

When Inca began his training with Walter, the hardest part of the German experience for him was coming into the height of collection with the more rounded, "gathered together" frame that is demanded in Europe. This was because of his long Thoroughbred legs and back—Inca was like an especially tall man practicing ballet. A large part of Walter's entire year of training would be spent in helping Inca to come into collection more quickly and to stay within this frame throughout his work.

"Make a spiral," I might be told as Walter walked to the center of the ring. There, he would plant himself like a tree and never miss a single one of Inca's steps. "Aufpassen" (watch out) he'd sing out. Here was a teacher who always caught me when I lost concentration and let incorrect things happen—even if only a few steps of unevenness. He gave me no slack. His commands would be coming at me as fast as I could translate them. "Keep the rhythm. Keep the bend. Now circle Inca in." I would circle inward until I was nervous about running him over. "Don't worry," he'd say, "I'll watch out for myself. *You* think about *yourself* and *your horse.*" During this moment he might be doing a bit of a light-footed jig, turning round and round on the spot, tapping Inca ever so lightly on the rump with his stick in order to intensify the way each hind leg came under and to increase crisp action in both hind legs.

Ever the perfectionist, after a minute or so I might be corrected with, "Now once again: Inca's left leg is lazy today—repeat the exercise." Then I would spiral out to the rim of the circle, and repeat the exercise. When a slight smile appeared on his face, I'd know he was pleased with my riding as well as with the way Inca was moving.

I had learned that this teacher was not one to talk theory during lesson time. For him, the flow of work was too important to interrupt. However, over a cup of tea after an early session together, he had explained that the spiral when ridden correctly, could put to work almost a dozen elements vital to dressage, leaving the horse and rider tuned and prepared for whatever the next moves might be.

How right Walter was. The quality of Inca's way of moving changed dramatically. His strides were rounder. There was a distinct "jump" to each step. If I had been watching I would have seen that in actual fact, Inca and I were spending more time in the air, as if we were marionettes being lifted by invisible strings off the ground. The first time I experienced this new sensation, I wrote in my journal, "We hadn't been in the ring more than a half an hour this morning, when Walter and Inca gave me an amazing gift—we became airborne and remained this way for another twenty minutes. When I got off the horse, I spent the remainder of the day dancing, convinced that this was a feeling that surely everyone in the world knew. Nothing like working with a Master!"

Always sensitive to the benefit of positive reinforcement, Walter would insist that I give my horse a "treat" whenever Inca and I took a step forward in our training: Back at home, a treat would have been recess or a tidbit of food, but at Tasdorf, I discovered that a treat such as "easy work" could be given within the framework of the lesson and without interrupting it. For most horses, a treat would be something simple, like a diagonal of forward trot or canter in order to feel freshened. But for Inca a treat meant doing two-tempi flying changes, where he changed leads with sheer delight every second stride. "Treats" like this were meant to be incorporated into the directional flow of the lesson and did not mean that we were permitted to lose attention. Mistakes were not allowed. We were instantly chastised if Inca's leading leg did not define the change every second stride. But if we kept focused, he seldom made an error.

Like a symphony, Walter's lessons built toward a climax. The climax varied with each day and could come in the form of a few steps performed with brilliant exactness or some moments of complete harmony between horse and rider. An observer watching such moments would see a horse who was totally giving himself, of his own free will, to the work in progress.

I would know that we were approaching the lesson's culmination when I would hear Walter slip into Morse Code. After riding, I drew up lists of these comments. They were almost a jargon, and I worked long hours translating them, determined that when his words next came at me machine gun style, I would understand and respond appropriately. There never was much time to think, only to act, with a teacher who seemed to be able to see both sides of the horse at one time and who held such high standards always in his mind's eye.

Like most students, Inca would attempt to evade difficult issues whenever he could, and it was necessary that I handle him correctly in order to progress through our work. At such moments, Walter would remind me, "*show* Inca he can do what we want him to do, don't force him." This particular quality of nonimposition was one of Walter's specialties. It was the reason why around the ring at Stall Tasdorf, I never saw a horse with glazed-over eyes, an ugly expression and laid-back ears. Walter looked for willingness to go along with the discipline, and tried to keep freshness in the training. This was not easy, and I thought it was very much to his credit that with few exceptions all of the horses in his barn looked happy.

There were times that I did not fare as well. I found it difficult not to reflect outwardly my inner pressures. I was plagued with a sense of being "put upon" by my own aspirations, by the way I assessed how I was coming along, and most of all by the sheer dailiness of the task. The highs and lows of learning were, in a subtle way, exhausting. My physical self struggled far less than my mental self. My mind's ear would ring with a chain of commands long after a lesson. I might be engaged in quite a different activity and an interior voice would call out, "Catch the instant, in the next stride get it right. *You* have to do it." Exasperation often assailed me, and for a period my riding would go straight down hill.

When this happened, Walter tried to ignore my unproductive frame of mind, but I could see that he was taken aback, because he would say very little and my lesson would seem less a symphony than a dirge. The inspiration that usually existed for the three of us would have vanished.

Left on my own to come to terms with myself, I turned to Kerstin. "Why is it that when problems arise, one is constantly told that it's the fault of the rider and never the horse? Can't a horse ever be wrong?" I asked. Kerstin was sympathetic. As a former jumping and dressage competitor, she knew the feeling. However, she didn't take my side. "Of course a horse can have his problems," she said, "but more often his problems are caused by the rider." The tone of her voice was so decisive that I ended the discussion there.

Later that morning, Walter himself substantiated her words of wisdom. He was having a problem with a horse and a junior rider, and was working out a difficult solution. Here for me to witness was just the type of situation I had inquired about, though perhaps not as dire, because even Tasdorf's young clients rode surprisingly well. The correction Walter was looking for was taking a long time in coming. He had been working intensely with the student and getting nowhere. Watching her, I could see from the look on her face that she had reached the limits of her patience and in her frustration had grown furious with her horse. At that point, in a dramatic gesture that was not typical of Walter, he threw up his hands and announced to everyone in the ring, "So ist das reiten!" (that's the way riding is). What he meant with this comment was that he, Walter Christensen, was not responsible for how enormously difficult work in dressage could sometimes be, exacting what could sometimes feel like the last drop of blood. What we all needed, Walter was implying, was patience.

I believed in Walter and trusted him implicitly, but there were times when, like Inca, I wanted to resist. My independent nature reared up its head and railed against being told what to do every single day. I longed for some space, some time alone, the chance to experiment on my own for a bit. I wondered if left to myself I could work things out faster and maybe . . . just maybe . . . give my teacher a surprise or two. Quite unexpectedly, the opportunity that I had been dreaming about occurred . . . or so it seemed.

Just as Walter and I were about to begin a lesson, Kerstin opened the casino door and called out "telephone!" Walter excused himself and went to the phone extension that was situated just inside the ring. After a short conversation, he announced that he had to leave and hurried off in the direction of his office with a look on his face that spoke of "serious business." I took it for granted that he would be gone for awhile and said to myself happily, "While the Master's away, this mouse will play," except of course I had no intentions of playing. Pushing Walter right out of my head, I went to work. My goal was to discover the balance and coordination I would need to refine the changes of directions in what is referred to as the "zig zag." This is a high-level lateral movement that is ridden from the centerline and calls for a required number of steps (either three or four) in the half-pass. It begins by tracking left, then goes right, and makes four counter changes before the end of the line. This movement is so lovely to watch that it belies the difficulty of riding it absolutely right.

At the time Walter introduced me to this exercise, we discussed the many necessary details it involved, such as balance, position, precision, and forward thinking. The morning I first began to practice it, he insisted on counting Inca's strides out loud in order to help me. I found his counting confusing rather than helpful and asked to count quietly to myself. Even then, Inca and I continued to take too many steps before changing direction, and when we did the change, we both had problems. Walter lost no time in informing me that I should try to just listen to what he had to say and then follow his instructions exactly. Under the growing tension of so much to do at once, all I could think about was how much I wanted to be left on my own. Then I'd be able to take the "zigzag" apart slowly, quietly, and peacefully and master it in my own way. So . . . after Walter was called away and his sharp-eyed bereiter had left the ring to change horses, I saw that at last—for the first time since my arrival at Stall Tasdorf—I was alone in the ring, entirely alone. There was no one around to say, "Priscilla, nein!"

"Come on, Old Trooper," I said to Inca, "here's our chance." For once, I went into the warm-up without thinking about how I was beginning the ride. In my head I was already "zigging" and "zagging," thinking about how to take each stride. A checklist of how I was sitting informed me that my position felt correct and no old habits seemed to be getting in the way. For a brief second I allowed myself the thought that Walter could have been wrong about me. Wasn't I sitting as tall as a Roman candle, weight evenly distributed, elbows at my side, legs long? Sure I was! As if I alone was about to execute this high-level movement, I turned down centerline and began. . . .

From the darkness of the entryway came a roar, "Pr-i-s-c-i-l-l-a! It was Walter stringing my name out in tones three times longer than necessary. "Was machst du?" (What are you doing?). The question really was not a question. The pain in his voice suggested

I'd let him down completely. "Have you learned anything since you've been here? So little preparation for your horse and then all of a sudden you ask him for the hardest things. Where are those building blocks we've been talking about?"

I had pulled up when Walter had started talking and found that I was unable to look at the man, so I looked at the ground.

"Sag mir," (explain to me) he went on, "was war in dein kopf?" (what were you thinking about?).

"Myself."

"Ich hab's gedacht" (I thought so).

Walter didn't give me a lesson that day, nor the next. He rode Inca himself and I sat on the bench and watched him train my horse in the areas he felt my fellow needed work. He performed the "zigzag" for me, taking it apart verbally first in slow motion then up to speed. On the third day, I was allowed back up in the saddle again—but no lesson. I suspected that Walter's assistant had been instructed to keep his eyes on me because I heard him twice say, "Gut geritten, Priscilla," (well ridden). During my usual lesson hour, instead of spending time with me, Walter schooled a member of the German Three-Day Event Team who had stopped by. Then, on the fourth day, lessons with Walter resumed.

That evening, I was invited for supper at the Christensen's home. During a moment of quiet, Walter touched me deeply. "Priscilla," he said very slowly so that I would be able to fully take in every word. Referring to my morning's ride, (in German, of course) "you know, I really did understand you. Once upon a time, I felt the same way myself." Then he told me how when he was a young apprentice, he had stolen into the stable late at night and taken out a horse he had been assigned to ride. He had wanted to be on his own and ride *his way* just as I had. It hadn't worked out very well, so he'd never done it again. Later, he discovered that his boss had been there all the time and knew exactly what he was up to.

Following my few moments of rebellion, I settled back into the discipline of my daily training with greater receptivity, more tolerance, and the hope that I could be more patient with myself. I was helped by the fact that Walter's teaching was progressively beginning to define itself within my being. My body was responding to the daily instruction as if by intuition, making the right demands of Inca as if by habit. My equine partner's neck, chest, and rump were taking on the look I'd come to associate with European Grand Prix dressage horses. Muscles were appearing in new places, so that he not only looked strong, he felt stronger. However, these physical changes were only a part of what was happening. We were being trained, honed, and inspired mentally as well.

Walter introduced more details and refinements into our daily sessions with each week. I was made to think about every dressage movement freshly, consider how best to prepare each one, execute it, and then bring it to a close. Not a single one of Inca's steps was to be ignored or left to chance. "Ride every stride," seemed to be the German dressage rider's motto. The meticulousness of Walter's work and the precision of his thinking reminded me of childhood hours spent at the piano muddling through fingering, trills, arpeggios, and two-handed scales. I'd learned a lot about the exact detail work at the keys, so in a sense I was primed and ready for Walter.

Never one to waste time, he put our detail work right to the test by adding one movement to the next and then the next. Within a bigger framework, we had to focus differently—see the whole picture, so to speak. This was when I had to put all the little bits of pieces we had practiced to the back of my mind and stay truly conscious of the way that Inca was moving. One of the most difficult things about dressage is determining where to focus attention first, since all the details seem to need perfect performance at the same time.

I learned that the way to handle this challenge was to think about my horse and to think ahead. For example, doing the half-pass to the right was harder for him than going to the left; transitions within the gaits as well as from gait to gait upward went smoothly; transitions downward were rough. Walter taught me that by keeping realities like this in mind, I would be ready to offer my horse support and encouragement. This meant that I should constantly be checking to make sure that he was listening, prepared to obey a new command, offering a steady rhythm, and keeping up a confirmed and even stride. I nicknamed these vital instances of communication, "Hello theres!"

It was because Walter called upon me to make instant use of the feedback from these "Hello theres" that I began to think not only in physical terms but in creative terms about riding. I made a point of anticipating beginnings and endings, sensing the moment that called for "freshening," and discerning the instant there was a need for restraint. Riding was turning into an art. Words like interpretation and presentation tumbled into my consciousness, while the labor, "the work" of dressage became less. Inca responded to the new approach with a buoyancy and an eager attention that he had never given me before. Walter noticed the change and said, "Inca's enjoying his work more now. That's what we want."

Encouraged by positive feelings resulting from Inca's new attitude, I acted on an impulse and prayed I was following along the pathway to progress. It was not an impulse to which I had actually given much thought. If anything, I had been pushing myself to do just the opposite—to be open, receptive, almost dependent, in effect be the best student I knew how to be. Thus the impulse I followed up took me as well as Walter by surprise. It was one of those occurrences that simply seems to happen of its own without prior planning or thought, which must have meant that the moment was opportune.

The weather was damp and dreary, the sort of day that tended to make you think nothing of any value could possibly come about, even though it was lesson time. We were past the warm-up, past a review of the preceding week and about to devote our energies to some fine-tuning of lateral work in the trot. Suddenly, the thought flashed through my mind that I needed some added suppling. Whereupon, I asked Inca for several repetitions of renvers left (steps in which the haunches remain on the track and the shoulders are brought slightly to the inside). Then I reversed it and asked for renvers right. Inca gave me such a perfect response that I almost believed he had read my firm, clear thoughts. I was thrilled. With an expression of profound pleasure, Walter said, "Now, you are becoming your own teacher."

Me? A teacher? Could this be true? These were precious words coming from someone whose own teaching I so respected. My heart leapt into the sky. Here was the breakthrough that I had come to think might never happen, the confirmation I never dreamt would come. "You are becoming your own teacher." The words repeated themselves, making a short, golden song and taking me back to my early student years. Hadn't I always turned to my special teachers seeking the inspiration that I needed? At last, and at this very moment, I was being told that I had climbed one step higher. What I had turned to in others was within me. Although I still needed help, I could begin to give back bits of what I had been given.

As is the way with dressage, before I could enjoy my mountaintop for too long, I fell off my peak, head first. I was faced with a challenge of a different sort than I had had so far while at Tasdorf, but one that was as inevitable a part of the riding scene as the ring itself—spectators. Lots and lots of them.

Beyond the spectators that sat in the casino at Stall Tasdorf and the few that wandered very occasionally into the ring, I was not ready for a group of people numerous enough to be called an audience. The incident began when we were deep into the essence of our lesson. Walter was working Inca and me in the transition phase of piaffe and passage (the highest form of collected, elevated trot done in place and then moving forward). The latter was mainly the problem. The three of us—Walter, Inca and I—were in our own world of intensely concentrated attention, when my focus was interrupted by an unusual noise. I stole a look to see what might be causing it. Standing just inside the entry door to the arena were at least fifty people who were silently watching us. I ceased work within the instant.

"Weiter gehen!" (go on) Walter ordered.

"Who are all those people?" I asked.

"Oh, it's only a group of riding teachers from Denmark, an association of some sort." Walter answered casually, his concentration still on Inca. "Forget them. Piaffe!"

"You didn't say they were coming," I persisted, "I wouldn't have ridden at this hour."

"That's exactly why I didn't say anything about them," he answered, "besides, I wasn't sure when they'd appear." His eyes were dark and serious. I knew he was testing me. If this had been the moment for tea and conversation, he would have lectured me firmly, insisted that I should not allow the presence of any one or anything to destroy my focus when I was on a horse. "Bist du bereit?" (Are you ready to go on?) was all he asked.

For Walter's sake, I wanted to, but knowing myself, I could not. I had not yet become comfortable enough in this European environment to wish to be in the center of the stage—perhaps later I might be able to remedy these deficiencies. For now, I was too busy translating fifty riding teachers into a sea of one hundred professional eyes—all experienced, all critical, all knowing how to ride perfectly. The weight of these conjectures was overwhelming. I wanted to leave the ring with the speed of a meteor.

I prayed that this once—perhaps, just this once—he'd relate to me as he did to himself instead of answering to the "shoulds" of his profession. Here was a human being who also had problems facing the public, most certainly when unprepared and taken by surprise. The identity he was comfortable with was as a teacher of people and a trainer of horses, not a performer or a competitor.

In some way, what I had said or the look on my face must have reached that personal side of Walter, because he held up his hand as if he were standing in a pulpit about to deliver a blessing, and in his kindest but most definite tone, ordered me to take the reins, sit deeply and quietly in my saddle, and he himself would take care of the rest. Whereupon he turned to Inca, spoke his name, attained the horse's fullest attention and commanded him to piaffe. He touched my fellow high on the rump with his stick as much as to say, "begin the piaffe back here," and then continued to tap out the steady beat of the piaffe itself. Immediately, Inca lowered his haunches and began flexing his hock muscles. I was amazed and thought, "good heavens, Inca is going to piaffe on his own without any guidance from me at all." Sure enough, I could feel his back begin to roll and his hooves leave the ground, and by degrees he lifted his legs higher and higher. I found Inca's response hard to believe—he was behaving as though he and Walter had been practicing this sort of thing every single day.

Then I heard Walter command, "Jetzt, Inca Passage!" (Now, Inca passage!). Out of the piaffe we moved effortlessly forward right into the passage, with huge, round, even steps. I stole a look at Walter and saw that he was no longer tapping Inca's haunches but was right there close beside us, halfway between a walk and a run, making passage steps himself.

The crowd came out of its silence, and like a church organ breathed with the greatest respect a word that I took to mean "b-e-a-u-t-i-f-u l," perhaps even "awesome."

While the instructors were shaking their heads with the most profound approval, Walter issued his final command "Genug," (enough) and then right away praised the horse, "Schone, Inca, schone" (well done) as if the intimate conversation they had been having had come to an end. I received a pat on the boot for having sat still. Off Walter went to take the instructors on the tour of the stables he had promised them. But before they had all left the arena, I overheard one of the Danes say to Walter, "I had no idea that the American horse would be able to passage like that."

"He's a good horse. He can do everything." Walter said to the man, and turned to me with a look that said, "We did it!"

How right he was! Except it wasn't "we" it was he. I cannot remember when I was ever more grateful to both my horse and to my teacher. They had managed to fulfill expectations beyond bounds and taken care of me into the bargain. Now my new goal had become to participate in the exercise, to become the effective rider who could initiate piaffe and passage regardless of outside distractions. What the three of us had "pulled off" was in fact a kind of circus act which is not at all real dressage, and which could never happen in competition. That Inca had acquitted himself so well was without a doubt a tribute to Walter—teacher to us both.

On a day when the stable was quiet, the Danes having gone off to tour Germany, their visit long forgotten, I witnessed another side of Walter that demonstrated his patience, his intuition, and his wealth of experience in dealing with animals. This time, Walter had decided he would himself ride a young horse that had been sent in for training instead of handing it over to an apprentice.

It was the hour for Stall Tasdorf's cook to announce lunch. The

Inca was everybody's friend. Sue Blinks in the foreground, Cathy Hooper in the background, and my grandson Robby Miller sporting new cowboy boots and thrilled with his ride.

Walter might be thinking, time for lunch yet? Sue Blinks, who eventually trained under Walter in Germany and then returned to teach at The Ark, and her dog Jessie, await the master's verdict. Photo: Carole MacDonald

Final moments with Inca in the warm-up before competition.

Volker Brommann wins the contest for happy smiles. Can there be a better moment than being pleased with your horse after a good ride—especially when you have just finished an important test in competition? Photo: Carole MacDonald

Note the focus and total concentration on Sue Blinks' face as she rides. It's so wonderful to see that even though she is riding for all she is worth, there is no tension or stiffness in her body.

On this occasion, Walter and Inca demonstrated some of the highest-level movements required at Grand Prix. They really brought the house down! Many of the
spectators had never seen anything like it. When they were finished performing,
dozens of people understood for the first time why some of us were making such a
serious commitment to learn what we could of this combination of art and sport.
Photo courtesy of Mrs. Edward Emerson, Jr.

Here Louise is aboard Inferno
(the horse she took to her first
Olympics) doing an exhibition
ride at the Benefit
Performance for the New
England Dressage Association
at the former United States
Combined Training
Association headquarters in
Hamilton, Massachusetts.
Looking on (left to right): Jack
Burton, Denny Emerson,
Renate Lansburgh, Walter,
and the announcer for the
NEDA exhibition. Each one
of these professional horsemen
gave a commentary to a large
and enthusiastic audience who had assembled to watch a program devoted to dres-
sage. Photo courtesy of Mrs. Edward Emerson, Jr.

Louise with two of her top horses. Dante on the left (successor to Inferno), and the stallion, Chirac, on the right. Two impressive mounts. Chirac was almost too hard to handle before he was sent to Louise—notice how knowingly she is in charge.

Lars Andersson, formerly on the Swedish dressage team, and Louise's life partner, takes a rare moment in the spotlight along with Louise and Walk On Top, her thirteen-year-old Hanoverian. Lars is her "eyes on the ground" both at home and before she enters the competitive arena. Louise speaks out openly about her need to have experienced eyes and good support. Lars fits this bill generously.

Denny Emerson in the middle of a lesson with Walter. Note his deep concentration. At this moment, he is totally unaware of the audience he always attracted at his lesson time. People admired him for many reasons (among them that he was an international three-day eventer), however, he came to his lesson without any ego. He brought his current international three-day horse and tried with every bone in his body to take in what Walter was teaching him. It was so clear to everyone how much Denny respected Walter and his profound knowledge of dressage. Photo: Carole MacDonald

Louise and Walk On Top have just taken top placing in the final competition of the 1998 Volvo World Cup in Gothenberg, Sweden. The audience is going wild with excitement as she makes her victory round to music and clapping. In the past fifteen years, no Swede has had such an important international dressage win. Here is a horse who knows he has won! Notice that Louise is holding the reins in one hand while she asks for the passage—no mean feat. Photo: Jan Gyllensten

A beautiful moment. Sue Blinks is wearing a smile that must have begun in her toes. For her, there is nothing more wonderful than when she and her horse are doing well together. Photo: Phelpsphoto.com

stable crew had finished their morning's labors and were lined up, hungry and anxious to eat. I was interested that Walter was absent, remaining behind all by himself out in the ring.

"We will start without him," Kerstin decided. "I know my husband well enough! He won't get off until that young horse he is sitting on decides to listen to his rider."

"How long have they been out there?" I inquired.

"Too long," was her answer, "already almost an hour." She explained that the horse was new to the place and that Walter had probably decided it was too important a moment to stop his work with the youngster. It could very well be a decisive time in his training, she informed me.

That bay horse is being made to stay after school, I thought. A good many trainers I had known would have become irritated by this extra effort. Some planned their days by the clock. This, however, was not Walter's way. His attitude was that other matters could wait, you can't work with animals and look at your watch. Looking through the casino window, I saw that he was wearing the concentrated look of a teacher so focused on his pupil that nothing else mattered. Typical of this man, he was making no unusual use of the whip or the spurs, he was just sitting quietly, but he was, as always, cool and insistent. His four-legged student (who had not as yet *agreed* to be Walter's partner, or for that matter anybody else's) was as wet as if he had been for a swim. The sweat, along with a bug-eyed expression that fairly shouted the sentiment "damned if I will!" gave evidence of what Walter was up against. I could see that this new boarder might be hard work, but on second thought, I knew I need not feel sorry for Walter. He'd said himself that above all other kinds of work, this was the kind he liked the most.

A short half an hour later, when the stable "family" emerged from the dining room, Walter and his pupil were no longer in the ring.

While the others headed off in different directions, rushing to get in a long midday nap, I went straight to the stable's unsaddling area to look for Walter and the young horse, curious to find out what had happened. At lunch, I had listened to the lehrlingers discuss the horse. They spoke of how fearful the animal was, how he rejected those who cared for, fed, and rode him. He kept everyone at bay.

I found Walter giving the horse a final brush. The two looked as if they'd been having a quiet conversation. "The change happened quickly when he finally realized there was nothing to worry about," Walter commented when he saw me. "All of a sudden 'the penny dropped' and he was willing to do everything I asked of him. Clever fellow." He went on to explain that finally they both had to reach an understanding of one another. "But," Walter added, "a long day once in awhile doesn't really matter. It makes for shorter days later on, especially when things work out the way they did today."

All the while we were talking, the horse was gazing at Walter intently without a single iota of fear or animosity. Although he was on the cross-ties, he kept trying to turn his head in Walter's direction, as if he wished to make small advances. In place of the solid hunk of somewhat defiant horse I'd spied out in the ring, he now appeared to be somewhat vulnerable, young, and innocent. His eyes were livelier and brighter than before, and the look of his total body stance was soft and reachable—even grateful—as if he'd been lost and now he had found a place he could be. He had made a friend, found someone he could trust. And that very same someone had been experienced enough to invite him to move in ways that turned the training itself into an open door.

As I watched the pair, I looked at Walter and thought, this is a very special man, a knowledgeable horseman and a unique teacher. Here is a human being who cares so deeply about his profession that there is no beginning or end to where he picks it up or sets it down. It *is* him. This is why both man and beast are so willing to work for him—are in fact inspired. This is why, in his hands, during those daily lessons, I am inspired and can outride myself. We can remove limits. I am able to make progress and move slowly onward. With Walter's years of experience and innate understanding always there for me to count on, we can truly work together. Although I am not yet allowing myself to think about training after I leave Tasdorf, in my heart he is teaching me for as long as I am able to climb up on the back of my horse.

≈ 14

Master Student

When Walter had come to my farm in 1979 to teach his first American dressage clinic, he brought Louise Nathhorst with him as his assistant. She turned out to be not only one of the most endearing guests who would ever visit, but an unusually knowledgeable horse person and Walter's more than capable interpreter and translator. On meeting Louise, I had been immediately struck by the quality of her presence—she had the serene, stylish femininity of an Audrey Hepburn. Though small in stature as a woman, as an equestrian she had big talent—the kind of shiny, confident ability that rivets the eye of every beholder. I was not surprised to learn that she was Walter's most gifted student.

During that year and for the next fifteen years, I too became a student of Walter Christensen and over time Walter and Louise would come to represent for me just how much a brilliant teacher and an equally brilliant student can achieve working together. It was a realization and inspiration that began with meeting the two of them, continued throughout my year at Tasdorf and is still with me today. My relationship with Louise and her influence on my riding was to extend over many years.

I was curious about Louise from the first moment I met her, but when I asked Walter about her, he was characteristically closed-mouthed. He told me that she had been his student for many years and that she had talent, a statement that I was to discover he made very seldom. He didn't like to talk about her very much, any more than he liked talking about his wife, or the horse he loved most. One didn't talk about treasures—one protected them.

On the other hand, Kerstin loved to talk about Louise: she was very proud of her compatriot, and was quick to brag that Louise was considered to be one of the most accomplished young riders in all of Sweden. "Some day," Kerstin would say with a pride that inflated her country to the size of the whole continent of Europe, "she may ride in the Olympics for Sweden."

Kerstin often referred to Louise as "Little Louise." The tone of her voice informed you she was talking about someone who was not only small physically but who was special to her. "Little Louise," Kerstin told me, had been coming to Germany for her school vacations since she was old enough to be the driver of a horse trailer. Her father was a doctor, her mother a collector of contemporary art, and her older sister had interests that were quite different from those of Louise. No one in the entire family had ever had anything to do with horses. From childhood on, however, Louise had pursued her passion for riding quite independently, quite determinedly, on her own.

This independence was apparent whenever she entered the practice ring. She carried an air of aloneness straight into the group, dispensing with the smiling, nodding, and socializing that were the norm for the rest of us. I used to think that when Louise was with her horse, her involvement with the animal was so total that people were no longer very real to her. She meant no offense. Our identities simply faded away in her mind, to return some time later.

Most of the apprentices were outspoken in their admiration of Louise. They watched her closely and would have given anything to be like her, but a few who were jealous of her made it quite clear that she was no role model for them. One of them even brought this sense of rivalry into the ring, riding up to her and throwing out the challenge, "Some day, Louise, I'll meet you in competition. Wait and see. I will be the winner." Thus Louise had to survive her existence at Stall Tasdorf in her own special way. Having talent didn't always make life easy.

Walter had said Louise was "talented." Watching her ride, I learned the meaning behind his words. Talent was more elusive than I had expected. Some aspects of it were like coming upon lovely, shining bits of mica in the sand, others took more time to appreciate and became apparent as I evolved in my own process of learning. Louise's talent was great enough that in the end I ceased analyzing her and found myself swept away by her art. Being at the stable when Louise was training was like being in an artist's studio when the artist was hard at work.

She began her rides just as if she and her horse were two best friends heading for a leisurely walk. They might have been going to the beach or a pine forest or some place equally delightful. It was easy to imagine Louise and her horse as two people, walking along companionably, taking the same length step, their right legs going forward simultaneously, their arms occasionally touching, absorbed in quiet, intimate talk. The pair were striking in their harmony, which went beyond synchronized motion: it was more that each could sense the essence of the other's thoughts.

Sitting there on her horse, body relaxed, saying "oh-o-o-o-o-o-o" at the walk, telling him by her wordless toning that he was a good fellow and that he need not be anxious, Louise confirmed her total presence to the animal. She was letting him know that not only was she entirely in charge of the moment, but that he was in safe hands. She would take care of everything: horses can feel nervous in the ring, and Louise understood that. Terrifying things can happen. Horses in for training often have a past that is as hard for them to forget as their old habits. Memories can scare them; rehabilitation takes time. In most cases horses are incredibly peaceful, generous creatures, it's humans who rile them and drive them senseless. Louise understood all these potentials for trouble. She intuited the atmosphere of the ring and then picked the way she wished to ride with boldness.

The first time I watched Louise train with Walter, I noticed how differently the two related and worked together than anyone else. To begin with, unlike many of Walter's students, I noticed that Louise didn't look to Walter to begin the lesson. She knew what she wanted to accomplish with her horse that day, and when she picked up her reins she started right in. For a time, Walter looked on in silence. I could see that he respected the plan that she must have in mind, her judgment, and the way she was starting her horse.

Watching most people in the warm-up isn't very interesting. There's nothing much to see but a horse and a person getting started; beginnings and stiffnesses being worked out. This was not the case with Louise.

"You have to think about starting your horse each day," Louise once told me, "as if both of you are in an exercise class. Start off easily but consider the different parts of your horse's body just as you would your own. You know where you're stiff; try to feel where he's stiff. Let what your own body tells you be your guide. Feel your horse's body out as you go along. Remember not to rush so you get tight, and above all, give both of yourselves time."

Watching Louise in the ring, I couldn't take my eyes off her. She was so incredibly natural, without an iota of artiness or posturing. She was, as the Germans put it, "echt," (authentic, genuine, and pure). While everyone else had their early morning wish-I was-still-in-in-my-bed look, Louise was blooming like a flower in the first rays of sun. Her whole being was expressing joy!

The expression of joy, I realized suddenly, is a talent too. This was a new way for me to view dressage basics. Getting my ABCs right had always had a hard edge to it—"Do it now!" or "Be exact." Inside me, a long-handled whip was continually snapping, reminding me of the urgency of discipline. In Louise, I saw that joy was a defining part of her equestrian presence: her shoulders back, chest open, eyes-straight-ahead public persona, individual and distinct, were infused with it. In future years when she stepped out into the big time competitions, this special quality would become even stronger and more defined.

It fascinated me to notice how Walter began his training session in a way that was different from Louise. Walter's style was to start off quietly, just walking his horse and making use of the time to smoke a cigarette and watch the training going on around him. Then, finally, he would take more of a hold on the reins and, still in the walk, go to work.

Few riders have the kind of talent that Walter seemed to have in abundance—the ability to bring his horse to a physical and mental peak without ever leaving the walk. His thoughtful, quiet manner revealed his method of training, which seemed to be based on a series of questions and answers between himself and the horse. He asked the horse to walk with energy, to march right along, to be alert, and to answer to the leg pressure and the weight of his seat. He worked every part of his partner's body until the animal's muscles had become supple and elastic. As the minutes went by, the movements that he rode became progressively more complicated—but only as complicated as Walter, judging from the responses, felt the animal was capable of handling.

Louise, on the other hand, chose action—she took only a few walk turns around the arena before proceeding into the trot. Perhaps it was her youth that made her want to get out there and start going. She wasn't much more than a young filly herself. But the difference between Louise and her teacher was due to more than age. Movement suited Louise just as the walk suited Walter. For each, the choice of gait was a demonstration of personal essence. Movement was so natural to Louise that Walter never had to say "Vorwärtz" (forward) to her as he did to his other students. He didn't have to repeat, "Sei fleissig" (be industrious, diligent, hardworking) because there was already enough energy in Louise's riding and she was already deep into her work.

I watched with acute interest to see the difference in how Louise spent her time in the ring compared with how I did. It was the difference between how a master student goes about her craft and how a relative beginner learns. From the beginning of the session, Louise was already concentrating on an altogether higher level of riding, on developing quality, precision, and refinement. My student-like "how to" had long before become an integrated part of her riding. However, she took nothing for granted and was always humbly eager to acknowledge how much more there was to learn.

As the lesson I was observing continued, I saw Walter lean forward, elbows on his knees, eyes intently watching Louise. She was deeply concentrated but she included him in her awareness. Though she clearly knew through a kind of sixth sense where the other horses and riders were in the ring, this knowing did not disturb her focus, which was Walter, her horse, and herself. If one hundred people had appeared in the entrance of the ring, she would have known that too and it would not have disturbed her: she was beyond that. Louise was well aware that Walter expected a lot from her but no more than what she expected from herself. A special line of communication existed between the two, a bit like a private telephone line with an unlisted number. Each seemed to know what the other was thinking.

Louise rode a 15-meter circle directly in front of Walter, then made it increasingly smaller. Immediately, he noticed that she wasn't sitting absolutely straight. Her upper torso was leaning ever so slightly to the side. Walter had the eyes of a surgeon, seeing through vests, sweaters, saddles, muscle, and bone. He looked for balance. At a word from him, Louise made a correction. I had not seen the fault at all.

No need to explain theory to Louise; in most cases Walter's observations and reminders sufficed. She glanced at him often for further direction, knowing that watching him helped her to keep her eyes up. She had a tendency to look groundward. It was a habit that riders who train alone often fall into, and back home in Sweden, Louise spent many months riding on her own.

Walter seemed to have an endless list of requirements for this session: he was choosing Louise's agenda for her, which wasn't always the case. On most days, she simply did her own schoolwork while Walter would nod his head affirmatively, encouragingly and make suggestions once in awhile—his usual method of teaching. Today, however, he couldn't get his words out fast enough.

Louise and I had talked about this rapid-fire delivery of his. During my first six months at Stall Tasdorf, I cringed at such outbursts: when Walter fired off words very fast, I could hardly ride at all. True, I was learning the language, but translation takes time and in the trot and the canter, there isn't any time. On the other hand, on days that he merely nodded his head and made one or two suggestions, I wasn't comfortable either. I felt abandoned.

Louise understood. She said that when she first came to Tasdorf, she became so frightened when the instruction was intense that she could hardly eat or sleep. She became quite ill. It was not that Walter was angry when he taught, like some instructors who really hate teaching, are burnt out, or believe that they deserve better students. We felt that his intensity was rather the natural outcome of a profound yearning for perfection in the world.

When Walter's responses were delivered slowly, Louise waited for his wise words. She believed in him implicitly as a trainer. If someone were to tell her that another instructor might help more, she would have shaken her head "no" without hesitation. Unlike some riders with an eye on the international competitive field, Louise made it crystal clear to everyone that she would never change her loyalties, would never leave Walter. They were a team and would go as far as they could together.

Now, as she completed her circle exercise, she asked for his help, welcoming the sound of his voice. "What do you think?" she asked.

Walter rose from the bench and went to the center of Louise's circle. He urged her to demand from the horse the fullest orb of action possible, making the canter stride both bigger and rounder. Once she got the canter stride for which he was searching, she was to make a flying change and keep that same roundness while performing the exercise in the opposite direction.

Louise was able to respond to Walter's direction so rapidly and instinctively that I couldn't help but wonder if she had intuited what his instruction would be before she actually heard it. Without disturbing her horse in any way or appearing to do anything special, she enabled Inferno to produce the exact canter stride that Walter was looking for.

It was at this moment of fluidity and intuitive communication between Louise and her horse that I fully realized the truth of what I had so often heard—men and women ride differently. Louise's feminine style was epitomized by the sensitive way she was able to elicit a response of such extraordinary willingness and immediacy from her horse.

Part of the difference in riding style between men and women is due to differences in body build and fundamental strength. On the average, women have less bone and muscle strength. Because of this they tend, like Louise, to invite and encourage their horses to perform. Men, on the other hand, usually have greater physical strength, which they can summon with relatively little effort, giving them a propensity to demand and command.

If a male rider has been riding for a period of time and has a deep and confirmed seat and strong muscled legs, he can almost force a big stride out of a horse, or demand a higher-level movement than the horse is trained to know how to do. Both in work and in competition, the male rider and his horse have a distinct "persona," one that is forceful, full of power, dynamic, and exciting. A woman rider, on the other hand, has a lighter, softer manner. She has established her own kind of subtle communication and (if she is like Louise) has a well-developed intuition about the best way to get the job done. In essence, she suggests or *asks* the animal to do what she wants. The effect of an experienced female rider on her horse can be powerful and exciting, filled with a uniquely breathtaking tension, but mainly, it is beautiful to watch. Perhaps that is why in Germany, I frequently heard it said that men should do the training and women the performing.

The seemingly "effortless" beauty of Louise's style played a great role in her later success at competitions like one I saw in Amsterdam. Louise had entered the ring appearing confident, radiant, and in her element, riding straight down the centerline. As the class was for the Kur (musical ride), she had the benefit of strong rhythmic music to buoy her. I watched as Louise and her black stallion, Chirac, swept across the ring in a design that was unusually creative and grabbed the eye. From the first moment on, spectators and judges alike leaned forward expectantly. She embodied variety, surprise, and small themes within her main idea—all within the limits posed by the strict requirements of the Grand Prix Freestyle. Each figure was shown as a piece of great art. The result was flawless, seamless, without force, and filled with a kind of vibrant exhilaration that made me believe that this resilient pair were about to take flight at any moment.

When the judges' scores flashed on the electronic board overhead, Louise and Chirac had won. Before the show, Louise had confided to me that as the only competitor from Sweden she would be riding more for her country than for herself. She smiled as the crowd cheered, the Swedish flag was hoisted for all to see, and everyone stood as the Swedish national anthem was played. I watched Walter standing at the entrance of the arena clapping so hard that his face turned beet red.

That first time at Tasdorf, as I observed Louise and Walter working through their lesson together, I saw not only that Louise's persona and femininity defined her own individual riding style, but also the selflessness of Walter's teaching, how clear and pure he was in recognizing, supporting, and helping her build that style. Of course, the world of dressage training was as full of difficulties and pitfalls as any other, and though master teacher and student strove for perfection, there were times when it eluded them. The tough reality of competitions could present challenges and setbacks not met at home, as I was to discover when Walter and Louise invited me to accompany them to a big international competition in Belgium. I was delighted at this unexpected opportunity and totally unprepared for the testing time that would follow.

For this show, Louise would be riding her Oldenburg gelding Inferno, whom she had bought from Walter when the horse was very young. At that time, no one had known whether he would be anything special. It is hard to tell talent at an early age. In buying an adolescent horse, you take a long look at his conformation and hope the creature will gain a bit here, lose a bit there, knowing that inevitably he will change. You judge his personality as best you can, studying the traits of the sire and the dam.

As it turned out, Inferno started off well and kept going well. Early in the training, Louise had trouble with a lazy streak, but as soon as she and Walter began working the horse at the highest levels, he had a change of personality: he stopped being lazy and stood up to the challenge of being a rising star. Louise's judgment on Inferno was that though he wasn't truly "international" material, he was still very good—in fact, he was just a little short of great. She loved him just as much as if he was indeed "great," and felt that with him she could gain the competition mileage that she needed.

So with Inferno in the horse trailer, the four of us left Tasdorf for Belgium. From the moment we arrived at the competition hall a day before the show, I felt that this experience was going to be different than other shows I had attended. There were no parking attendants standing around giving information, no flashing, spotlit entrance signs, no islands of little trees or potted plants to greet us. A single piece of paper stuck on a post indicated where to go to find van parking.

Perhaps it was sheer exhaustion, but what turned out to be the back entrance seemed to me as dreary as a tomb. It was obvious we were there to work—along with the bakery man, the cold meat and sausage man, the fish man, the cheese man, the purveyors of alcoholic and soft drinks, the salespeople for cars, horse equipment and riding attire, the electrician, the engineering crew, the electronics specialist, the lighting technician—and of course the other competitors. It was a change coming in at the back, but unlike most American competitions, European shows are not volunteer affairs—they are big business and like all the other workers, we were there to support it.

We were not alone in the stabling area; there were other arrivals like ourselves. Some had come earlier, settled their horses and gone away, others were right behind us, leading their animals and bringing in all the equipment that they would need for the show.

We found that the stalls came in sections to be bolted together at the joints. The wood had been used so many times that it was dry as old bones and didn't yield easily. With such old timber it was important to check carefully for splinters, a danger for a horse who might try to loosen a tight mane braid or scratch his chest against the door.

Horse people learn by instinct and experience to be aware of hidden dangers in unfamiliar stabling. They search the inside walls of the portable stalls and the ground for nails left by careless people. Walter's exploration yielded a piece of old wire and a nail. He raised his eyebrows with an angry growl—how impatient he could be with carelessness—and how right he was: the wire and the nail could easily have become lodged in the horse's hoof and lamed him perhaps for life. Then the six years or more that had gone into his training would have been for nothing.

Take a horse traveling and you discover how dependent horses can be—a bit like children. They are easily afraid in new places. Louise understood these feelings well and Inferno was her child. She could skimp on doing things for herself, but she never skimped on caring for her horse. She went right in that twelve by twelve space

260

and walked him around to let him know everything was just right for him. She took off the leg wraps that protected him during travel and removed the white bandage that bound his tail. Then she pulled off the blankets one by one. Every action was done in slow motion. This was her ritual, her ceremony, not just a job to get through.

Inferno watched every procedure with undivided interest. His ears were forward and turned in their sockets a bit, with the furry, open part toward her. He was ready to listen to anything she might say and even pretended he was going to bite when she undid the straps that held the blankets tight across his chest. But you could see that nipping her was a cock-and-bull story; he was just pretending to live up to his name. She laughed and I knew they had done this before. It was their game. Inferno's eyes were fixed upon Louise as if there was nothing else in the place worth looking at. When she moved around, he'd follow her as far as he could.

After Inferno was settled, I went with Walter and Louise to the secretary's office to get a pass that would permit me access to all show areas. The woman must have recognized Walter, because she greeted him with unusual pleasure and respect. "It's wonderful to go anywhere with Walter," Louise had told me earlier, "And especially to a competition, because everyone treats him with such respect."

True, Walter could have been attending a business conference from the look of him, but it wasn't his clothes that impressed the person behind the desk. Judges, officials, riders, and trainers of all kinds were hurrying in the door, equally well dressed in the European tradition. What was different about Walter was his manner.

Unlike the nervous energy exuded by others, Walter gave off an inner calm that encompassed the ringing phones, the whirring fans, and the clatter of office machines. Yet his quiet equilibrium did not imply that he was either important or unimportant; it went deeper than that.

The lady in the office informed Walter that Hermann Duckek had been preparing the footing for the warm-up area and the competition arena for several days. Walter could not have been more pleased. In Europe, experts work endlessly on the problem of preparing an optimum base that will hold up for jumping, dressage, and whatever show numbers the manager has planned. Drainage is no problem for the indoor winter-spring circuit, but there are various ways of using sand, sawdust, and other man-made or natural fibers, as well as plastics.

The Danish Herr Duckek is one of the best known of the international experts who prepare the footing for the Olympic Games, World and European Championships, and the large national shows in Europe, Canada, the United States, and Korea. In short, he is unique. There's a story that when Duckek was in one country where he didn't speak the language and could not find enough laborers to work overtime, he stayed up every night of the weeklong competition to replace and rake the turf himself.

As we walked through a subterranean tunnel in search of the warm-up area, the chilly dampness of concrete walls and the cheerless wattage of the electrical light bulbs, made me think how hard it must be as a competitor to work oneself up to ride in the morning. I wondered if you ever get used to conditions that aren't easy or whether you just learn to ignore them. From the titles of several books that I had seen on Louise's bedside table back home, I knew that she "worked" on the thoughts and the feelings that surround competition.

The warm-up area was a cramped hall. Louise was worried. Inferno needed space, she said, he grew distracted and tense when surrounded by other horses in a tight area. Walter reminded her that there would be time enough to let him out for some big strides just before her bell rang; then she would have that entire auditorium to herself. "Und nicht krumm machen," (and don't sit hunched over) he added, pulling his shoulders forward and folding himself up over his left rib cage in exaggeration. Clearly, he wanted to make her laugh with him, but she wasn't ready for that.

Though Walter and Louise kept reassuring each other that it would all work out, I watched Louise biting her lip, a habit she sometimes had when things got serious for her. It was not up to me to say anything, of course, but I was thinking that there was no such thing as an easy show.

On the first day of competition, the big ring would be open to all competitors at 5 AM for an hour-and-a-half, and then closed, raked, and prepared for the show. Louise said she would need enough time to allow Inferno to get used to everything in the area, from the commercial sponsors' billboards that lined the sides of the arena to the banks of decorative flowers and the platforms with the table desks set up for the judges and their scribes. One never knew what might catch a horse's eye. Walter reminded her that if she remained positive and quiet herself, the horse would take his cues from her.

I wondered if the fame of some of her fellow competitors was making Louise nervous. When I asked, she said that she tried not to think about them. Instead, her effort was to stay wholly concentrated on riding, on the test, and on her horse. After all, she pointed out with her little smile, Inferno wouldn't know the winner of the European Championship or the members of the German Olympic Team. Louise might not have wanted to think about those top performers, but they could not, and indeed would not be ignored, as she was soon to discover.

At 5 AM on the morning of the competition, I went with Louise to the warm-up area. The plan was that she would begin walking Inferno with a loose rein and then after a few minutes, Walter would be along to work with her. As the minutes ticked by and he didn't appear, she kept looking over to the entranceway of the arena to search for him. I wondered whether he had overslept, or whether his transportation from the hotel to the show had failed to show up.

I could see that Louise was distressed and unconcentrated. All of the riders had someone working with them. It was easy to pick out these coaches, trainers, wives, husbands, and helping friends from the few spectators who, like me, were merely behind-the-scene fans. The important ones, mentors to the famous, stationed themselves at a distance from each other, probably so that their advice couldn't be overheard. They stood stolidly, their eyes fixed steadily upon their riders, exuding a certain air of status. Actually, they reminded me of generals whose commands were unquestionable. They communicated with their riders in monosyllabic commands and occasional nods. Each rider listened to his or her advisor's voice and kept an eye on that one person.

What was surprisingly apparent to me was that the combination of horse, rider, and "anchor man" seemed to confer a power that gave them the right to claim space. These trios seemed to state to any other equestrian pair approaching, "Eyes up, we have the right of way." The competitors rode with assertiveness and confidence, emphasizing the directions that they chose to ride in and the preparation methods that had won previous victories. Their approach must have felt to Louise like a winter wind. Less famed riders, like smaller ships, had to change course and upon occasion simply get out of the way fast.

Eventually, Walter appeared in plenty of time to give Louise the help she needed before the arena was closed off. The footing was a good consistency for Inferno and as far as either she or Walter could determine there were no discernible distractions to take his attention off the Grand Prix test. Of course anything can happen once you enter the ring. An uninformed tourist might take a picture, a lady sitting in the costly seats nearest to the ring could stand up, turn her back to the arena, remove her coat and not notice she had caught the horse's attention, the heavy show program could slip off a lap and land with a disturbing slap on the concrete floor. Riders try to keep their mounts concentrated, but, like the competitors, horses can shift their attention, lose it, or even fall apart. This is when the five, six, seven, or more years of day-to-day discipline that have gone into dressage training can provide such a solid grounding that the unexpected will be ignored.

In spite of a good work out, the vulnerability that Louise had experienced that morning had lodged deep. It may have caught her with her guard down and ignited old feelings of insecurity or brought new ones up to the forefront. Her face had a pallid, inward look, different from her usually shiny-eyed, self-possessed appearance. When she took out the little book that contained her test, it was her way of telling everyone that she needed to be left alone by her stall.

It was one of those times when you want to help out and you don't know how. Eva, her groom, offered to go to the restaurant to get Louise a cup of coffee but that was turned down. Walter put his hand on her shoulder to say something but couldn't find the words and ended up asking her if she wanted his jacket to keep warm. I looked at my watch and saw that she had six hours and twenty-three minutes to wait before she would enter the ring.

At the competition, there were several options for whiling away those hours: one could watch dressage, or inspect the dozens of shopping concessions that offered anything from the latest in horse equipment to rainbow-like arrangements of candy. One could drink draughts of beer drawn from barrels and eat all sorts of goodies. Though I took advantage of many of these choices, I was haunted the whole time by an image of Louise, just as I had left her, wrapping silence around herself, sitting on a bale of hay, half looking at the test. Inferno was standing behind her as close as he could, his head lowered to the level of her head, eyes intent upon her.

None of us felt much joy that day at the show. The hours of waiting and the tensions seemed to isolate us, making conversation out of the question. Even Eva, who normally had a smile for everyone, went quietly about her work as if she were shut off in a separate world. Walter wandered off to drink tea with friends, called Stall Tasdorf to check on what was happening at home, read and reread the posted order of rides, and kept returning to keep an eye on Louise. Finally, I heard her call his name and I could see he was glad she had spoken. We had all been bothered by her unaccustomed silence: it was not the best kind of silence to keep before a ride.

"Walter, can we talk?" she said, drawing in her breath as if she had a desperate truth to utter. I moved quickly away to allow them privacy, but Louise later told me what happened.

It had been a very strange day for her, beginning with the early morning warm-up when she had started alone. Instead of being able to concentrate solidly on the riding, every question that she had ever asked herself came to her, demanding an answer right then and there. Every goal that she had dreamt of put in an appearance; every choice demanded commitment.

As an international riding competitor reaching for the pinnacle of success, Louise was facing enormous pressures. In order to qualify for the Olympics she would be returning home after this competition to ride the circuit of national shows and try to win a place for herself on the Swedish Team. If she performed well enough, her federation would then send her to all the other countries to ride for Sweden. Getting to the top was a step by step procedure like the training she'd been having in dressage.

Louise was no doubt thinking what her life would be like: the goals that she had cherished for such a long time may suddenly have appeared frightening, perhaps even appalling, making her feel incredibly lonely. Finally, her anxiety became so strong that she had called Walter over. "Walter, I can't do this by myself," she had told him.

"If you are talking about my being late this morning, I am really sorry," he had replied. There was a kind of pause, "I was tired," he said. Then he held up his wonderfully big hands in a gesture that was both understanding and pleading. "I will be there for you next time," he promised.

And he was. Walter was Louise's Rock of Gibraltar, standing by at any ring that she was competing in, giving her courage by being there. Her talent attracted international attention for him as "the new trainer on whom to keep a close eye." Master and pupil were of vital importance to one another.

If Walter were to set out with Louise on the timetable of her competitions, I knew the changes in his life would be as extreme for him as they would be for her—in his work, his lifestyle, and himself. Like Louise, he had not as yet had his name in the headlines. On the other hand, he had trained and sold horses to competitors whose names were household words. He had trained winning riders who had brought him a solid and even outstanding reputation and apprentices that stable owners were eager to have. None of this was any small achievement in a country where the horse industry was so competitive and such big business, a country toward which other countries looked for quality and talent in the horse world.

Instinct told me that I had witnessed two beginnings right there at the show: that of an international trainer and of an international rider. How much more could I experience in the year that I was having? Seeing that such horizons could appear further underlined for me how amazing it was that my year of training had happened at all. I had come so innocently to a place that was to hold so much for me!

The Belgian show was not one of Louise's most distinguished competitions. In her tests each day, she placed somewhat lower than the middle of the long list of riders. Of course she was disappointed. She expected so much of herself and took the entire burden of showing upon her shoulders. But she had muscle in her soul for a time like this and could endure it.

"There will be other opportunities to prove yourselves," was Walter's wise reminder. And, indeed he was right. There were other times and other shows and Louise and her horse did prove themselves; they became members of the Swedish Dressage Team. As often as was humanly possible, Walter was there at the competitions with her. He had kept his promise to her.

For me, another image remains indelible—one that is not public—an image that defines her spirit for me better than anything else I can remember. It came to me like this:

It was evening at Tasdorf. Louise had been staying with me and I was worried because she was several hours late coming home. Thinking that a horse might have become ill and she might need help, I went back to the stable. I found the main barn dark, but a single light shone in the annex out back, and there I discovered Louise. She was standing companionably with her horse Inferno in his stall.

Louise had been concerned about her horse, she explained. He was scheduled to train with a new bit for the first time the next day. Higher-level competition requires certain pieces of equipment and excludes certain others—this was a bit she thought he might have to get used to. Wanting to make it easier for him, she had thought that if she put the bridle on him while he was comfortable and happy in the stall, it would give him pleasant associations to help him accept it. She had decided to stay there with him, and while she was massaging his gums, his lips, the sides of his mouth, his face, his ears and his neck, she had lost track of time. She looked complete and happy, smiling as if to say that for her there could be no better place or moment than this one. That is my image of Louise.

$$\approx 15$$

We Won't Say Good-Bye

I threw off the down comforter that last morning just as the alarm announced 7 o'clock, but I needed no reminder. Packing into the late hours of the previous night had caught me up in the excitement of going home and had driven away almost all possibility of sleep. Even so, I was less exuberant than I might have been on that mid-March day, 1980. Going home meant leaving Tasdorf—and part of me didn't want the change.

Part of me wanted to stay; to stop time. Would I be in this town or sleep in this bed ever again? Was my German dream truly coming to an end? I had been at Stall Tasdorf for a year and though logic and fact told me otherwise, it didn't feel possible that the last day should ever come. How could I leave when every voice and every fiber within me was saying, "You have now learned enough to realize you've merely begun!"

Suddenly all the details of my German life were important, even my narrow beds. Hadn't they been my comforting nest for hundreds of nights? To think that my first challenge on foreign soil had been not how to sit on my horse, but how to sleep in my bed. Those first nights in the Park Hotel could have been yesterday. The hotel bed had been narrow like this one. It had the same wooden frame that nicked my shins when I climbed in. The standard German bedding had been so totally foreign. The down comforter was so spare in size that there wasn't an extra inch to grab on to. It literally sat, feather-fat and encased in its coverlet, on top of the mattress, allowing for no tossing and turning of the sort I indulged in at home. Within two nights, I had trained myself to sleep sentry-still and believed down puffs to be among the best things in life.

And how could I forget the pigs that I had gotten to know from my window view the last six months? Was this the last time I'd listen to pigs scream for their breakfast? For once, I hated to close my window. Every morning early, I had listened to their squeals, but as pigs don't smell and these made pleasant baritone noises during the day, they were good neighbors. In any case, their pen across the street had been my view and they were a part of daily life as well as an essential part of Tasdorf economy. Yes, I would miss the pigs.

I had written about these animals in my letters back home, making them my light topic when I felt heavy and couldn't put my feelings into words. Living in a foreign land and studying dressage had connotations of glamour and high purpose. Pigs were a wonderful contrast, and making people laugh was a way of keeping them from noticing what I wasn't saying. I was living out my dream, which made me feel I owed my well-wishing correspondents back home good news, but often reality was more complex. Too, no one at home had a view like this.

Even more than the world outside, the inside of my own particular room on the second floor mattered to me. It had been my home for many months. Every time I had put my key in the front door, removed my boots in the entry, climbed the stairs, turned right between Frau Sievers' two children's rooms, to finally open my door, I'd felt stress drain away. The tension had been most intense in the first months, grew better, but never quite disappeared. However, when I closed the door of my room behind me, I entered a space that was all mine. I was never lonely there. Hardly anyone ever came in but me, and my room became my renewing place, like a gentle, inviting, and familiar friend.

Actually, I had very few personal possessions to spread around. My clothes were out of sight, shut away in the cupboard, but I had placed strategically the few momentos and objects I did own in order to make my space welcoming, as if my room waited for my return. I wanted to see that I had projects afoot, not emptiness. However, once a week, my landlady cleaned. She methodically returned the place to its neutral, stark state, piling my letters, books and photographs, private journal, magazines from America, and papers into a single pyramid on the coffee table or else putting them into the dresser. I had heard that in Germany, leaving one's belongings around in one's room was considered messy, even dirty. Apparently, my landlady thought that I was typically American in this respect. We had never discussed this silent battle even when I went to pay the monthly rent. Talking to someone who was seldom without a broom in her hands, who must have risen every morning with a master plan for scrubbing, seemed useless. We simply saw things differently. On this March day, everything I owned was packed into suitcases except for the clothes that I was to wear. I hoped Frau Sievers would be pleased right down to her polished shoes.

Still, I'd miss the place. I'd even miss Frau Sievers. Our minor complications had been so predictable, so silently manageable. Patterns of sameness and places that were familiar had held a comforting feel for me. They had been my treats, my candy. I had grown accustomed to the entire rhythm of this tiny town. It moved with the predictability of my clock.

I dressed quickly to ride and went out on the street. This was a morning when every thought and even the smallest actions seemed full of significance. Spring was in the process of giving the area an extended embrace. I had never known such a glorious spring, but people at the stable claimed it was like this every year. Perhaps it was. Yet I had noticed that the words they were saying and the conversations they were having sounded lighter and more hopeful than I had ever heard. It was true that a season of so much greening could make the whole world seem a promising place. I, for one, felt buoyed up. Walking down the street, I listened intently to the sound of my footsteps and knew I would remember the sights and sounds of the life around me.

Before I came to the stable's high wooden gate, one of the town's huge farm tractors came rumbling down the road. A raised finger inside a gloved hand had always been the driver's only salutation, his only recognition that I was there. All I had ever seen of him was the side of a felt hat with a feather stuck in the wide brim. He had always appeared to be deeply studying his fields. This day however, the farmer turned right around on his high metal seat and with the smile of one with whom I might have recently shared a meal, called out over the thunder of his machine, "Guten morgen" (good morning).

I responded in kind and added a wave. "God, I'm happy here." The words rose up in my mind so spontaneously, I hardly knew they were mine. I hadn't ever had such a thought before, or at least not consciously. Then, a second thought came: The fight was over. I was on my way home. Fight? I asked myself. Was that the right word? Was that how it had been? Who had I fought? Not being one who believed that I could have easily gone to war, I was startled to have come up with such a word.

Images tumbled into my head like pieces in a puzzle, scenes that brought back memories of the year past: my inability to speak the German language, lack of knowledge, fear of the unknown, distress over mistakes, insecurity, and loneliness. These images were not about my riding—they were about how I had lived my life here. Who had been the enemy? Plainly, it had been myself.

Now the battle was over, and strangely, it seemed to me that it was in leaving that I had finally arrived. To be greeted on this morning was a gift. Seeing the farmer face to face was like a sign of welcome. Of course, my departure was not exactly a secret. I had been told that in Tasdorf, everyone was acquainted with every one else and many of the inhabitants were related. I knew the town had no newspaper and would never need one: the events of each day were communal business to be shared verbally and with great energy: head shaking, large arm movements, and dramatic hand gestures. Events were the reason for human contact amongst the townsfolk: across the fence, in the field, or at the kitchen table over beer or coffee and cake.

The town folk seemed to take an almost proprietary interest in me. That we were curious about one another had been obvious to me from the start. We observed each other surreptitiously, I peeking from behind my window curtain, and they with veiled glances whenever they encountered me. My German teacher, Frau Kunze, had always referred to me as "My Mrs." when she spoke of me, but in her case, I could understand her sense of possession, since I had actually sat at her table over soup, and had studied German with her as her paying student every Monday and Thursday afternoon from 2:00 to 3:30.

How well I knew the stretch of road from the Sievers' house to Stall Tasdorf. I could have walked that dead-ahead macadam straightness with my eyes closed, right to its farthest point. Over the last months, I had grown to love the sky above that road, too. The sky had invited me into the universe and opened me in ways that my earthbound feet could not. Mentally, pursuing this higher route, I had entered an endless continuum, and had thereby, been instantly transported home to America. No need to cross an ocean. I felt I could look down on whatever and whomever I longed to see; no matter that with the time difference, people were in their beds, or that back home my dogs were sleeping. I could check the flowers in their pots, sit in my chair, the one with arms at the end of the kitchen table, remember the smell of coffee beans being ground, the sound of heat coming through the old pipes, the taste of salad the way I make it. The family always ate up every scrap even when I put together twice too much. They made me feel pleased with myself. They didn't have to tell me that I was important to them. Like the pot on the stove, I had my place. Gazing up into the German sky had brought my family's warmth to me on cold winter mornings when I was a newcomer far from home.

The last months had become progressively easier. Change had come so gradually that I didn't even notice it until I suddenly realized things were different. Then, the next time I looked, change had occurred again, bringing me a new life, like the subtle advance of spring.

Everyday happenings—my early morning walk, flicking the latch of the stable door and entering, moving quietly in case there was a horse in the aisle, hearing Walter say "Moyn, moyn" to the farrier, a visitor, or a customer, shaking hands if there was need for that, checking on the hour of my lesson, inhaling the odor of urine, manure, and golden fresh straw, leading my horse out of his stall, and tending to every detail of preparation for our upcoming work— all this and ever so much more, had changed over time from being merely automatic actions to becoming the consciously observed components of my day.

When I arrived at the stable, Lothar Kohler, the official county veterinarian, had already come to take care of the procedures and documents Inca would need to travel home. Volker, the young apprentice who had started at Tasdorf a few months earlier (see page 149), assured me that all of the required documents were in order. Within the week, Inca would fly home.

"You must be happy to leave today," said the lehrlinger who was the newest apprentice and must have been feeling the yoke of the next few years.

"Nicht so ganz," (not so entirely) I replied, in the shorthand stable jargon.

"Ja, I understand you," put in Halle from Denmark. "I have finished my four years and last night I sat down with Herr Christensen and asked if he'd keep me on. I have to learn more. Once I leave here, I'll be on my own. Right now, I'm not good enough."

"Did you hear that Dieter has been offered a job at a private breeding stable where he will break young horses?" put in blonde Hanna of Sweden who had recently come in for the spring school break. She had brought her pony to sell and wanted Herr Christensen to find her the right young horse. In a discussion about what she wanted to do with her life, he had suggested that she might support herself as an instructor. She had a particular way with people and she both thought and spoke clearly. Her talent as a rider was good but not great. If she wished to compete, Sweden would be the best place. She had accepted his advice and was thinking about teaching.

"What will you do when you get back to America?" Volker asked me.

"Compete," I said not even needing to watch their reactions. To these young people, America was the land of milk and honey. They pictured the United States to be like Las Vegas and Hollywood, like Florida and California, where there was eternal sun. They thought everyone in America was rich. How many horses did I own, someone wanted to know. Every one of the apprentices had plans to come to America some day. They had been told that dressage was just catching on there. Would it be all right to give me a call they wondered, and then there were handshakes and they all wished me luck. "You'll do well," one of them said.

Suddenly, it was time for the last lesson of my year at Tasdorf.

Walter was sitting on his bench in the arena helping his riders. The radio was on as it often was in the early mornings before the customers arrived. The stable people claimed that whether it was riding or cleaning, music made their work easier, possibly better. I couldn't help but feel the peacefulness in this place.

I led Inca to the center of the ring. Tightened the girth the customary two holes. Dropped the stirrups and mounted.

Walter was watching me. He made a familiar sound in his throat, a kind of low, guttural, clearing tone that I had grown to love because it expressed a deep level of wordless feeling, leaving me to guess just what that feeling was. This day he invited me to choose how I would like to use my last lesson. Would he take charge or would I?

Knowing that I would soon be on my own, and feeling the need to begin the process of letting go, I told him that I would like to work as though I were already at home but with him sitting right there by the arena with me. I would do my warm-up and then ride the movements of the Grand Prix test in whatever order felt right to me as we went along. I wanted to feel free of any sense of hurry, or the need for one movement immediately to follow another. And I requested that he critique me as I went along.

My suggestions appeared to please him.

As I picked up my reins and began the walk, I was unaware that this last lesson was to be even more special than I had imagined. I was to overcome a hurdle that had haunted me from the time of my earliest lessons at Tasdorf.

I had set myself a high goal. There would be no hiding behind the easier figures—we'd do the hard ones. No part of the work that we had been doing together would be left out. Sitting astride Inca, I felt no nervousness or tension, only a deep sense of respect and gratitude toward the man who sat there waiting to correct me. To ride well was the best way to thank him. "Weiter," (let's begin) he said, and I knew that he meant I mustn't just sit there on my horse doing nothing. In spite of his quiet, almost laid back nature, Walter had always insisted that I "get going."

After a few minutes of silence, Walter called out, " Ubergange," reminding me to work with more transitions. Then suddenly, there was a second command, "Energie!" spoken out emphatically. This "forward energy" aspect of the work was so vitally important to Walter that words alone were simply not enough. To emphasize his point as one that I should implant in my brain forever, he made a gesture as if pushing everything in the world out in front of him. I urged Inca to reach even more underneath himself and give me livelier, bigger steps.

During the last month we had established a good pattern for the warm-up which we now employed. We began with short sessions of the walk, trot and canter. Once I got Inca's three gaits established and moving, I alternated between lengthening and shortening his strides. It didn't take long before I could feel with an almost certain confidence that I had gained both my horse's attention and his obedience. Only then, as I had been taught, could we move on ahead.

Looking at Walter's familiar figure brought home to me just how enormously I would miss him. If only I could take not just Walter, but all of Stall Tasdorf, back home. How often the other good riders and their fine horses had unknowingly been my teachers and now, once again, a glance in their direction was all it took to remind me to check myself and the correctness of my own position. I did not, however, linger to watch anyone else. In fact, I hardly looked left or right. I was riding for all I was worth. Twenty spectators could have come and stood in the ring and I wouldn't have noticed them. Even if I had happened to glance their way, they wouldn't have disturbed me. My concentration was as protective as a suit of armor and as liberating as an opened door.

Gone was the self who had fled from the practice ring at the advent of spectators, who had dreaded the critical eyes of the Sunday crowd peering down from the casino window, who had been distracted by the movements and exercises of other riders. Now finally, in my last lesson, I had achieved a new level from which to work, operating not just from my head or from my body, but from a deep-down, gut sense of rightness that sprang from total focus.

The disparate bits of information I was receiving gathered and became unified action. Messages telling me what I needed to do surfaced in my mind in a voice that I recognized as Walter's. My instructor's voice and my own were melding—I was on the way to becoming my own teacher.

Inca too, appeared by some instinct to know that this morning was not just routine. He came quickly into his magnificent self. He was excited and a bit hot, rings of wet had already started at the base of his ears and the little black points on their ends headed straight up to the sky.

"Bleib ruhig im tact," (keep a steady rhythm) shouted Walter.

Yes, the rhythm! My fault. The canter had turned into an explosion. My intensity had caused us to rush. I half-halted three times, insisted on several steps of walk, and then began again. This time we breathed our way quietly into better strides.

"Aufnehmen. Gross werden" (collect the horse. Sit up), was Walter's next directive. I turned on the centerline and Inca's body dove downward. I corrected the axis of his balance, rode him upward, and grew tall myself. The two corrections and Walter's words were simultaneous. Our thinking was alike. Precisely what I needed to see to feel secure that I was learning. I checked: was Inca's body straight, his neck positioned?

Then I began a simple sideways movement with Inca's long Thoroughbred legs reaching far under his belly and crossing one over the other. I followed this with the Grand Prix version, the "zigzag": two steps forward, three steps right, six left, six right, six left, three right and once more forward to the finish. I had discovered that the exercise would flow smoothly if I thought of it as an entire line of music in which not a single note could be omitted.

"Nicht schlecht," (not bad) was his comment, and then, ever the perfectionist, he added that my body position was out of line and too far forward. He demonstrated my angle and the degree I was to change to correct it.

I had now gained more courage than I had when the lesson began, and was ready to try pirouettes. We had practiced pirouettes dozens and dozens of times in the Tasdorf ring. At first, they had worried me. For a while I had avoided them. Finally, I faced them fiercely, head on, every day, determined to learn to ride the canter-on-the-spot-360-degree-circle in six to eight steps that were small but distinctly on going. Eventually, I actually grew to like the taste of being airborne and suspended. I felt I was riding the air. It took real self control to sit quietly, to neither twist nor turn, to guide the action, hold the regularity, ride the stride; in other words, to make the horse do his work.

"Gut," was Walter's comment, and I allowed myself for one instant to feel proud. His confirmation of my growing ability was important—necessary. I needed to know I had developed an instinct that I could rely on back home.

Still fully focused, we went right to flying changes. It was a good exercise to choose after the tight pirouettes. Inca's body was now primed for these moves and best of all, he adored them. He performed with an air of exhilarated abandon, a kind of take-a-look-at-me-if-you-want-to-see-something-well-done attitude. From the bench, Walter counted out the fifteen flying changes required by the Grand Prix test.

Elated, I asked for extension, forgetting for a split second that I had a horse who liked to run and that asking for an extension was likely to be interpreted as going to the races. "Nicht so viel!" (not so much) Walter shouted.

We flew past our final point with an exuberance I couldn't control. Quiet restraint was a point that Walter had worked on especially with me, but on this particular morning, quiet restraint was a quality Inca and I didn't have.

However, we re-established ourselves quickly and changed gaits, with Inca trotting as if his life depended on it. Walter smiled his approval from the bench and told me once again that I had "the horse of a lifetime." Inca was buoyant and, though I still found it hard to believe, during the final months at Tasdorf I had finally learned to sit to all his spring.

Remembering one of my teacher's most often spoken dictums, "Don't get stuck, if an exercise is right then go on with your work," I didn't ask Inca for a repeat, although I was sorely tempted to luxuriate in another good extension. Instead, I took a deep breath and faced my next move—the passage.

What I had in mind would be great for me both as a rider and as a confidence builder. I prayed we could pull it off. I had only re-cently begun to get Inca to give me the movement totally unaided by my teacher. Bolstered by the work we had just completed and by my sense that at that moment Inca had built up the ingredients we needed (he was in fact asking me through body language, "What do you want next?") I sat deep, gave a slight thrust forward with my pelvis, a gentle squeeze with my calves, and an ever so slight up-ward motion with soft fingers.

The response was right there. Inca began in what felt like slow motion. Released by excitement, power surged through him, filling him until his body felt twice its normal size. Sitting quietly on his back, it seemed I was being raised into the air—held suspended while Inca lifted his legs alternately, effortlessly, and rhythmically. So all-consuming was this motion, I only half registered the thought, "Was sitting on a horse more like being in heaven than being on earth?"

"Jawol!" (Yes!) came Walter's benediction from the sidelines. He stood up on his feet as if to encourage me onward.

I turned up the centerline, keeping the passage, and when I stood aligned in front of my teacher, maybe twenty feet away, I decreased Inca's strides with the tiniest of half-halts, shifted my weight by mil-limeters, moved my legs ever so slightly, and inwardly whispered "piaffe."

We got it. Twelve high piaffe steps almost in place. No outside reminders this day. Inca had not needed the small tick-tick of Walter tapping his boot with a whip or my "giddy-up."

"Loben!" (praise him) Walter called out instantly. He came over and patted the horse and then he patted me. His face was all smiles.

If I rode the way I had ridden that morning, he told me, I'd do well back home. Then he said that he had been doing a lot of thinking in the last days and that we needed to talk. Would I let one of the apprentices put my horse away and sit down for a cup of tea in the casino?

I was both delighted and curious.

Kerstin came to join us. She offered to translate for us, even though she actually knew that Walter and I had learned to manage quite well.

Though I've forgotten most of the exact words of our final conversation, I will never forget their impact on me. With the air of a "fait accompli," Walter announced to me that in the future he would be happy indeed to come to America and teach as often as he could. Though the decision would mean he would have to give up his beloved annual deer hunting forays, if I could accommodate him he would like to schedule a fourteen-day stay for the coming fall. That was all the time he would be able to spare from his own stable and responsibilities. He was eager to teach Americans, he said, and interested in working with our Thoroughbred horses. And of course, most important of all, he wanted me to be able to continue with the training that Inca and I had begun. He paused to look at me. Well, what did I think of his plan?

Think? There was no need to think. I knew what was in my heart. Listening to Walter's words, I realized to my joy that although my year was at an end, there would be no end—just a pause. The dream that had begun on my first day in the Tasdorf casino had taken root. "The end" would become a new beginning.

Before we parted, he presented me with a pair of spurs. "They're not new," he said somewhat apologetically, explaining that he had tried to polish them and make them look better.

I have used them occasionally," he said, "but I thought they might be good for you with Inca."

Studying his gift, I saw that the spurs were not the usual German type that I found to be somewhat frightening with their long, cruel-looking shanks. Instead, this pair was well-constructed, balanced, strong, rounded at the end, and of less than medium length. They were better in every way than the ones that I had been using. How could I thank him, I wondered? How could I find the right words to tell him that they were the best present he could have given me?

Twenty years later, I still have those spurs, and while looking at them brings back rich memories of my days in Germany, more than anything it is Walter's voice that endures and his words that go on ringing in my ears. In moments of frustration, in times of discouragement, I hear him clearly. "Always ride the very best way that you can," he says. And that, after all, is all there is to do.

⌒16

Afterward

True to the promise he made to me on my last morning in Tasdorf, Walter began coming to America. The news that he planned to come to The Ark twice a year and give clinics spread quickly.

Upon my return home, I found out that interest in dressage was in high gear—growing even more rapidly than when I had left. Riders were especially eager to receive European training or at least be able to watch and thus learn from such a high caliber of instruction. Dressage enthusiasts from everywhere, even as far away as Canada and Bermuda, tried to get in touch with Walter. They wanted him to extend his normal stay in America and include their area for training sessions.

Walter was eager to help as many Americans as he could. While initially he did travel around the country, he later turned down requests to visit anywhere other than The Ark. He found that his business responsibilities in Germany allowed him to spend only a limited time in the United States, and he concluded that he did not wish to divide the days he gave us with anyone else; those who wished to work with him could come to The Ark. And people were so eager for his instruction that in the end they did haul their horses to us from all over the land. Looking over his roster of students, I'd hear him say on occasion, half seriously, half in jest, that perhaps we should give our place a second name—"Tasdorf West." Needless to say, the loyalty and the commitment this man gave to those of us who trained with him at The Ark was deeply treasured.

In no time at all, Walter's name became legend. For those of us who made up the core of his serious riders, he became an institution of the highest learning. Though his day of lesson giving never extended beyond seven hours, with each visit his audience grew larger. Popular demand would have detained him months longer than his prescribed two weeks, and aware of this, Walter occasionally did give us an extra visit, especially to aid us in a competition. It was obvious that he was deeply moved by the enormous appreciation that was shown for his work. In Germany, he explained, his instruction was simply "expected." In fact, he was so impressed that he once told me that if he were a younger man, he would have thought seriously about moving to Massachusetts for part of the year.

I am quite sure no one looked forward to Walter's visits more than I. As the clinics were so important, preparation for his coming began weeks in advance. As far as I was concerned, the entire farm had to be perfect. Those German fraus out on the stoops with their mops and scrub buckets had found a permanent niche in my thinking.

When the grand day of Walter's arrival finally did come around, the farm was breathlessly ready. I had seen to a special cleaning of the house and the stable and Russell had "made up" the two dressage arenas to look as if they had been laid out with clean sheets. The family silver had been polished, the garage vacuumed, the hayloft tidied up, and the tractor shed swept. The six horses, two dogs, one barn cat, the rabbit, and the seven sheep had all undergone a major inspection, and when needed, had been groomed, washed, clipped, pouffed, or newly shod according to what was deemed most appropriate. Even the driveway had been raked. By the time we brought Walter home from the airport, the farm had settled back down into a deceptively peaceful appearance—one that would change entirely over the following two weeks.

Our labors gave Russell and me a great sense of accomplishment, but what we looked forward to most was the look on Walter's face when he arrived. We never wanted a single thing to mar that. The happiness of his expression matched by the way his body seemed to visibly "open up" was our reward. That precious moment always reminded me of all things natural, beautiful, and good—the sun, the earth, and a warm relaxed spring day. And if by chance I was feeling stressed, none of the things that had worried me remained important.

Walter was not your everyday guest. To begin with, upon arrival, even before entering the house, he'd insist first upon a visit to the stable. He'd unfurl his long legs from their cramped space, stride with a somewhat stiff but determined step toward the stable and say, "I hope you don't mind if I say 'hello' to my friends." All the while, he'd be searching for lumps of sugar he had pocketed during his travels. Once in the barn, he'd go right to Inca, who having intuited what was happening would be at the front of his stall, wide-eyed and impatient with waiting. Walter was not one to be satisfied with thrusting treats through stall bars to a pal he'd known so well, so he'd slide the door open and go all the way inside. Then he'd stroke my fellow with a firm hand and study him intensely, giving him an overall "reading." Next would come a specific examination of Inca's legs. Most likely he'd pick up a hoof and have a close look at the shoe. Walter liked our farrier's careful work—it was different than that in Germany, but he appreciated it just the same. Finally, Walter would look across at me and comment "Ist gut"(it's good) as much as to say Inca had passed scrutiny with flying colors. The look on Inca's face would be stating quite blatantly, "Of course. What did you expect?" Inca's moments of cockiness made Walter smile.

Following his visit with Inca, Walter would always stop by the other stalls and have a chat with each one of the inhabitants, all of whom he'd come to know well. Then, he'd walk back up the aisle, taking in the brush cabinet with its cleaning equipment, leg wraps, and liniments, and everything that was required for daily care-taking. He was curious and interested in each detail of horse care and stable management, and had questions about many of our American products. "What is this used for?" he'd ask, and "Last time, I took a jar of that home and it worked well. Might I try another?" The freshness of Walter's curiosity was a delight. I used to wonder if there was any detail that would escape him. Furthermore, it was obvious that he felt a certain horseman's responsibility for whatever pertained to equine life on the farm, because he'd check out the tack room, the feed room, the shower stall, and the hayloft. He repeatedly marveled at the quality of our green American hay. Eventually, we'd head up to the house for supper.

At Walter's suggestion, most of the slots in the clinic were given over to professionals. He felt this was the most practical way to spread his teaching. But, whether an amateur like me or a professional filled the hour, there was no difference in the style or tenor of Walter's teaching. Aside from recognizing that we varied in our natural talent, he saw every one of us as unevenly educated in dressage, and at worst, as completely uneducated in his field. But our lack of competence never seemed to bother him, in fact it made him more determined to give us a basic foundation. Never once did he talk down to a student. He took us on as we were and sincerely tried to make us understand the "correct way." His aim was to give each one of us a goal for ourselves and our horses—a goal to strive toward for that hour, the next day, the following week, and until his next visit.

Today, times have changed, but in the 1980s many of the riders who came to The Ark brought American-bred horses with them. Thus the mounts that were presented to Walter were utterly unlike the European warmbloods that he worked with everyday at home. He enjoyed the challenge and one could see him trying to get right inside the head of a particular horse so that he could help him understand what was being asked of him. Occasionally, the temperament or the conformation of a horse made training very difficult for Walter, but he was not one to give up easily. He firmly believed that work in dressage would improve any horse both mentally and physically, no matter in what discipline the animal would ultimately be worked. Although I never heard him blatantly tell a student that his horse was unsuitable for dressage, I did hear him point out to one or two that if they wished to reach the middle or even the higher dressage levels, they needed to have an animal who was appropriately equipped for the challenge. His honesty, his experience, and his sincerity appeared always to be accepted with gratitude.

Truly, the appreciation that flowed out to this man was unusual. Aside from the riders who expressed their thanks after each lesson, the spectators, too, often demonstrated their sentiments by bringing gifts—a painting for Walter to take home, photographs, flowers, foods, and numerous items that were typically American or especially useful for a horseman. Walter was amazed to be thanked so profusely by those he was teaching and was profoundly touched by the gratitude and obvious eagerness and interest in dressage evident among the spectators. "You Americans!" he'd say to me on occasion in a tone that indicated he didn't know quite what to do with the reception he was getting.

Yet there was never any doubt in this man's mind about how he should react to the presence of an animal. Take our stable cat, for instance, who was clearly positive that Walter was just the right person to be at The Ark. One early spring morning I was riding for Walter in the outdoor ring. He was sitting on our old wooden church bench by the side of the arena taking in a rare treat for him—the sun. Neither of us took too much notice of my black and white about-to-be-a-momma kitty when she appeared at his feet. She took a long look at him as if she had something important to tell him and then with one jump she was by his side. Ever so carefully and quietly, she curled up as close to him as she could get. All of a sudden, I heard Walter say, " Priscilla, kuck hier!" (look here). There was the cat, giving birth to her kittens, one after another, right on the skirt of his jacket.

"Wait! Don't do anything," he called out when he saw that, horrified, I was beginning to dismount. "It's all right, my coat can be washed." He was surprised but entirely comfortable and did not wish to have his feline friend disturbed in any way. "Let's get on with the work," he said calmly.

My lesson that morning was the kind one wished could be repeated every single day. I wondered if I had been influenced by the magic of the moment—the cat and her demonstration of utter trust in our friend. Inca's flying changes were fluid, forward, round, and absolutely even in rhythm. Walter said that if we were in competition I'd surely have gotten a 9. The "zigzag," pirouettes, passage, transitions, halt, and rein back went just as well. All I heard from the bench were short reminders and then the statement after one real correction, "But you know about that now." What a banner day!

Although competition was not what we riders were primarily thinking about during the clinics (we were far too focused on using each precious moment to learn), those of us who were serious competitors were making substantial improvements in our scores. Over time, some of us were able to report major "wins." Such news always elicited Walter's sincere congratulations, but what pleased him most and brought out the biggest smile was when a student's horse made a giant step forward in a clinic. Then a clap on the back might even be in order.

My time at Tasdorf had taught me the importance of daily work with an instructor, and I had also come to value the opportunity to watch excellent riding on a regular basis. While I was still at Tasdorf in that memorable year of 1979 I had offered Louise Nathhorst, Walter's talented student, the instructor's position at The Ark. Louise had already come to America in the fall of 1978 to work and compete in company with trainers Michael and Tom Poulin in Fairfield, Maine. Walter had been influential in urging her to take the position, believing that the time on her own would be a maturing and useful experience, helpful in preparing her for the rigors of a future life devoted to European competition.

So when I returned home from Tasdorf, Louise came to The Ark and I had the great good fortune to be able to continue my daily lessons with the best instructor possible. We worked together for over two years and shared our eagerness for Walter's reinforcing visits. Louise enjoyed her stay in America and placed well in competition, but missed her family and felt pressed to return home to fulfill her childhood dream—that of becoming a member of the Swedish Dressage Team and riding for her country.

When the summer of 1981 drew to a close, Louise headed home to Sweden, and immediately thereafter to Germany. After months of intensive training, she entered in what is referred to as "the Tour," a succession of European dressage shows in which she confronted a caliber of competition that she had never faced either in Sweden or America. Her talent was quickly noticed, and within a short period, she captured her dream—a place on the Swedish Dressage Team. In 1984, she made her debut in the Los Angeles Olympics. Her Team came home with a bronze medal. When it was time for Louise to leave, I asked Walter, "Haven't you got someone at Stall Tasdorf who could come to The Ark and stay and instruct us all year long?"

The idea was interesting to him, and he said he'd give it some real thought. It would have to be someone who would be willing to leave Germany and move to America, someone who spoke English, rode well, and who could teach. Perhaps, if he was able to come up with such a candidate, that person could return home periodically, not only to visit family but to stay a bit for some intensive personal riding work. Walter was emphatic about the necessity for a professional not to grow stale. Everyone, even the most experienced of horsemen, he believed, needed occasional supervision if not inspiration in order to be an effective teacher. Eventually, Walter thought of Volker Brommann. Did I remember him? The "new boy" who had begun his apprenticeship while I was at Tasdorf (see page 149). Walter volunteered to have a talk with him.

In the late fall of 1981, Volker came to The Ark to train horses, teach students and to be Walter's translator at the clinics. He has a quick sense of humor, and if you were to ask him how he came to be in this country, he might very well reply, "Priscilla imported me." Volker remained with us for almost three years before moving out to be on his own.

As it did for his teacher, Walter Christensen, competition has played a secondary role for Volker Brommann. Up to now, his professional career in America has centered primarily on instruction and training, both of which he claims bring him profound satisfaction. He lives in Carlisle, Massachusetts, gives regular clinics in New England and across the country, and teaches at The Ark.

During his initial stay at The Ark, Volker, always one to appreciate correct classical training, urged several of his most earnest students to go to Germany for instruction. One of these was a young woman who was determined to undertake a career with horses. Her name was Sue Blinks.

Sue was so serious about learning to ride well that she hardly needed much urging, and in 1983, she went to Germany. Once there, she threw herself into the "student" life at Tasdorf and remained with the Christensens for fifteen months. While she was still at Tasdorf, I sent her an invitation to come back to The Ark as our instructor, to keep us riding "the Christensen way." During the ensuing five years she spent with us, Sue not only taught and trained, but she competed in all the main shows on the East Coast and became a certified "R" level dressage judge.

Today, Sue Blinks makes headlines in the dressage world and has proven both herself and her horses. She wears the USET emblem and represents America in competition. While on the Florida circuit in the winter of 1997, a prominent dressage judge made the kind of comment about her horse Flim Flam that totally thrills a trainer—"this is a horse with no gaps in his education," was the judge's opinion.

Walter's career also broadened and headed skyward. In addition to his American visits, he was regularly giving clinics in Sweden, hosting forums for dressage judges in Tasdorf, offering short courses of instruction for young north German dressage riders, and training members of the Swedish Dressage Team. He attended Louise's competitions, assisting her as well. In 1989, Walter was named the official dressage trainer for the Swedish Team. The doors of the newly formed International Trainers Association opened to him and he joined an impressive roster of the world's best trainers.

But, just at the time when Walter's life appeared to be coming to its fullest and happiest fruition, he was diagnosed with lung cancer. He was too ill to attend the 1990 World Championship in Stockholm, where his student, Louise Nathhorst, received one of her country's highest honors. To commemorate that World Championship, the Swedish government issued a stamp bearing the image of Louise riding the stallion Chirac.

Walter died in August of 1990, and the loss of her trainer, friend, advisor, and second father, all in one, was almost more than Louise could bear. After facing a period of reassessment, she became a master trainer herself and began regularly training members of the Swedish Dressage Team. By the time she was in her early 40s, she had fully trained twelve horses to the Grand Prix level. Competitively, she has chalked up an impressive list of achievements. She is a veteran of three Olympic Games, two world championships, four European championships and three World Cups.

Walter's working years left behind a rich legacy in the host of Tasdorf graduates who now hold responsible and important positions in Germany's equine world. For example, Klaus Rat, the assistant that I had the most contact with during my years of visiting Tasdorf, now trains in a stable located in the neighboring town Boostedt, and ranks high among Germany's top professional competitors.

Walter's wife, Kerstin, continues to live in the town of Tasdorf, but Stall Tasdorf is no longer a small, private dressage stable. The daughter of Walter's original partner is reorganizing and rebuilding it into a large equestrian business, so Kerstin boards her horse with Klaus Rat and now rides solely for pleasure in the beautiful woods nearby. She has replaced the responsibility of running Stall Tasdorf with a part time job for the city of Kiel's busy Tourist Bureau, putting to good use her ability to converse in three languages. Kerstin keeps in close contact with Louise and tries to attend most of her shows, major competitions where Kerstin is often invited to be a scribe for the most highly respected judges.

Kerstin and I have kept up our friendship, and every second year or so, she comes to America and visits me here at The Ark. Though I no longer import and sell European horses the way I did during Walter's lifetime, The Ark remain an active stable with visiting instructors, clinics, and an occasional dressage schooling show. In the tack room, prominently displayed, are a number of beautiful photographs of my friend Inca who ruled the roost and remained in fine health until the age of 22. He died in the same year and month as Walter Christensen—in August of 1990. My present horse—the last one that Walter found for me—is a Grand Prix level Danish warmblood named Demian. He has won my heart, but no horse will ever replace Inca.

For many of us, Walter Christensen became not only our most important riding influence but a special friend and even a mentor. I am aware that whenever a group of his riders meet, we are bound together not only by his training but by our common memories of him as a man—there is a special connection between us, a feeling of family. Naturally, our main subject is our horses and how they are progressing. When we discuss exactly what one of us is doing in detail, someone invariably makes the remark, "Do you remember what Walter used to say?" And of course we all do!

It is now twenty years after that lovely autumn day in 1978, when Walter Christensen first invited me to train with him at Stall Tasdorf. I remain forever grateful to him for encouraging me to "take up the reins" and for setting me so firmly on the path of one of life's most fascinating adventures—the fine art of dressage.